My RACE

*A Jewish Girl Growing Up Under
Apartheid in South Africa*

Lorraine Lotzof Abramson

*DBM Press LC
Springfield, VA
2010*

Dedicated to the memory of my parents
Sadie and David Lotzof

First published in 2010 by

DBM Press, LC
6412 Brandon Ave, #123
Springfield, VA 22150
dbmpress@yahoo.com

See our catalogue at http://www.dbmpress.com

For quality used and rare books, go to:
http://www.usedhistorybooks.com

Library of Congress Control Number 2010929016

ISBN-10: 0-9816102-3-4
ISBN-13: 978-0-9816102-3-8

First Edition

1st Printing
10 9 8 7 6 5 4 3 2 1

Interior Design by AuthorSupport.com

Printed in the United States by BRIOprint

TABLE OF CONTENTS

PROLOGUE

This book would never have been written had it not been for an email I received from my son Gregg, on November 2004. He wrote: "Ma, click on this link. Does Grandpa know him?"

Upon opening the link, I began to read about a Jewish man who grew up in a small town in South Africa. As I read his story, it was as if I were reading my own.

As it turned out, my father didn't know the man, but the message got me thinking. My life growing up was so vastly different from my children's and grandchildren's. Shouldn't I record it? The idea of putting it all down on paper was born.

With encouragement from my family, especially my children, I started to dig down into my memory bank as far back as I could go, and I began to put a frame around the portrait of my memory. This allowed me to travel back in time and to zoom in on certain people, places and events that I hadn't thought about in years. The project gave me an opportunity to reflect, and to explore my own thoughts and feelings at the most important moments in my life.

I started to look back with renewed appreciation at my brave grandparents, who left Eastern Europe to escape oppression and anti-Semitism.

Throughout history the Jewish people have had to flee their homelands due to oppression. They went to North and South America, Europe, Israel, Australia and other corners of this world in search of the freedom they longed for. However, the Jews who went to South Africa found themselves in a unique situation. In their new adoptive country, oppression was alive and well, but there was one huge difference. By virtue of their white skin, the Jews found themselves on the same side as the oppressors. The way we dealt with this situation is part of my story. It covers the time period from my father's arrival in South Africa with his family in 1921 until I left the country when I married my American husband in 1968, and it continues to the present day. It has been an exhilarating journey. I offer this memoir humbly, knowing that everyone has a story.

This book is for you, my children and grandchildren, and for anyone else who might be interested. You've already heard some of the stories, but I hope this will help you comprehend part of your roots, so that you won't have to say as I so often do:

"I wish I had asked my grandparents more questions."

CHAPTER
One

Reitz

"On a clear day you can see a long ways back."
ADELA ROGERS ST. JOHN, *The Honeycomb*

rs. Duminee clutched the Bible to her chest.

"Children," she intoned, "God is speaking to us in these verses. He's telling us that He wants us to keep our white race pure. That apartheid is good. That, with His help, we will keep the races in this country separate." Her voice was flat and rough as sandpaper. She stood in front of our fourth grade class, explaining the verses from the New Testament. The single word BIBLE was embossed on the cover of the brown leather volume, and she held the weathered book so that we could all see the word. Each page had a gold edge, which was hard to see, but when the Bible was closed and all the pages came together, it looked like a shiny gold band. Mrs. Duminee's steely gray hair was tightly pulled back into a bun and her eyes behind the thick glasses looked much too large. She reminded me of a scary old owl. The bright South African sunshine flooded in through the open window. It was October 1956 — springtime in the southern hemisphere — the springtime of my tenth year.

Fourth Grade Class in Reitz

She continued to clutch the Bible as if it were a protective armor, but it was, in fact, her weapon. Everything we learned about apartheid in those early years, we learned in the name of God. We were never allowed to argue with, or question, God, the Bible, or Mrs. Duminee. Even at the age of ten, I knew that her words were dark and ugly, but I also knew better than to contradict her. I sat chewing on the back of my dark green Venus No. 2 pencil, watching her mouth move, and thinking of all the things I was not supposed to say out loud. I wanted to ask, *"Did God really say that?"* But I didn't. I wanted to tell her, *"Mrs. Duminee, my mother said that Afrikaners like you, who support the apartheid regime, twist the word of God to suit your beliefs."* But of course I didn't. I kept my silence.

Each morning our class, like all the other classes, started with a prayer and a Bible story. I was the only Jewish child in the class, in the entire school, for that matter — because my brother Selwyn was still too young for school. So I had no choice but to join in with the rest of the class. We lowered our heads but I kept my eyes open, as Mrs. Duminee began to pray in Afrikaans, "Liewe Jesus..." The prayer always ended with her thanking God for making us white. I wanted to ask, "*Didn't God make the black people too?*" But I knew that if I asked that, I would surely get my knuckles rapped with the wooden ruler.

The ruler lay, forbidding and prominent, on her desk. She employed it to instruct inconvenient questioners with the same measured pace she used for those who made a spelling mistake. She would call us to the front of the class, and we'd hold out our hands palm side down to receive the two raps on our knuckles. By the faces the boys made, I was sure she hit them harder than she hit us girls. Sometimes she would make them touch their toes and then, with the ruler, she would hit them on their rear. My friend Anid told me that some of the boys put a thin book inside the seat of their pants when they knew that they were about to get hit so that it didn't hurt as much. Anid and I had been in the same class every year; this year we were in the fourth grade. Her real name was Dina, but she hated that name so she reversed all the letters and became Anid.

After Mrs. Duminee closed the Bible she said, "Today we're going to talk about what you want to be when you grow up."

She started to go around the room. I told her I wanted to be a teacher. Most of the girls wanted to be either teachers or nurses. The boys said many different things. Jannie said he wanted to be a doctor. I noticed how the sun played on his golden hair, the same color as the silk spun by my silkworm collection. If he ever became my doctor, his piercing blue eyes would be all the medication I'd need to feel better. I would rather have died than let him know what a big crush I had on him. I was way too shy. Then Mrs. Duminee came to Albert. When it was his turn, I couldn't believe what he said. He answered in Afrikaans, "Ek wil 'n polisie wees. Dan kan ek die Kaffirs donner." My jaw dropped: He wanted to grow up to be a policeman so that he could beat up the blacks.

Had he really used that derogatory Afrikaans term, Kaffir, right in front of the teacher? My eyes darted in her direction to see what she'd say. Her reaction shocked me even more. She laughed. So did the rest of the class. Mrs. Duminee must have spoken like that in front of her own children too, since she found his comments so funny. Albert said his father told him that becoming a policeman would give him all the authority he wanted.

This was the same Albert who, the day before, had stuck my long dark braid into the inkwell on his desk. His desk behind me was pushed right up against mine. My desk had a lid that lifted up, revealing a storage compartment below, where I kept my pencil box, a sharpener and a few extra nibs that went in the front of my dipping pen in case one nib broke. Someone had carved a heart in the dark wood with the words, "Koos loves Sannie." Cupid's arrow pierced right through the heart, dividing the two names. On the right top corner was a hole where the inkwell was placed.

Why didn't they make desks for us lefties, with the inkwell on the left? I had to reach across my desk when I needed to dip the nib of my pen into my inkwell to get ready to write my name at the top of the page. I held the white blotting paper in my other hand, ready to blot the page so that the wet ink wouldn't smudge. Ballpoint pens had just been invented, but we weren't allowed to use them. "They'll ruin your handwriting," my teacher said. Suddenly I had felt a tug on my right braid. I'd swung around to see Albert laughing. I felt tears well up in my eyes when I saw that the bottom of my braid was wet, covered in dark blue ink. I'd felt crushed, but we weren't allowed to talk in class, so I had just suppressed my anger and hurt. My mother had to cut an inch off my hair that night to get rid of the ink.

———⊰◆⊱———

WE LIVED IN a dry, dusty little town called Reitz, a tiny dot on the map. It was founded in 1889. When I looked at the atlas my father bought me, I saw that it was located in the eastern part of one of the four provinces in South Africa, the one called the Orange Free State. Reitz lay in the cradle of the agricultural and animal farming center of the country. The land was dry, with vast grassy plains on the outskirts of the town, and so flat that you could almost see the next day. Miles of golden grasslands separated Reitz from the neighboring towns, and there was a huge emptiness and silence in the countryside when we drove from one town to the next. The only sounds you heard were the crunching of the tires on the gravel of the dirt roads as they kicked up dust and stones behind us.

I know now how ironic it was that this province was called the Free State, because it was anything but free. We lived in the heart of South African bigotry. The population living in the actual town was about two thousand whites. The apartheid laws dictated that the black Africans, numbering about five thousand, be relegated to a separate township just out of town and known simply as "the location." Even its name sounded isolating.

On the beach in Durban with my nanny

There was an exception for the domestic help, who lived in a separate structure called the servants' quarters in the back of the main house in town. I thought nothing of it. This had been the law of the land all over South Africa since the ruling Nationalist Party came into power in 1948, and I knew no other way. That was just the way it was. I had no connection with any black African children. They all went to a separate school in the location. That is, *if* they went to school. Education was mandatory and free for every white child, but the African children had to pay for their education and didn't have to go to school if they didn't want to. Whenever I had a big exam, I thought how lucky African kids were that they didn't have to go to school and study for tests. Once I said this right out loud, but then my mother responded, "Lorraine, they're not lucky at all. This is the government's way of keeping them illiterate, poor and dependent."

She went on to explain that the government was concerned that if they became too educated and worldly, they'd become a threat to the apartheid regime by wanting to take over and rule the country. So the only way the white minority could rule the black majority was to keep them illiterate and dependent.

———◆◆◆———

LIFE WAS YAWNINGLY quiet. Nothing much happened to disrupt our calm, predictable journey through each day.

That standard rule of childhood, "don't talk to strangers," was something I never heard when I was growing up, because there were no strangers. We knew everyone in my drowsy little town. "Goeie more Oom" or "Goeie middag Mevrou" was the way my friends and I greeted the grownups as we walked past them on the sidewalks. In Reitz we were one of the very few families that spoke English at home, but in the outside world we spoke the same language as the majority of the white people in the town, which was Afrikaans, the language of the Afrikaners.

White South Africans were divided into two main groups: the Afrikaners or Boers, descendants of the Dutch settlers, and the English, descendants of the British settlers. The English were further divided into the Christian English and the Jewish English. Even though the Jews came mainly from Eastern Europe, we spoke English at home and our political views were more in line with the more liberal English than with the conservative Afrikaners. The Jewish immigrants to South Africa came mainly from Lithuania and Latvia, fleeing oppression in their Eastern European countries. They had to struggle to find their place in the complex web of people in South Africa. The Afrikaners made up the majority of the white population, and they claimed that the country belonged to them. They said that it was the way God wanted it. For all other ethnic groups, like Italians, Greeks, English, Irish, French — even though we were born there — it wasn't really our country. We were citizens yet outsiders. Because we were white, we could enjoy all the privileges of the land, like voting, owning property, running businesses and so forth, but it wasn't really our country. The country belonged to the Afrikaners, the supporters of the apartheid regime. "Die ware Afrikaners," the true Afrikaners — that's what they told us all the time, and that's what we learned in school. According to them, it said so in the Bible, their chief weapon — the same Bible from which all their apartheid beliefs flowed.

For the purpose of segregation, all the whites were referred to as Europeans, while other ethnic groups like Chinese, Japanese, Indians, Cape

Malays, Blacks and people of mixed races (known as coloreds) were classified as non-whites or non-Europeans. All privileges were denied these people, and they lived in a separate area. Everyone was neatly grouped according to skin color. We were a nation of separate and unequal people.

Our house on Convention Street was a modest home, built from yellow face bricks, and it had windows with curly white wrought-iron burglar proofing. The burglar-proofing, seen on every home, was a signal to, and a strategy for protection against, the Africans. It was a message: keep the Africans out and the whites in.

There were kids living in every house on the street, and I had lots of friends on the block. Everyone spoke Afrikaans. Some were a bit older and some younger, but we all played together in the middle of the un-paved street; there were hardly any cars. We were playing in front of Anita's house when she said, "My mother's baking cookies. Let's go inside and get some." Mrs. Muller was well known as the best baker on the street. The smells of her baking beckoned us inside. Her specialties were Milk Tart with cinnamon on top, Romany Creams held together with a chocolate filling, and the best of all; the six inch long, syrupy braided Koeksisters, which were made of fried dough, soaked in sticky syrup. One bite of the crusty Koeksisters released the sweet liquid into my mouth, and the Milk Tart was smooth and rich on my tongue.

Anita's parents always said bad things about the Africans. Whenever we walked into the house her mother was usually yelling at the maid.

"What do you mean there's no more soap? Why didn't you tell me yesterday?"

"Madam, yesterday there was soap."

"They're all so stupid," her father said. "They can't be trusted. If we gave them an inch they'd take over the whole damn country. You'd think they'd be grateful that we give them jobs, but they're not."

"The Kaffirs are all the same," her mother added.

I tried not to look at their maid when Mr. and Mrs. Muller spoke like that in front of her. The maid stood with her back to us, busying herself at the sink with the dishes, but it must have been a terrible thorn embedded deep in her heart, hearing this kind of talk day after day. I never heard my parents say things like that.

I wonder if Anita's parents say bad things about the Jews when I'm not there. I wouldn't be surprised. What would I do if they said something against the Jews in front of me? Would I stay quiet like the maid? I can't argue with a grown-up, so I probably wouldn't say anything ... but I'd tell my parents.

At home, I told my mother what Mr. and Mrs. Muller said about the Africans.

"Lorraine, don't listen to that kind of talk. They don't think of the Africans as people with feelings, but they're human beings just like everyone else," she said, shaking her head.

"Yesterday in school Kobus told me that his father said they're different and don't have feelings like us." Kobus lived behind us. The Mullers and Kobus's parents weren't the only ones who spoke like that. I heard that kind of talk everywhere.

My father seemed less forthcoming than my mother during conversations like this. When he did join in, it was to remind us that the whites are outnumbered twenty to one.

"If we gave them the vote, it would be the end of us," he said.

I was always aware of the slight difference of political opinions that existed between my parents. Neither of them supported the views of the Afrikaner Nationalist Party, the supporters of apartheid, and neither of my parents ever voted for them, but nonetheless my mother was far more liberal (by South African standards, at any rate) than my dad. I was always torn between the two as I listened to their views. Both made sense. I agreed with my mom: "Of course they're human beings with feelings." Then I heard my dad's voice in my head, "They outnumber us twenty to one. So be careful about giving them power."

—⊷⊰⋙——

ELSIE LIVED NEXT door to us, and even at the age of five I wished I could replace my dark straight brown hair and brown eyes with blonde hair and blue eyes like hers. We were always in each other's homes. In Elsie's house, however, something was different. Besides the Springbok and Impala heads mounted on her walls, with long horns and glassy dead eyes that looked right at me and gave me the creeps, there were empty glasses all over the place. In her parents' bedroom there were bottles of brandy on the nightstands. Her mother, whom I called Auntie Martha (Afrikaans children referred to any adult as "Uncle" or "Auntie" as a sign of respect even if they weren't related to you), was a friendly lady, but I noticed that her face often looked red and puffy and her eyes seemed dazed and unfocused. The house reeked of brandy.

I smelled the same smell on her breath when she kissed me hello. I politely asked her, "Hoe gaan dit met Tannie vandag?" She answered my question by saying that she was fine. In Afrikaans one never addressed an adult with the pronoun "you." It was always in the third person. Elsie's mother didn't look fine. She swayed slightly as she spoke to me. Then Auntie Martha and Oom Jan went into their bedroom and shut the door for hours, just the way they had done many times before. Elsie never dared to knock on the door. It was a barricade, like the curly wrought-iron burglar-proofing on the windows. It seemed to say, "What's inside stays in and what's outside stays out."

I told Elsie that I'd ask my mother if she could come to our house for supper.

When we walked into my house, I could hear my mother humming *When Irish Eyes Are Smiling*. (If it wasn't an Irish song, my mother would be singing Doris Day songs like Que Sera Sera.) We found her busy creaming butter and sugar in a bowl, preparing to make cinnamon buns, known in Yiddish as Bulkalach. She was about to add the flour, cinnamon, raisins and nuts when I asked her if Elsie could stay for supper.

"Yes, of course."

While we were waiting for supper we played our favorite game on the front lawn, spinning around and around with my full skirt flared out like a tent in a fluttery ripple and counting to twenty. Bonzo, my black Terrier, barked, yapped and jumped up and down as we spun. My arms were stretched out sideways for balance, like the whirling Dervishes in Turkey, and the goal was to see who could stay standing the longest before we collapsed in dizzy heaps of giggles on the freshly mowed, sweet smelling grass. The grass felt soft under my bare feet. We never wore shoes. All the kids loved to walk barefoot. The warm earth greeted the soles of my feet with a kind of do-it-yourself massage. My soles were as tough as a pony's hooves, just as a country girl's should be. Whether it was a surface of hard pebbles, soft grass that tickled, or just the sand, it always felt good for me to be in direct contact with the ground.

As we lay there on the grass, the flower garden swirled around me in a blur of snapdragons, pansies, roses and sweet peas with colors of bright scarlet, pinks and mauve, and they offered their sweet perfume. Piet, our "garden boy," was watering the flowers the way he did at five o'clock every afternoon. He was called a boy, even though he was a grown man of about forty. All the Africans were referred to as "boy" or "girl" even if they were grown up. This condescending way of referring to a black adult was so common that we didn't even notice it. I wonder now if Piet felt insulted by being called a "garden boy." He always kept the smile on his face, revealing teeth that looked even whiter against his dark brown skin; but who knows what he was really thinking. Maybe he, too, was so used to the term that he accepted it. The Afrikaners called the Africans many worse names than that.

We lay on our backs on the lawn that day, and noticed the shapes of the clouds. "Daar is 'n hond!" I excitedly pointed out the shape of the dog. Elsie said, "kyk na daardie ou man se gesig." Sure enough I saw the perfect shape of an old man's face. One wispy white cloud looked like a bride's delicate veil. We watched until gusts of wind blew away the cotton-like shapes.

The garage door was open and I could see the biltong, a South African delicacy of cured dried meat, hanging from the hooks along the wire that my father had strung from one wall to the other. My dad made his own biltong. He seasoned the raw meat with kosher salt, vinegar, coriander and black pepper. Then he stuck an "s" shape wire through the raw meat and hung it up to dry. After a few weeks, when the biltong was ready, he would slice it into thin slices with his silver pocketknife, balancing each slice on the blade as he brought it to his mouth. It always made me nervous when he brought the razor sharp blade to his mouth like that. I was afraid he'd slice his tongue one day. Sometimes we'd just take the whole ten inch long piece of biltong, hold it in our hands, and rip off pieces of the dried meat with our teeth, like a cannibal. South African mothers often gave their babies a chunk of biltong to chew on when they were teething.

It was October, and the blossoms on the trees were pink and delicate as butterfly wings, with the aroma and promise of spring. Soundlessly they fell from the branches. In our dry little town, with 340 days of sunshine a year, rain was precious. The week before, however, we had gotten a good soaking rain. The unpaved roads, with their cinnamon-colored, powdery sand, were turned to mud. Elsie and I squished through the warm mud puddles, which looked and felt like chocolate pudding as it seeped between our toes. The flowers always seemed so grateful for their rain bath; I noticed the drops glistening on their delicate petals.

We heard my mother calling and went inside. The aroma of cinnamon buns baking in the oven engulfed the house. She loved to bake, and there was always a large tin of cookies in the sideboard. There were ginger cookies, shortbread, and my favorite, chocolate cookies. (I spent a great deal of time as a young child trying to figure out how to take a few without it looking as if any were missing.)

14

"Lorraine, I need you and Elsie to pick some vegetables for the salad."

We went to the vegetable garden in the back of our house, basket in hand, to "pick our salad." I plucked the peas, tomatoes and cucumbers right off their vines, while trying to dodge the ever-present Kelly-green grasshoppers. Our vegetables always came fresh out of God's earth. I remember the anticipation of getting ready to tug a carrot out of the rich, dark soil and hoping it was nice and fully-grown, so I didn't have to feel guilty for yanking it out before its time. As I tugged the carrot, I dislodged a dark pink, almost transparent earthworm from its hiding place and watched as it squirmed around making S shapes as it wiggled. After that, we picked fruit for dessert. I reached up and plucked a luscious fig right off the branch and took a big bite. We laughed as the sweet juice oozed from the fig and ran down the sides of my mouth. I wiped the juice with the back of my arm. Piet had to help my Dad put up stakes to support the branches of the fig and peach trees, which were so heavily laden with fruit that the branches bent under their weight, brushing the ground below.

"Be careful not to spoil your appetite for supper," Gracie, our maid, said as she walked past us to the chicken run, collecting fresh eggs for our breakfast the next morning.

Because of the meager salaries that the Africans were paid, every white family could afford at least one servant, regardless of their economic level. Most had two.

When we sat down to eat, Elsie said she liked my mother's Jewish cooking, especially the beetroot soup and sour cream. She laughed at the name "borscht." We both tried to copy my dad as he used his knife to peel the skin off the boiled potato for the soup. The soup was followed with crispy fried fish and chips. The chips were wedges of fried potatoes, smothered in salt and vinegar. My father ate chicken skins called "gribbenez." Elsie laughed when she heard the word "gribbenez." "Wat is dit?" she asked. My dad explained that it was pieces of chicken skins that were deep fried until they were brown and crispy — a kind of Jewish bacon. She watched as he smeared a thick layer of schmaltz on a piece of rye bread. Then he sprinkled this layer of chicken fat with salt, put on the gribenez and topped it off with greasy fried onions. Looking back, I realize that it was a meal that would make any self-respecting cardiologist cringe!

I felt like gagging when I heard my mother on the phone, giving her weekly order to the butcher.

"Hello Mr. Michaelson. I'll have one oxtail, some kidneys, a tongue, calves' liver, some chicken livers and a few marrow bones." My stomach churned as she read out her order of body parts.

———

ELSIE WAS THE one who told me that the soft pink meat in my tongue sandwiches was actually made from the tongue of a cow. I didn't believe her. The next day, when Gracie handed me what had up to that point been my favorite sandwich, I asked her whether or not it was true.

"You mean this is actually a cow's *tongue*?"

Gracie laughed. "Yes, it's a cow's tongue."

I was shocked.

"From *inside the cow's mouth*?"

She was really laughing now. I never ate it again.

I remember the day I went with my father to the farm to bring Gracie to our house. We drove in my dad's rattling old lorry with its open "bakkie" in the back. The lorry was a sad metal structure held together by luck and a prayer. My dad's big hands circled the steering wheel with fingers that looked like bananas. There was no air-conditioning, and the open window offered little relief from the sweltering heat. It also allowed the dust from the dirt road to settle all over us. I was wearing shorts, and my bare legs were sticking to the vinyl seats as the lorry bumped along the uneven dirt road. I looked out the side window at all the small clay huts that dotted the landscape of the farms as we drove by.

Suddenly my dad braked hard, and I jerked forward. There was a herd of fifty or so sheep taking up the entire road. They walked as though they had the whole day, which they did. We had to sit and wait until the man with the long stick was able to herd them off the road.

"A farmer must have just bought them from the livestock sales," my dad said as he wiped the sweat off his brow with the back of his sleeve. When the road cleared, the lorry groaned and sputtered into action again.

"How can one man control all the sheep? How do they know to stay together?" I asked.

"They just do. They all follow the one in front. That's why they say that people who blindly follow others are like sheep," he said laughing. I could see the heat waves in the air in front of us, yet I had to turn up the window every time a car passed and kicked up dust and pebbles against the windshield. When we arrived at the farm I saw six round, dark brown clay huts with pointed gray, dry thatched roofs. Thomas was there to greet us. He clapped his hands, just one clap, bowed his head slightly, the way they all did when addressing a white person, and greeted us with a big smile that revealed a space between his yellowing teeth.

"Goeie dag Baas en Miss Lorraine." It sounded like, "Mees Lorraine."

Thomas was the head worker on our farm, where my dad raised cattle and sheep. My dad would buy the animals at the cattle sales and transport them to the farm, where they stayed until they were fattened up and ready to be shipped to the meat market in Johannesburg.

Thomas lived there with his wife, his many children and his extended family. Whenever the daughters on the farm reached a certain age, they would be sent to work as domestic help in the homes of white families in Reitz. Gracie was Thomas's oldest daughter and the first one to leave.

Thomas's khaki shirt hung loosely on his bony frame and there were a few buttons missing. He took off his hat and crumpled it in his wrinkled dry brown hands, hands that looked like leather, as he listened to my dad's instructions.

"Ehh ja baas," Yes boss, he responded dutifully nodding his head while he looked down at the ground. The Africans did not look a white person straight in the eye while receiving instructions. They had to look down at the ground. This was the way it was, all over the country.

It was a typically sweltering day, and I saw that the women were walking around in long colorful skirts with bold geometric shapes. Some were walking back from the river, balancing large clay pots of water on their heads. One woman had a baby sleeping in the sling of fabric tied around her waist, a quiet bulge in the bright hammock of cloth on her back. The little children ran around stark naked, no shoes and no clothes, except for a string of colored clay beads around their necks. Their brown bodies and potbellies were covered in dust. They were happily playing under eucalyptus trees, which offered some respite from the torrid sun. The trees filled the air with pungent eucalyptus aroma. The children stopped and stared at my father and me, not quite sure what to make of us.

I couldn't talk to them because I didn't speak their Bantu language and they couldn't speak Afrikaans or English, but my dad brought some sweets and gave the bag to me to hand out to them. They gathered around me and clapped their hands, one clap and then cupped them together to receive the sweets. This was the way they said "thank you." I noticed a few old men wrapped in blankets walk by. Their thin, mangy dog wandered toward me. Thomas scolded the dog and yelled, "Voetsek!" The dog scurried away.

The long wheat-colored dry grass swayed slightly in the breeze, looking as if it was waving to us, but the heat was smothering. I felt thirsty, and Thomas's wife invited me into the hut for a drink.

"Come inside, Mees Lorraine."

She was bent and frail, with cheeks that were withered like a bad apple. I stooped down so I wouldn't hit my head on the low entrance, and then I blinked for a few minutes as I adjusted to the darkness inside the hut. Soon shapes swam out of the grayness and formed into four small stools and mats on the floor. The mats served as a place to sleep and a place to eat. I noticed that it was spotless. The clay floor was swept, and the makeshift shelves with the tin plates and cups were all clean and neatly packed on top of each other. On the shelf was a jug of water covered with a doily. She poured some into a tin cup and handed it to me. It tasted cool and refreshing as the water ran down my parched throat. After giving me the drink she resumed her task of sweeping the area outside in front of the hut. The broom was made of long dry grasses, held together at the top with string and beading, and it made a swishing sound. She hummed an African song as she swept. The copper sun was starting its descent, and it was time to leave.

Gracie dutifully climbed onto the back of my dad's lorry. As the lorry rumbled to life, I waved to the children as they started to run after us, smiling broadly and waving wildly. I couldn't believe how long they kept up with us, running right behind the moving lorry.

"Look at them! They can really run!" I was astonished. The mangy dog barked, the running children finally receded, and we were on our way.

"Daddy, why do they wear blankets when it's so hot?"

"Because they believe that the blankets keep out the heat. They also drink hot tea because they believe it cools the body." I didn't understand the logic.

As the lorry chugged along the dry dirt road, the wheels spat pebbles up behind us. We drove past the field of mielies, with their green leaves covering the stalks of yellow kernels inside. "The mielie crop looks good this year," my dad noted, nodding his head in satisfaction as he eyed the corn. We saw some of the women at the nearby stream doing their laundry. They were rubbing the clothes on a large flat boulder that rose out of the water, and we could hear them singing mournful African songs. They piled the washed clothing into baskets and placed the baskets on top of their heads, ready to carry back to the huts.

"Daddy how do they balance those baskets on their heads?" My dad laughed. "I don't know."

This was the first time that Gracie had ever left the farm. When she stepped into our house, it was the first time she walked into a brick house with separate bedrooms, bathroom and kitchen. When she entered our home that day, she immediately turned around and ran out screaming.

"Oh Meeses, I can't work for you. There are ghosts in your house."

Mystified, my mother asked her why she was screaming and why she thought there were ghosts. She was wringing her hands nervously and replied in a quivering voice, "Meeses, your furniture is talking." Gracie had never before heard a radio.

My mother calmed her down and coaxed her back into the house. She was fascinated by the way water flowed out of the faucets, and we had to show her how to flush a toilet. That night she blinked as her eyes made their first acquaintance with electric lights.

CHAPTER
Two

The Farm

"I hated that farm," said my mother, chewing her thumbnail.

My parents were married on August 13, 1944, and for the first few years of their marriage they lived on a farm in the Orange Free State. Throughout her life, my mother made no secret of the fact that she had detested living in that desolate, isolated place. Reitz was about an hour away, and Johannesburg, where my mother grew up, was a three-hour drive. She was an active, energetic city girl stuck in the middle of nowhere.

It happened like this. One day, during her single years, her friend Ann said, "Sadie, I want to introduce you to someone. His name is David Lotzof. He's a farmer who is visiting his family here in Johannesburg." As soon as she set eyes on him, she told me, his rugged good looks, his wavy brown hair and the sparkle in his blue eyes attracted her.

"You must have really loved Daddy to have agreed to go and live on the farm," I commented to her while I sat at the kitchen table. I had a photo album open and even at the age of ten, I loved to look at family photos, and I loved to hear her tell me about her earlier life.

23

My parents' wedding

"When Daddy proposed to me," she said, "he promised me we would only live on the farm for one year, and then, when he harvested and sold the crops, we'd be able to move to the nearby town, Reitz, and buy a house. I agreed, and we were married in Johannesburg the following year."

"So what happened?" I asked as I turned the page of the album and saw the photo of them, a young bride and groom on their wedding day.

"The plan didn't quite work out that way." She was mashing hard-boiled eggs, first the yolks and then the egg whites, which she would use to decorate the chopped liver; but I could see her agitation in the way she mashed those eggs a bit harder than necessary. "A drought killed off all the crops of mielies and buckwheat. Even the cows and sheep were suffering. It was three years before we were able to leave the farm."

She put her hand in the pocket of her dress to get her keys, and then she called, "Gracie, where are my keys?" With Gracie working right in our house all day, my mother, like all South African housewives, had everything under lock and key. She had a big ring of keys like a jailer. The only problem was that she never remembered where she last left them. Several times a day I heard her call for her keys and Gracie would dutifully bring them to her. "Here's the keys madam," she would answer in her soft voice. I don't know why my mother bothered to lock anything, since it was Gracie, and not my mother, who always knew where the keys were. Although my mother always spoke of treating her servants with respect, I wonder now whether she ever thought of how insulting it was to Gracie to lock up everything. I believe she was oblivious to this. All South African drawers, cabinets and closets came with a lock and a key. The assumption was that the African servants routinely stole things that weren't locked away: another not so-subtle insult. Why *should* my mother have thought about this? While I was living in South Africa, I never thought about it.

My eyes followed as my mother unlocked the kitchen cabinet to get the salt, and I noticed the neat rows of groceries. I scanned the canned fig preserves, canned fish called Lucky Star Pilchards in tomato sauce, sardines, Marmite to spread on toast, a box of Post Toasties cereal, and Tiger Oats with the familiar tiger's head on the front. She relocked the cabinet, put the keys in her pocket, and continued her story.

When she lived in Johannesburg, my mother was a legal secretary and used to volunteer for the Red Cross. But on the farm, instead of typing lawyers' letters, my mother spent her time drawing water from a deep well in the ground because they had no indoor plumbing. She would then carry the bucket of water to their dilapidated stone farmhouse with its corrugated red tin roof.

"You were too young to remember this," she said. She explained how she panicked as she watched the level of the water in the well drop lower and lower due to the drought. The water had to be boiled in large tins on the big cast iron black stove to make it safe for drinking.

I turned the pages of the photo album while she spoke, but I was listening with interest. When she was finished with the hardboiled eggs, she began pushing the fried liver into the grinder and continued to crank the handle as she recounted her miserable life on the farm.

"We used oil lamps and candles at night. I was lonely and I missed my friends in Jo'burg. I missed the library and I missed the active life I had had, celebrating all the Jewish holidays with my family and friends and the charity organizations that I belonged to. There was nothing on the farm. There were no people for miles around — except for the African workers."

"Didn't you have a car? Couldn't you drive to Reitz?" I asked her.

"We had an old car but we couldn't afford to waste petrol, so we only used the car when we really had to. I was stuck on the farm. I couldn't even talk to the African women because their huts were a long distance away from the farmhouse; and besides, I couldn't speak their Bantu language and they couldn't speak English."

Me at eleven months

"If you were so poor, how could Daddy have people work for him? How did he pay them?"

She explained that the Africans lived on the farm and were paid in kind. This meant that in return for the work they did on the land, they got a small portion of the crops for themselves and they had a place to live. The wives and daughters helped in the houses. This was the way it was on most of the farms in the country.

There was sadness in her voice and a dull ache in my heart as I listened to her. For a minute she stopped cranking the handle, and with the back of her hand she wiped away a stray lock of brown curly hair that had fallen over her pointy glasses. Her stories could go off on many tangents as she strayed from the point, but she always reeled them back, and I listened. I turned to a page in the album where I saw a photo of her as an attractive young woman, with a slim body, nicely shaped calves and thin ankles, smiling with a group of her friends. When I looked up at her in the kitchen, I saw an unhappy woman with nails bitten to the quick.

She told me that two years after their wedding, as the summer months drew to an end and my mother's due date for their first baby (me) got closer, she and my father drove the three-hour trip from the farm to Johannesburg. The plan was that she would stay with her mother and un-married younger brother Seymour until she gave birth. My father would return to work on the farm until he got word that I was born. Then he would drive back to Johannesburg to bring his wife and new baby home to the farm. When she went into labor, Seymour took her to the Florence Nightingale Hospital.

There was always a special bond between my mom and her brother Seymour and she spoke of him often. "Uncle Seymour was born when I was four. He became "my baby" and I loved to play with him," she said with the same smile she had whenever she spoke about him.

But it was different with her older sister Becky. From a very young age she always felt inferior to Becky.

"Becky was my father's favorite. He would always announce "Quiet everyone, Becky's talking." There was much resentment in my mom's voice when she relayed these occasions to me. My mother subsequently left school before she matriculated because she wanted to work and earn her own money.

"I was tired of wearing Becky's old clothes," she told me. "I loved my job as a paralegal."

Now she was telling a different story.

"Uncle Seymour was twenty four," she said. "As we entered the maternity floor, a woman was just about to give birth, and she let out a piercing scream. Uncle Seymour grabbed me by the arm and all the color drained from his face. 'Sadie, I'm not leaving you here. Let's get the hell out of this place!' His voice was filled with terror." She told this story often and always laughed as she recalled the look of horror his face.

March 6, 1946, was not a very significant day in the annals of history. World War II was over, President Truman was in the White House, Jan Smuts headed South Africa, and Israel was not yet a state. But it was a very important day in the lives of Sadie and David Lotzof. That was the day they became parents.

"It's a girl!" my mother said in an excited voice over the phone to my father, who was still on the farm. There was a moment of silence from the other end.

"A girl?"

She could hear the disappointment in his voice. Whenever she told the story she was always quick to add that once he held his seven-pound daughter in his arms, he looked at me, stroked my dark hair and said, "They can all keep their boys."

———<>———

I WAS NAMED after my mother's father, Louis. His Hebrew name was Leib Arieh, which means lion. My Hebrew name Livia means lioness. Most Jews have an English and a Hebrew name. Tradition has it that we're named after a deceased relative to keep their memory and name alive. My mother's father died on December 26, 1939, five years before she got married, so my dad never met her father.

Soon after I was born, my parents drove back to the small rundown house on the farm. "I had to stuff newspapers into the cracks in the walls to keep the draft off you, a newborn baby," she told me. "The wind would whistle and howl as it leaked through the spaces in the walls at night."

These were only the first of many unhappy stories my mom told about my early childhood. One morning while I was having my usual breakfast of Tiger Oats cereal and milk in our kitchen in Reitz, she pulled up a chair and said, "Life is much easier now. The thing I really hated the most on the farm was the outhouse. I was always afraid that a spider would bite me on the behind."

I laughed.

"It wasn't funny, Lorraine."

I cupped my hand over my mouth trying to stifle my giggle fit.

"What did you do in the middle of the night if you had to go?" I asked, "Did you have to go outside in the dark?"

"No. That was the worst of all. We had to pull a chamber pot out from under the bed in the middle of the night."

The chirping of the nocturnal insects and crickets scared her too. She was used to the sounds of people, cars and buses, not animals and insects. "I don't think I was a very pleasant wife in those days. I hated my life." As I read between the lines, I detected the strain that must have existed in their young marriage. On the opposite wall hung a picture of me sitting on a tractor with my father on the farm. I glanced at the picture and realized that growing up on the farm was the only way of life I knew, so I was perfectly happy.

Insects and crickets were part of my life, and I wasn't afraid of them at all. I recalled how every morning, as the sun peeked over the horizon; the "cock-a-doodle-doo" of the rooster announced the start of each new day. Soon the mooing of the cows and the bleating of the sheep reached my ears. The farm was waking up. My friends were the animals and my toys were the rocks, sticks and sand. I had a red leather bunny rabbit and one doll that I put in a stroller. I don't remember any other toys, except for my mother's glass jar filled with hundreds of colored buttons. Whenever she got ready to iron the clothes, I sat at her feet on the faded, cracked linoleum floor, sorting out the buttons. She heated two flat irons; one would remain on the stove to stay hot while she used the other. She sprinkled water on the clothes and I waited for the sizzle as the hot iron met the drops of water on the fabric. As she ironed, I grouped the buttons first by color, then by size. In my imagination they became animals on the farm. The big ones were the cows and bulls, the smaller ones, the sheep, rabbits and dogs, and the tiny ones were the chickens, turkeys and birds. Every half hour or so, she'd open the black heavy cast iron door of the stove to shovel in another pile of black coal. The coal was kept in a grimy shed outside near the kitchen door. She opened the oven door with the long metal stoker, carefully putting its tip into the hook and lifting it up. The yellow flames of the fire bellowed out, screaming hot. The open oven looked like an angry mouth as it swallowed up the black coals my mother fed it. I always backed away so that it wouldn't swallow me too.

My father, my pony and me at age two on the farm

The warm sun streaked orange across the sky the morning my father kissed me and said, "Happy Birthday, Lolzy." I had just turned two. It was March 6, 1948. "Come outside with me. I want to show you your birthday present." As I reached up, his huge hand engulfed mine. He pushed open the rickety kitchen door and we stepped outside. I could smell the farm, the eucalyptus trees and horse manure. There stood a beautiful pony with big brown eyes and long lashes that blinked at me as if to say "hello." I squealed with delight and hesitatingly reached out and patted him on his thigh. That was the only place I could reach. The hair felt smooth and warm. My heart was pounding fast as my dad's large, strong hands hoisted me up onto the back of the black and white Shetland pony. It seemed so high, but I wasn't afraid because he was right there next to me. I was never afraid when I was with my dad. I knew he would always keep me safe.

With my mom on the farm

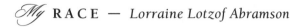

I named my pony Berry. I sat perched on Berry's back and because there was no saddle, his hair tickled my bare legs; when I held onto the bridle, the brown leather reins felt hard in my hands. My father took the reins and led me around the farm. Berry was moving his jaw as he chewed on the bit. We passed the field of green mielies and the grazing cows. I heard their long, low, deep call: "Moooooo." They swished flies off their backs. All day swish, swish. We passed the old rusted plow and the broken-down tractor that I liked to climb on. Then we came to the huts where the Africans lived. Thomas and his children waved to me but I was too afraid to let go of the reins to wave back. It was early in the morning, but already the heat from the sun was breathing down my neck and Berry's hooves made a loud clopping sound on the dry mustard-colored earth. I tried to imitate the sound of his trotting hooves by clicking my tongue, first with my lips wide like a smile, and then by forming my lips into a small circle. "Click clock click clock." Life for a two-year-old on the farm was complete bliss, and all I could ever want.

CHAPTER
Three

A Fool's Paradise

"Guess what, Lorraine. Today's the day we're moving away from this miserable farm. We're going to live in Reitz!"

I was about four years old when my mother began joyfully packing up the house with their few meager belongings. I didn't quite understand all the excitement going on. Reitz was a half step better than the farm. Its population was about two thousand — a real metropolis by comparison. Even after we moved there, though, my father kept the farm and continued to raise cattle and sheep.

I don't remember the first year in Reitz but I clearly remember the following year. A few days after my fifth birthday, my mother came to me and said, "We have a special surprise for you. We're going to have a baby."

I jumped up and down clapping my hands. "Yea!" I shouted. All my friends had a brother or a sister. Even my cousin Rikki, with her curly red hair and her face sprinkled with freckles had a baby brother Larry. I was the only one without, and I often asked my mother when I was going to have a brother or sister. Once they told me a baby was on the way, I started to count the months. My mother let me choose the name for the baby ... from a list of options she and my father had created. I chose the name Selwyn.

I was five and a half when Selwyn was born on September 16, 1951, weighing nine pounds. When he first came home, my mother laid him down on the bed with a hill of pillows on either side so he wouldn't fall off. I uncovered the blankets so that I could carefully count his fingers and toes. Ten of each: A perfect baby! I was allowed to sit in a chair and feed him a bottle. I was even allowed to brush his duck-fluff newborn hair gently, of course.

How proud I was! Now I too had a baby brother in my house, just like Elsie and Rikki. Elsie came to see my new brother, but soon we were more interested in joining the kids outside. We played outdoors in the warm weather all year round, until the moon replaced the sun or until hunger pangs insisted it was dinnertime.

Five and a half was a great age for me: Not only did I get a new brother, but I also started primary school. The first grade was called Sub A. Primary school lasted for seven years: Sub A, then sub B, followed by standard one through five. I felt very grown up in my school uniform. I looked in the mirror as I smoothed my green gym tunic with my hands. I checked my white shirt and straightened the green striped tie. What I didn't like was that I had to wear shoes. I pulled white socks over my heels every morning and pushed my feet into black lace-up shoes.

"My toes feel smushed together," I complained to my mother. "I wish I could go to school barefoot."

Those strange-feeling, laced-up shoes walked me to the single storey school building with its whitewashed walls and red tin corrugated roof. Other kids on the street joined me as I went by. Even with shoes on, I always walked faster than my friends.

———⊰•⊱———

"Indians are never allowed to be here in the Free State," my mother told me one day as she walked me home from school. A car with an Indian family inside had just driven past us.

Me at age five in my school uniform

"They look like the people we see in Durban," I told my mom.

"Yes," she said. "They must be on their way to Durban. They can only drive through on their way somewhere else." She said this in a matter-of-fact way, as if resigned to the laws of the land.

Although apartheid echoed from one end of the country to the other, its ideology was carried one step further in the Free State, the geographical heart of South Africa. It was the only place in the country where no Indians were allowed *at any time* except to drive through on the way to their destination elsewhere. As we continued to walk, my mother recalled how the Indians were brought to South Africa originally to help chop the sugarcane in the fields in Natal, all around Durban. "We're living in a fool's paradise," she said. "How long does the government think it can get away with suppressing the blacks and all the others who are not white? We're such a small minority. They outnumber us twenty to one. How long can they get away with it?"

I didn't understand what she meant. Did she want an answer from me, or was she just thinking out loud? I heard her say things like this to my father a lot. He would just tell her that there was nothing we could do about it. If we spoke out against the government, he constantly told her; we'd be arrested and sent to jail. He reminded her that we were living in a police state, where we could be jailed with no trial. He warned my mother to be less outspoken. "You can get into trouble if the wrong person hears you and reports you."

Looking back, I realize that my mother struggled with the notion that her grandparents fled Eastern European oppression — only to find themselves living under another oppressive regime. This time, their white skin put them on the side of the oppressors. My mother might not have been able to say anything about her surroundings out in public, but she certainly spoke her mind at home. I heard this ongoing conversation between my parents throughout my childhood, and I, too, learned from a young age to hold such conversations quietly — or in the privacy of our own home, behind the closed doors and the curly white burglar-proofing.

My mother's distaste for the South African government could only be matched by her strong love for the State of Israel. No one ever dared to say anything against Israel in her presence or they would have to deal with her wrath. Arafat is lucky he never came face to face with my mother. She bought me many picture books about the Israelis and how they were building up the young country and turning the desert into a garden. I too, developed a strong admiration for those pioneers who bravely toiled the desert and made it bloom.

Later, as an adult, I would read how the European Jews of the first Aliya immigrated to a vastly under-populated Palestine, and the land onto which they moved was bought primarily from absentee landlords and real estate speculators. This region was an appropriate place for the Jewish refugees for two reasons: first because of its close connections to their history and ideology: and second, because of the demographics of the land to which they were moving. The word they used was *"returning."* My mother dreamed of moving there and spoke about it often.

"We should move to Israel," she would say to my dad.

"I'm not moving to Israel." My father's answer was always short, emphatic and unwavering.

"Why not?" she asked.

"Because I can't speak the language and what would I do there?"

"We could live on a Kibbutz or a Moshav and you could continue farming," she answered.

"I'm making a good living here and I'm not moving."

She spoke often about how the Jews, after the terrors of World War II and the unspeakable events of the Holocaust, found themselves at the mercy of other countries. Would these countries allow the Jews to immigrate into their borders or not? Some let them in, and some refused them entry. "With the existence of the state of Israel," she said, "no Jew will ever again be without a homeland."

What she was referring to was the policy whereby no Jewish person in the entire world would ever be turned away from Israel if they wanted to go and live there. They'd immediately become Israeli citizens. Even though I had a high regard for the young State of Israel, and an enormous admiration for its people, I had to agree with my dad. South Africa was the only home I'd known, and that's where my friends and family were. I didn't share my mother's idealism of wanting to move there.

"I don't know what we're waiting for," she continued. "One day there'll be a bloody uprising in this country. Remember the German Jews said it could never happen to them."

This parallel about the German Jews was her mantra. I heard her repeat it many times.

"We're not moving," was the response from my dad's corner.

That was always the end of the discussion — for a while. Inevitably, it would come up again.

40

WHEN WE REACHED our house, after the short walk from the school, Gracie was waiting to give me a fish paste sandwich and a glass of milk. After kicking off my shoes, happy to be barefoot again, I sat down to eat. I watched as she rinsed out the empty milk bottle and placed it at the back door, where Oom Koos, the dairyman, would take it as he did early each morning, and replace it with a full bottle of fresh milk. I loved Gracie. She was kind, with a soft voice. When she smiled, her teeth, with the space in front just like her father Thomas had, flashed white in contrast to her dark brown face. Gracie rubbed Vaseline on her arms and legs, making her skin look shiny like the glaze on a chocolate cake. Her hair was always covered by a colorful headscarf that she called a "doek".

I did my homework quickly each day so that I could meet the kids outside on the street. Our games were simple and unsophisticated. We divided ourselves into two groups and played cowboys and crooks or hide and go seek. The way we chose the one to be "it" was to stand in a circle clenching our fists, thumbs turned upwards. Then one person would go around the circle touching each fist as he said "Ickle ockle blue bockle, fishes in the sea. If you want a pretty one, please pick me. Ickle ockle out." Whoever was "out" was "it".

Andre, my friend Anita's older brother, taught me how to take a branch from a tree, one that was just thin enough to bend. Then we would tie a piece of string to each end, making a bow. For the arrow, we used a straight stick, and I learned how to take a stone and file the tip into a point. We would line up some old tin cans and aim the arrows at them from a distance to see how many we could knock over. When we heard a "plink" we knew we had hit a can. Andre also taught me how to take three thin, pliable branches from the willow tree and braid them into long strips. Elsie's brother Johan had an even better trick: he could take a long piece of wire and bend it into the shapes of cars and lorries.

———◆———

"YOU CHEATED," THE boys shouted at me.

"I didn't cheat," I protested, feeling tears stinging the corners of my eyes.

The accusation came one afternoon as the annual sports day at school was nearing and we decided to play "Olympics" in front of Anita's house.

Andre had drawn a line with a stick across the dirt road to mark the starting line, and another about sixty yards ahead to mark the finish. There were about ten boys and girls, ranging in ages from five to eleven years old. I was five and a half. I remember I was wearing my favorite yellow sundress, the one with the straps at each shoulder tied in a bow.

I felt the sun-baked earth under my feet. A row of bare toes lined up just behind the starting line. Andre was the starter. He said "Op julle plekke, gereet ...!" I waited while he said on your marks, get set. When he said "gaan!" (Go!), I shot out like a missile, as fast as my five-year-old string skinny legs could carry me. The skirt of my sundress flapped wildly in the wind and I pumped my arms as hard as I could. I crossed the fin-

42

ish line first. The boys, most of them much older than I was, were angry because I beat them.

"You must have cheated and started before Andre said go. How else you could you have beaten Koos and Jakob, who are eleven?"

It hurt to be falsely accused. They said we had to run the race over. So, we lined up again, and I beat them a second time. I didn't mean to make them angry; I was just as surprised as they were that I had won. But I felt glad and proud to have beaten them a second time, to show them that I hadn't cheated the first time. They couldn't have been *that* angry, because from then on, whenever we played games where we had to be divided into teams, they chose me first. Little did I know it at the time, but that race would be the first of hundreds more to come ... and running would eventually change my life completely.

We were so busy with our races that none of us realized how late it was. I didn't start walking home until it was already dark. When I got home, my mother was furious. "Where were you? We've been waiting for you for supper." She ordered me into her bedroom, where she took my father's brown leather belt off the hanger and made me lie on the bed on my stomach. I cried even before I felt the first smack. My dignity was much more hurt than my butt. She always spoke during the spankings.

"Don't," *smack*, "ever", *smack*, "do", *smack*, "that", *smack*, "again", *smack*.

I was glad her sentences weren't longer. I always felt that my mother's spankings were much less effective than my father's very different way of disciplining me. Because of his strength, he was afraid of really hurting me, so he left the spankings to her. Instead, when he wanted to make a point or punish me, he would sit me down, look me straight in the eye, and tell me how disappointed he was in what I had done. I felt so bad that I had disappointed him that I swore I'd never do it — whatever "it" was — again.

After winning my first race at age five

After my mother spanked me, I was usually left feeling angry and resentful. But not today. My mind was consumed with that race. I couldn't believe I had beaten all the big boys. I had no idea I could run as fast as that. I was excited about the upcoming school sports day, and I was chomping at the bit, ready to seize the next opportunity to race again.

———⊰•⊱———

OVER THE BLARING loudspeaker, Afrikaans Folk music filled the air for miles. All the farmers and their wives had come into town and set up "braais" around the field. Smoke curled up to the skies from these barbeques, where lamb chops and boerewors sausages grilled all day long. The sports day had finally arrived, the highlight of the year, and the whole town joined in the festivities. The school was divided into teams of different colors. I was on "die geel span." The yellow team — which made me happy because yellow was my favorite color. With bare feet, and wearing a rosette in our team color, we marched around the dirt track. Left, right, left, right, behind a banner, as if it were the actual opening ceremonies at the Olympics. I was in first grade and was going to run in the "under six race".

The day before, I had come home from school and told my parents, "We practiced running at school today, and I won all my races. I want you to come and watch me run tomorrow in the sports day."

They didn't pay too much attention. My mother stopped singing "Daisy, Daisy Give Me your Answer Do", and casually said, "That's nice, Lorraine. As soon as I'm finished feeding Selwyn, I'll walk over." Conveniently, the track was across the street from our house.

The silver steel of the starter's gun glistened in the sunlight as he raised it above his head for the start of my race. I lined up with the other five-year-old girls on the dirt track, and when the gun sounded, I took off like a rocket, with my bare feet eating up the dirt on the track and my white knee length skirt flapping around my legs. I heard my mother's voice calling, "Go, Lorraine!"

Age eight, running my first relay race

"You won by about twenty yards," exclaimed my father with a broad smile on his face.

"You ran so fast that if you had a ponytail, it would have stuck straight out," he said laughing. The next day I was excited to see my name appear in the local paper:

"Winner of the under 6 race, Lorraine Lotzof."

Running turned out to be my means of winning a sense of belonging. I wasn't exactly fully accepted by my teachers, peers and the town's folk, but my ability to win races elevated me to a level of importance in their eyes. I was different — the only Jewish child in the school — but that became secondary to my ability to run fast. It was a very big deal to people that I earned points for my school. This was because we lived in a sports-crazy country. I'm sure if I had been a great pianist or artist, it wouldn't have been the same. I was good at what the town's folk considered important.

Not only had I found an avenue to acceptance ... I loved running. It gave me a feeling of exhilaration and personal expression, a special kind of freedom in what I could tell, even as a child was a stifling and oppressive society.

Elsie phoned me the next day to say "good shot" for winning my race. It was easy for Elsie to remember my phone number. It was 364. It was even easier for me to remember hers. It was 25. No one in the town had a phone number of more than three digits. I cranked the handle on the heavy black phone and waited to hear Marie, the operator, ask "Nommer asseblief." Whenever she asked me for a number, I would imagine my voice snaking through the phone lines. We were very fortunate to have our own private line. Many of my friends shared a phone line with other families. In those cases they had to pick up the receiver and listen to hear if another family was using the phone. Then they'd hang up and wait until the line was clear before making their call. I was always very careful not to mention any secrets to my friends over the phone because their neighbors could be listening in.

My father never had to worry about people listening in to his conversation when he phoned my grandparents, who had moved to Johannesburg. He spoke to them in Yiddish because they couldn't speak English. No one in Reitz spoke Yiddish. We were one of just three Jewish families. He would phone the operator, and book the trunk call. Local calls went through right away, but trunk calls to distant towns required my father to hang up and wait about an hour until Marie called back, connecting him with his parents. I heard him say;

"Vos machs du?" He was asking about their health. "Ich zoched, vos machs du?" He repeated his question louder the second time. Then he filled them in on our news and told them that we were all healthy, thank God. "Alla bees zeier goot, adank Got. Der kinder bees ech goot." After more yelling so my grandfather could hear him, he'd finally end the conversation by saying "zai gezund," keep well. From these conversations I learned to understand Yiddish.

The next call was from Elsie.

"Howzit?" This was the South African way of combining the three words, (how is it?) into one.

She asked me to walk with her to the café to buy a loaf of bread and some milk for her mother. She had two shillings and a sixpence in her pocket to get some black flat licorice and toffees too. Our currency was the British pound, shillings and pence. South Africa was a member of the British Commonwealth, and we sang "God save the Queen" before every sports event and before every movie showing.

With her coins tied to the corner of her white handkerchief so she wouldn't lose the money, we were off on our fifteen-minute walk to the shops, kicking pebbles with our bare toes as we went. Even though Elsie was five and I had turned six, we roamed around the town without any grownup supervision. It was perfectly safe; the town was so small that we could greet everyone by name. It was also safe for a young child to cross the street alone, because there was rarely more than one car an hour. As we reached the shops, the sun sat high in the sky, it was about 1.30pm. When we got to the store, a sign on the door read, "Out for lunch between 1 and 2 pm." How silly of us to forget that every store and business closed so that the employees could go home for lunch and take a nap. Only the Greek café owned by Maropi and Jimmy Pappadopolis was open.

"They work like dogs," my mother had once said about Maropi and Jimmy, because of the long hours the café was open. The café was our refuge that day; we sat eating the licorice, waiting until Mr. Brummer woke up from his midday nap to open up his grocery shop. I don't know why everyone in town was so tired that they needed a nap, but that is what they all did every day. If the pace of life was any slower, we'd all have been standing still.

When I got home, it was time for my favorite radio show: John Saxon's "No Place to Hide." There was no TV in South Africa yet. I had to use my imagination as I listened to stories on the large brown wooden radio, transporting me to other worlds. I never knew what John Saxon looked like, so I had to form a picture in my mind around the sound of his voice. He had to be very handsome and brave the way his spaceship flew to other planets. After that show I turned the knob and watched as the red dial moved from one number to the next, listening to the crackling sounds of the poor reception, making my way through the chopped off sentences until I found the right station. The FM had much better reception. The radio station known as LM was in Lorenzo Marques in Mozambique, and played pop music all the time. The announcer would say "This is Lorenzo Marques for happy listening." Happy listening for me was Elvis Presley ordering "Uh uh, honey, lay off of my blue suede shoes," and Pat Boone writing love letters in the sand. I often saw Gracie dancing to the music as she dusted the furniture in the living room, introducing an African style of dancing to Elvis's songs. Gracie was no longer afraid of the radio. Some of my friends' parents said that listening to pop music could lead to sin. The Afrikaner farmers said that pop music was anti-God. We listened anyway.

The apartheid laws specified that the African servants weren't allowed to sleep in the house or sit at our table for meals. So Gracie and Piet, our garden boy, ate in the back yard near the vegetable garden. They slept in a separate structure behind the main house, just like the domestic help in every other house in South Africa. This was just the way it was; none of us thought of living any differently.

The servants' structure had two bedrooms and a bathroom. Gracie's room was sparse and her bed had a coir mattress. Coir was a kind of horsehair filling that caused the mattress to sag in the middle. Like everyone of her culture, the four legs of her bed were raised up on at least three bricks. When I asked her "Hoekom is jou bed so hoog?" she explained that the bed needed to be high enough so that the "Tokkalossie" wouldn't catch her while she was sleeping. The Tokkalossie was a little demon, supposedly about two feet high, that the Africans believed might come into their room at night.

I was allowed to eat outside the house with the servants, and did occasionally, but not vice versa. I remember one night when I decided to have supper outside with Gracie and Piet: we sat on large over-turned cans, around a three-legged black cast iron pot that rested on a small prymus stove, which was basically a hot-plate with a flame under it. They spoke to each other in Zulu and occasionally laughed as the other told a funny story. I wished I could understand what they were saying. They could understand my language, but I couldn't understand theirs. They weren't trying to exclude me; it was just natural for them to communicate with each other in their native language.

In the pot was beef or lamb swimming in gravy. In another pot Gracie cooked "mieliepap." This was a maize mixture that you mushed in your hands to make into a ball. Then the "pap" was dipped into the gravy. Delicious.

After my meal with Gracie and Piet, I went back inside and sat down at the table in the kitchen to do homework. I swished away a fly from my book and Gracie picked up a fly swatter and started to chase it. Flies regularly found their way into the house. The windows were open all day and there were no screens. The curly burglar-proofing kept out burglars, but not flies. We got rid of the flies by hanging sticky curly orange paper from the ceiling where they would land, never to leave, or else we swatted them. Gracie and I played a game to see who could swat the most flies. First she covered the jug of water on the table with a doily, which had beading around the edges to give it weight so it would stay covered. Then she handed me a fly swatter and took one for herself. "Een, twee, drie vier, vyf," we counted in Afrikaans. Piet just took off his shoe and killed them with one hard swat. He never missed. The small black flies were bad enough, but I hated the big green ones. Their loud, constant buzzing was grating to my ears. I went for them first.

When my "huiswerk" was done, I put away my schoolbooks and it was time for my bath. My mother never forgot her days on the farm, and as she turned on the tap she often said in an excited voice, "Such luxury.

I can turn on the tap in the bathroom or kitchen and clean clear water comes pouring out. One tap for cold and the other for hot with just a flick of the wrist. Remember how we had baths on the farm?" Before I could answer she continued. "On the farm if we wanted to have a bath we had to take the silver zinc bath and fill it with water that was drawn from the well." She said the water was first poured into large paraffin cans and heated up on the stove and then poured into the bath. "I kept the stove hot with coal and always opened the stove's door very carefully, so the heat that escaped wouldn't hit me in the face."

After Gracie was finished washing the dishes, she went to her room. My father drank down the last drop of scalding Rooibos tea, just the way he liked it. He then put his favorite long-playing records on the record player in the living room. He stacked a few LP's on top of each other, and I watched with fascination as they dropped down one at a time. The arm with the needle at the end would automatically swing to the first groove of the black plastic disc. Doris Day's velvety voice oozed from the record player singing "Once I had a Secret Love," and then telling us in the next song that whatever will be, will be. I could almost see the Spanish woman with the bright red flared skirt, in the painting above the couch, come to life and dance to the music.

"Come here Lolzy," my father said. "I'll teach you how to waltz."

I stood on the top of my father's shoes as we waited for a few beats, and then we danced around the living room. My feet fit perfectly on the front of his shoes. My hand was completely swallowed up in his, and I noticed the veins on the back of his hands. They looked like winding rivers on a map, dividing into smaller streams. We floated around the floor with great ease, in time to the music. It wasn't until I was about ten that I graduated to standing right on the floor while we waltzed. His smile went all the way up to his eyes as he counted, "One two three, one two three. That's it; you've got it, my girlie." After our dance I kicked off my shoes and walked in my socks.

"Take off your socks!" my father exclaimed. "Don't you know that you should never walk in socks? It's very unlucky." This was just one of my father's many superstitions. According to him, bad luck would follow us if we left a loaf of bread upside down, opened an umbrella indoors, put shoes on a table or walked around in socks. If I spilled some salt, I had to immediately throw a few grains over each shoulder into the eyes of the devil.

"David, how can you believe in God *and* in superstitions?" my mother often asked him.

"That's what my parents told me," he'd say, in defense of whatever strange rule he'd just laid out for us. "And you never know. I'm not prepared to take a chance," he answered.

The only superstition my mother had was her love for the number 13. She was convinced that it was a lucky number in our family. She was born on September 13, engaged on February 13, married on August 13, and she could name many other happy events associated with 13.

I took off my socks so that bad luck wouldn't follow me, and was quite happy to be barefoot again. I was always amazed that my dad was such a smooth dancer and so light on his feet, considering how big and strong he was. After our dance my dad went to sit in his favorite chair to smoke his pipe. He had a brown leather tobacco pouch and a chocolate colored wooden pipe. I loved to put the tobacco in the bowl of the pipe for him.

"Remember; don't pack it too tight or too loose. It has to be just right," he instructed me.

I opened the pouch and the powerful tobacco aroma escaped and filled me. I took some dark tobacco in between my forefinger and thumb and stuffed it into the bowl of the pipe. I continued until it was filled just enough. Then I handed it to him, noticing his teeth marks on the tip where he chewed on it. He took it with his yellow stained fingers, and after close examination he said, "Perfect." There was a warm feeling in my stomach knowing that I had done a good job for him. He settled down into his big chair, and I watched as he sucked on the tip of the pipe, inhaling deeply and suppressing a cough, while small puffs of smoke escaped from the sides of his mouth. The twisting smoke and the aromatic smell of tobacco wafted into the house.

Soon it was my bedtime. My father came into my room every night before I went to sleep. He'd sit on the side of my bed, put his big hands on each side of my head, and kissed me on my forehead as he went through his usual unique routine.

"Good night." *Kiss* "God bless you." *Kiss* "God look after you." *Kiss* "Pleasant dreams." *Kiss* "I love you." *Kiss.* I was aware of the faint smell of tobacco on his breath, but I didn't mind because it was just part of my dad. I went to sleep every night wrapped in my father's kisses. I knew I was loved.

In the middle of the night I heard him coughing, hacking, spitting and choking. His coughing fit lasted for hours. In the morning I heard him tell my mother, "I thought I was going to die. I couldn't catch my breath." That same morning, I watched as he unceremoniously threw his pipe and leather tobacco pouch, along with a few cigarettes, in the rubbish bin. He never smoked again.

———⟫•⟪———

MY FATHER POSSESSED the strength of a far younger man, and because of this, all the workers on the farm used to call me "tombi skethla" which in Zulu means "daughter of the strong master." One day when I was about eleven, I was outside our house and I called the garden boy.

"Piet."

He continued walking away.

"Piet," I repeated louder this time.

With his back to me, he continued to walk as if he didn't hear me. I was close enough, and I was shouting, so I knew he heard me. Neither Piet nor I saw my father come out of the house. In a thunderous voice, one that I had never heard before, my dad yelled,

"Piet kom hier!"

He swung around when my dad told him to "get over here", and walked toward him. Three hard punches landed right on Piet's face. Pow! Pow! Pow!

My father was crimson in anger, and he yelled in Afrikaans, pointing his finger right at Piet as if he was poking holes in the air, while his voice rose uncontrollably.

"Don't you *ever* ignore her like that again. Do you hear me?"

Like a marksman, his words hit its target.

"Ja Baas."

Piet lowered his eyes as he said yes boss. Then my father turned, and walked back into the house.

I stood frozen.

My heart thumped hard in my chest. I was holding my breath, and stood rooted to the ground like a tree. It was the only time I had ever seen my father lash out in such a violent way.

I was unable to move. Thoughts darted through my head. *Why did daddy snap like that? I know he loves me and maybe it was because he saw Piet being rude to me by ignoring me when I called him. I'm sure that was what triggered it. That's why he said, "Don't ever ignore her like that again." Piet must have felt so humiliated to be hit in front of me. And what about the way daddy turned around and walked right back into the house; he must have been embarrassed that he lost control like that in front of me.*

The incident was never mentioned again, but it left an indelible mark on me. Had he said something like; "Lorraine, I'm sorry I lost my temper like that and I'm sorry you had to witness that scene," I might have discussed it with him and asked him what made him snap like that. But he didn't, and because I was used to suppressing certain things that I saw in that society, I remained silent. Silence was part of my coping mechanism. Looking back now, I realize that it was part of the country's coping mechanism.

CHAPTER *Four*

Jews in a Church

"We all have to go to church next Sunday," my father announced flatly. It was the day after the incident with Piet.

"What?" my mother asked, apparently as shocked as I was.

"Daddy, why do we have to go to church?"

In our often drought-stricken part of the world, rain was considered a gift from the heavens — one of God's wonders. After a particularly long dry spell, the town organized a special day of prayer for rain. The preacher of the church phoned my father.

"David, man, we need you to come to church to help us pray for rain. Bring Sadie and your children with you. If we have Jews present in the church, God will look favorably upon us."

I heard my dad tell my mother, "Cookie, we have no choice, we have to go and help pray for rain. All of us. They really believe that if we're there, God will send some rain! How can we refuse?"

They always called each other "cookie" or "cooks." In the fifty-seven years that they were married, I never heard my father call my mother by her given name. Even when he was angry at her he'd say, "Ag, Cookie man, how can you say a thing like that? You know you're wrong." The "ag" sounded like the first syllable in the German word "achtung."

The Dutch Reformed Church in Reitz

She'd answer, "Cooks, don't you dare tell me I'm wrong." Occasionally she'd call him by his name. But these were rare (and serious) occasions. Somehow they never stayed angry at each other for too long, because soon they'd be dancing in the living room to my mother's favorite Bing Crosby or Mario Lanza records.

"I really don't want to go to church," my mother said.

"Ag, Cookie man you have to go. It's important. If it doesn't rain, they'll blame us." He told her what the preacher said.

58

So on the following Sunday, we all went to church. The huge stone structure was the town's main focal point. It looked like a fort, and loomed over the town. I could see its tall bell tower, and I could hear the hourly church bells from all corners of the town. The rooster/weather vane sat on the very tippy top of the spire, and there was a large clock in the front of the tower. All the Afrikaners belonged to The Dutch Reformed Church, known in Afrikaans as "Die Nederlandse Gereformeerde Kerk." It was a strict Calvinist variation of Christianity. Its laws were unyielding, forbidding any public display of affection, any listening to rock and roll music (that could lead to sin), and any absence from church during Sunday services. If you wanted to go to heaven, you did not violate these or any other scriptures.

The English-speaking population belonged to either Anglican, Methodist or Protestant churches, with a small Catholic following. It was clear what the main religious force in town was, however. The only paved road in the town was the one that led up to the imposing Dutch Reformed Church at the top of the hill. On Sunday morning the bells tolled constantly, as they did each week, calling all the white Afrikaners to prayers. Only whites were allowed in the large "Mother Church." The Africans had their own church in their township.

We prepared to go to church; I wore my favorite pink dress with the tiny black polka dots and wide black patent leather belt. Under my flared skirt I wore my yards and yards of net petticoat. It was called "the thirty yards petticoat." My skirt stood out flared like a tent, just like all my friends' dresses did. Gracie would wash my petticoat in sugar water and let it dry in the sun. This made the net nice and stiff. With my full skirt and shoes on my feet, I was ready to go to church. The ceiling was the highest I had ever seen, and the sunlight cascaded through the stained glass windows, throwing a colored glow over a few of the pews.

"Lorraine, remember we're not allowed to kneel," my mother whispered to me.

I sat quietly, mesmerized, while my wide eyes traveled up the gigantic brass organ at the front. Its thunderous tones filled the church with the tune of something I remember only as Hymn 23. The preacher held a great Bible, bigger than Mrs. Duminee's. He went on at some length about the drought, and concluded the service by thanking God that they were all born white.

"Please dear Lord," he said. "Help us keep our white race pure according to Thy will." The congregation nodded in agreement.

I whispered to my mother, "I wonder what the black preacher says in their church?"

"Me too," she said, and continued, "It's hard to believe that the preacher would actually thank God for making them white." I remembered how Mrs. Duminee, just like the preacher, used religion to justify apartheid. The preacher and Mrs. Duminee hid behind their weapon, the Bible.

Considering the bigotry that appeared to flow so freely through the town's veins, it was amazing how peacefully my family and I lived in Reitz. My father was treated with respect, and I can't remember any serious anti-Semitic incident against me, although Selwyn had some problems at school when a few boys called him a bloody Jew. I do remember once overhearing someone's father telling his daughter; "I'll give you five shillings if you beat that Jewish girl in the 100 meters race." His comment made me more determined than ever to beat her. I did.

Even though I gained acceptance through my running, a comment like that would surface once in a great while. We were different; there was no doubt about that. We spoke English while most other white people in the town spoke Afrikaans. Our religion and our political beliefs set us apart. My parents never supported or voted for the Afrikaner apartheid government.

My family knew that anti-Semitism always lay just under the surface in South Africa. My mother told me many times that at the beginning of World War II, a lot of Afrikaner national-ists became German sympathizers; a referendum of some kind was held, and the country decided by just a few votes to side with the allies. Many wanted to go on the side of the Germans. We were never naive enough to think that the Afrikaners loved the Jews. We knew we were lucky that our skin was white. They were so focused on the black Africans and the danger of being outnumbered, that we lived a relatively peaceful life, even though we were referred to as "Die Jode." The Jews.

When we started to walk out of the church that Sunday, the most amazing thing happened. There was a very slight drizzle! I'll never forget that moment as we all looked up to the heavens in wonderment. I turned my face upwards, closed my eyes and drank the drops of rain. It didn't quite break the dry spell, but my father was elevated to a position of awe by the town's folk, who really believed that the drizzle occurred because Jewish people were in the church that day.

There had been quite a number of Jewish families living in Reitz when we first moved there, but within a few years they all left for larger cities and just a handful of us remained. Amongst those who stayed were Pearl and George Tobias, the Rabmans, Louis and Alma Lemkus and the Levins (Auntie Gertie, my dad's sister), her husband Uncle Harry and their children, Rikki and Larry — and us.

At the end of the week, every Friday night, I'd watch as Gracie spread the clean, starched white cloth over the table for our Sabbath dinner. She placed the shiny polished sterling silver candlesticks in the center. These were the ones that had been given to my mother, the ones with the engraving "To Sadie Faiga on the occasion of your engagement." For some reason there was no mention of my father. The silver wine "bechers" were put at each place and the "kitkah" (challah bread) was covered, ready for my father to make the traditional Hebrew prayer over the bread and wine. Our house was kosher, but my parents ate non-kosher food out of the house and in restaurants. My mom lit candles every Friday night, and the aroma of the chicken soup cooking in the kitchen filled the house as a sign that the Sabbath was upon us. The gefilte fish was ready in the fridge; each ball of fish had a slice of carrot balancing on the top. Other than the Sabbath meal, I don't remember religion playing a very dominant role in our lives. My mother *tried* to observe the Sabbath by not writing or handling money. "Only if I have to," she said. It seemed that she often had to.

My Dad wasn't at all observant. We only went to synagogue on the High Holidays like Rosh Hashanah and Yom Kippur, in a neighboring town called Bethlehem, or we drove the three hours to Johannesburg, where my parents' siblings and my grandparents lived. As a young child, and before I was required to, I used to see how long I could fast on Yom Kippur. It became a personal challenge to see how long I could go without food or water.

I always looked forward to my favorite holiday, Passover. My paternal grandparents' house on Prentice Road, Greenside, Johannesburg, was aglow with white candles. The festive Seder table, with its white cloth, matzah and Seder plate, snaked around the room to accommodate my father's seven siblings, their spouses and children. My cousins Marcelle, Victor, Rikki, Larry, Selwyn and I were at the far end. The house was filled with noise and chaos, and wonderful smells of chicken soup with matzah balls and brisket coming from the kitchen. We listened, as we did every year, to the story of the Jewish liberation from Egypt to freedom.

When I was a young child, my mother bought me a large, pictorial Bible with God on the cover. He was depicted as an old man with a long white beard and He sat dressed in a flowing red outfit, and from the wide billowing sleeves came two outstretched arms. Surrounding Him were pictures of the seven days of creation. She would read one chapter to me each night before I went to bed. I listened to the stories and stared for hours at the pictures of the separation of the land and sea, and the picture of Eve with her long flowing hair, holding an apple in her hand. My mother believed in heaven and all the literal texts of the Bible but my father was not spiritual at all. He said, "If you can see it, it's there, and if you can't then it's not." He often said, "When you're dead, you're dead." He referred to being buried as "pushing up daisies."

I loved all the Bible stories, but I soon came to see that grown-ups used these same stories to justify their own way of life. The Afrikaners interpreted certain texts in the Bible to mean that God created the white people as a superior race. I would later learn that other faiths interpret texts in the Bible as saying that God in fact created all men to be equal. As I grew older, I started to become skeptical of the Bible. I had witnessed so much twisting of God's words. I heard spiritual leaders of the same faith interpret the same text differently. So my own skepticism remained.

———◆———

In 1956, when I was ten, we moved to Buitekant Street; but Elsie remained my best friend. It was called Buitekant Street (outside street) because it was the last street on the edge of town. A large plot of empty land lay across the street.

Once, Elsie and I were playing outside in that vacant lot when she said, "Lorraine, remember when the elephant peed on your father?"

We each convulsed instantly into fits of laughter. We laughed until no sound came out. I could hardly catch my breath, and tears rolled down my cheeks as I recalled the incident. It had taken place a couple of months before, when the circus had come to town. I had called Elsie as soon as I heard.

"Howzit? Listen, Elsie, the train carrying the circus, with all the animals, is coming tomorrow. We have to get up early so that we can be at the station before the train arrives." I hardly slept that night. The next day, Saturday, we got up as the sun was just peeking over the horizon, and we ran all the way to the train station. We ran past all the Africans walking in the opposite direction, going into the town to start their day's work. Some women were balancing large baskets or suitcases on their heads. Every time I saw them balancing packages on their heads while they walked, I was amazed. I always asked myself; *How do they do that?*

The train rolled into the station like a majestic beast, spitting fat black clouds into the sky. Then, with screeching brakes, it shuddered to a halt and exhaled. Men started to unload all the animals. We followed the circus crew to the open field, and watched as they pitched the big tent. The air became engulfed with the smell of animal droppings; we had to be careful where we stepped with our bare feet.

"Guess what I have?" my Dad asked that night when he got home from work.

He opened his hand and revealed four tickets to the circus. "Four front-row seats for tomorrow night." I could hardly wait to get to school the next day, to tell everyone how lucky I was. Front row seats!

The following night, as we took our seats in row A, I was the envy of all my friends. The lights dimmed and the music started to play with earsplitting volume. I got shivers down my spine in anticipation. Eventually, it was time for the elephants to make their way around the ring; they thumped and plodded along as they walked. When the huge lumbering creatures came in front of the spot where we were sitting, one elephant stood in front of my Dad, lifted its leg and peed right on his lap! I gasped and slapped my cupped hand over my open mouth in horror. My eyes were glued to the stream gushing onto my father. I don't know the size of an elephant's bladder, but it kept gushing and gushing, as if it would never stop. My dad flew out of his seat. The entire audience, including my mother, went wild with laughter. When we got home my mother threw out every article of clothing he had been wearing. It took months for my father to live it down. The elephant incident was the most exciting thing that had happened in Reitz in a long time. Even though I laughed along with everyone else, I felt sorry for my dad because I knew he must have felt embarrassed. I loved him and always went along with everything he said, so I was perfectly willing to agree when he told me;

"That's the last time we sit in the front row."

———⟫◆⟪———

It was the girl who lived in the house behind us who told me how babies were made. Celeste was two years older than I. When I climbed over the fence to get to her house, I thought I was looking at an apparition from another planet. A huge tent-like dress was working in the garden. Inside that loose dress was Mrs. Fourie, Celeste's mother, a mountain of a woman and the heaviest person I'd ever seen. She could hardly walk; she wobbled from side to side on two tiny feet. I was sure that if she fell over, she would never be able to get up on her own. She huffed and puffed with each step.

She looked up at me and her moon-face said, "Celeste is binnekant in haar kamer." "Dankie Tannie," I added, politely thanking her for telling me that Celeste was inside in her room.

We were sitting on Celeste's bed when she decided, on her own, to give me a detailed account of how babies are made. I didn't believe her.

"Jy lieg," I told her in Afrikaans.

"I'm not lying," she said laughing. "Go ask your mother."

"My mother and father would never do anything like that," I said, getting ready to leave.

I thought to myself: *And your mother and father couldn't do that even if they wanted to.*

"Go ask her," she repeated as she got off the bed, opening the door for me.

As soon as I got home, I found my mother sitting in the living room crocheting doilies to cover the water-jugs and bowls, as a protection from the ever-present flies. As usual, she was humming a song. Next to her was a jar of her favorite hand cream, Ponds Cold Cream. Sometimes she just squeezed the juice of a fresh lemon right on her hands and arms. ("Lemon juice is very good for your skin," she told me many times.)

"You know what Celeste told me?"

My mother looked up at me. "What?" she asked.

I repeated Celeste's explanation. My mother looked stunned, and then she began paying very close attention to her crocheting again.

"Is it true?"

"Yes," she said quickly.

She was clearly uncomfortable discussing this topic, so I didn't press her with any further questions. My entire sex education from my mother was compressed into that one word:

"Yes."

To GET TO Celeste's house I had to walk past our chicken run in the back yard, with its smell and incessant clucking of hens. There were about ten of them. Besides the fresh eggs that Gracie gathered every day, the hens served another purpose. They became my four-year-old brother's pets. Because of the five and a half year age difference between Selwyn and me, we were both pretty much in different worlds with different interests. He was my little brother and he was always around, but we seldom did activities together because of the age difference. I did love to watch him chase the chickens. He would chase them all around the chicken run as I yelled, "Selwyn, c'mon, get 'em!" I would laugh as he scurried after the hens. When he caught one, the poor chicken would cluck and squawk, making a terrible noise and desperately flapping its wings, with a fountain of feathers flying everywhere. He could tell them apart, and he gave each one a name. The newly hatched chicks would scurry around like fluffy yellow balls with their high-pitched peeps.

Very rarely, my mother would have one of the chickens killed for our dinner. One night on such an occasion, while we were all sitting around the table, Selwyn announced;

"Tonight we're eating Goldeyes."

That was the end of my appetite. I couldn't take another bite. A few days before, I had seen how Goldeyes flapped around when he caught her, and now she was lying divided in pieces on each of our plates.

"Lorraine, stop that nonsense and eat your food."

I couldn't. It was impossible for me to eat anything that I'd seen alive the day before.

My dad wearing his felt hat, buying sheep
at the sale kraal

When my mother ordered chickens from the butcher, they arrived whole. Fortunately and mercifully, the heads and feet were removed and the feathers were plucked, but everything else was still intact. I watched as she placed the dead chicken on the kitchen counter like a patient on the operating table. Her whole hand disappeared inside the cavity of the chicken and she pulled out the heart, lungs, intestines and unlaid eggs. I tried to stay far away from the kitchen during these times. My squeamish stomach couldn't take it.

The week after the Goldeyes incident, I went with my father to the cattle sale, just outside of town, where he spent most of his time. The farmers sat on the hard wooden planks that made up the bleachers around the center kraal. Then the cattle were paraded two or three at a time, so that the buyers could get a good look at them. The auctioneer started the bidding by rattling away a mile a minute, while listening and watching for the bids. The farmers, including my dad, all wore gray or brown felt hats with wide brims to offer some protection from the scorching sun. I noticed a band of sweat on the felt around my dad's hat. The farmers carried walking canes, not because they had trouble walking but because they used the canes to prod the cattle, to move them along after they bought them. When my father clutched the ivory handle of his cane, I noticed the sunspots on the back of his hand, and the black onyx and gold ring that he wore on his pinky, given to him by my mother.

My dad's cane served another purpose too. He never called out a price during the bidding. He would subtly raise the tip of his cane, and the auctioneer knew that my father was raising the bid. I couldn't understand a word the auctioneer said. I could only understand the end when he said, "Sold to David Lotzof for twenty-five pounds."

After my father bought the livestock at the auction sales, the cattle would be branded with a long branding iron with the initials DL. They were then transported to his farm, where Thomas would fatten them up for resale at the future cattle auctions, or they would be shipped to the Johannesburg market for slaughter, to be sold to the butchers around the country.

On the drive home from the sale I asked, "Daddy, are we rich or poor?"

"Are you short of anything?" he asked.

"No."

"Then don't worry about it." That was all I ever got from him on that topic.

Although my father was the breadwinner in the family, at home my mother ran the show. She kept the books and records of the prices of cattle bought and sold. I often heard them discuss whether it had been a good month or not. She not only controlled all the finances, but she was at his side to encourage him during difficult times in his business. But it was not always smooth sailing. I remember a lot of bickering and arguments. Often the arguments lasted much longer than they needed to, because they each had to have the last word. Neither would give in.

"I'm going to the abattoirs," my dad said to me the next afternoon. "Do you want to come with me?" I was a bit reluctant to go to the place where the animals were slaughtered, but I had never been there before, so I agreed. Besides, I'd go anywhere with my dad, even to the abattoirs.

When we walked into the first area, large skinned carcasses of sheep and cattle hung upside down from hooks, their heads towards the floor, blood dripping. There was a sudden rise and fall in my stomach; I tried not to look at them. In the next area, people were chopping off the heads of chickens. Heads or no heads, though, their nervous systems still seemed to be working; the headless chickens were hopping around doing what looked like a dance. I noticed that there was, of course, no clucking sound from the hens. The place was silent; they were all dead. The smell of blood was everywhere, and the chicken feathers covered the floor. A wave of nausea washed over me. I put my hand up to cover my mouth in case I threw up. On one side of the room there were about twenty African women sitting in a row, plucking the feathers from the dead chickens. They worked with authority and conviction as they plucked away. This was the first time I noticed African women in charge and having the authority: over dead chickens. I pinched my nose closed as protection from the horrible smell. I couldn't wait to get out of there.

"This is the most disgusting thing I ever saw. I want to go home," I pleaded with my father, tugging on his sleeve.

"Just a few more minutes and then we'll leave," my dad said, while talking to a man in a white blood-stained coat.

Once we were back in the car I said, "I'll never eat meat again."

"Ag man, Lorraine, don't be so silly. You have to eat meat. That's how you get protein."

From that day on, I tried to block my day at the abattoirs from my memory, in order to get through dinner and to get my protein. But while some people see a piece of steak as something delicious, I see it as a piece of animal flesh, and the image of the sheep and cows hanging on the hooks jumps immediately back into my mind. I struggled to get through dinner that night and I wished I never had to eat meat again.

"Madam, I have pains in my chest."

A few weeks before our visit to the abattoirs, Gracie had been complaining about feeling tired. When we got home that day, her dark eyes looked anxious as she clutched her chest and told my mother of her condition. My mother drove her to the doctor, who said she had a heart condition and shouldn't do housework anymore. After working for us for ten years, Gracie had to leave and go back to the farm. When she left, it was like losing a member of the family. She wasn't there anymore to welcome me home from school with my sandwich and milk, or to swat flies with me. There was a void in our home. I missed her.

I realized that in all the years she worked for us, I never knew her last name or asked her questions about her life. She was just always there ... for *us*. I knew nothing about *her*. I didn't even know how old she was, or the date of her birthday. I remember how she used to bake delicious birthday cakes for me on my birthday. When was *her* birthday? I never asked and, as a result, never wished her a happy birthday during the entire time I knew her. I should have asked her about her brothers and sisters on the farm, and how she felt when we picked her up to come and work for us and she had to say goodbye to her family. I wondered if she was happy working for us, and if she missed the farm. At some point her father Thomas would have sent for her when he found her a husband. How would she have felt about that? I should have asked her how she felt about being black in South Africa, about working for white people. I think I know what her answer to this last question would have been. She would have most probably looked at me and laughed, showing the familiar space between her front teeth and asked, "Is there any other way, Mees Lorraine?"

If I had been able to have a deeper conversation with her, I would have validated her as a human being with feelings and opinions, and I would have shown her that I was interested in her as a person. But I didn't, and all these questions remained unanswered. I felt sad, remorseful and embarrassed when I thought about that, and I still do. I don't even have a picture of her. She and I were born into a system, and we simply took that as a way of life. We filled the roles we were born into.

———◆———

"Jesus loves me, this I know, for the Bible tells me so!"

A few weeks later, I came home singing this new song that I'd learned in school that day.

I caught my mother shooting a glance at my father that froze like winter. His brow was furrowed.

The next year I was sent to boarding school.

CHAPTER
Five

Eunice High School

"Lolzy, I have to talk to you," my dad said in a measured voice. I was finishing up my homework when he pulled out a chair and sat down. He put both elbows on the table and laced his fingers. He leaned forward toward me. Even before he spoke, I knew he had something important on his mind. I was aware of the faint smell of his Prep shaving cream. I had just turned twelve, and was in my final year in primary school. There were six months left before the school year ended. I had one more year to go before I entered high school. Selwyn was in his second year in school, known as Sub B. For a short time we were in the same school at the same time. "Ooh, this sounds serious," I said to my dad mockingly.

"It is," he said. "We're going to send you away from home."

At that point my mother joined us, but she let him do the talking. He couldn't hide the sadness in his eyes as he spoke, and there was something in his face that moved me. "Mommy and I have decided that we want you to expand your horizons beyond Reitz. We would like you to have a better high school education than this local school can offer. We've

75

heard Eunice High School in Bloemfontein is one of the best schools in the country. Its academic reputation is well known. In addition, we want you to be able to attend a synagogue and learn about our people and have Jewish friends, too."

Preparing to leave for boarding school,
age twelve

It sounded as if he had rehearsed this "speech" many times. There was a crack in his voice, and with the hug that followed; I knew that his big heart was breaking at the very thought of sending me away. My mother finally added, "Just remember we're not sending you away because we don't

76

love you. We're sending you away because we *do* love you." I swallowed hard and fought back the tears that were threatening to spill down my cheeks, but this news did not come as a surprise to me. I had always had a vague suspicion that this decision was in the works, because it wasn't unusual for Jewish boys and girls from the little rural towns to go away to boarding school, for the very reasons that my father had mentioned. "And we want you to meet Jewish boys, too," my mother added.

Even though I had suspected the day would come when I'd be sent to boarding school, there was a tightness in my stomach at the thought of leaving my parents and Selwyn. There wasn't much I could say, though. I had six months to get used to the idea. As uneasy as I was, I was also excited at the thought of moving away from our little town and going to a big city.

———————

THE FIRST WEEK in January, 1959, brought typically warm summer weather. The new school year was about to start. My mother and I packed my suitcase with my brand new uniforms. Each article of clothing had a nametag sewn on, in accordance with the school's instructions. The nametag had clear block lettering in red: Lorraine Lotzof. My father put the suitcase in the trunk of our big, shiny, black Pontiac, with its stylish tail fins. I knelt down and hugged our dog Bonzo, and told him not to worry; I'd be back on all the school vacations. With butterflies flapping around in my stomach, I jumped into the back seat of the car. Half those butterflies were nerves, and half were excitement.

———◆———

WE WERE OFF on the three-hour trip from Reitz to Bloemfontein, one of the capital cities of South Africa. The country had — and still has — three capital cities. Cape Town is the legislative capital, Pretoria the executive capital and Bloemfontein the judicial capital.

I had just completed my seven years of primary school and I was about to start the first of five years of high school, standard 6 through 10. My mother loved to sing on our car trips, and always encouraged us to join in, teaching us ways to harmonize a song; but this time she was uncharacteristically quiet during the ride. My father seemed deep in thought. I don't know what they were thinking, but I know the questions mulling around in my head. *Will I have friends? What if I get homesick? What will it be like to study from books written in English? Will it be hard to do math in English?* In English the count is twenty-one, twenty-two, etc. But in Afrikaans it's "een en twintig, twee en twintig": one and twenty, two and twenty. So I'd have to reverse my thinking when I did math in English. *How am I going to do that?*

Three hours later we saw the sign: "Welcome to Bloemfontein." All the roads in the town were paved and lots of cars were whizzing back and forth. People were coming in and out of the shops and everyone seemed to be in a hurry. There was a robot (our word for a traffic light) on every corner. While stopping at the red light of one of the robots, I heard a chanting sound through my open car window. It was a group of African workers digging trenches along the side of the road to lay pipes and cables. They were all lined up with picks in their hands. They sang in Zulu, and chanted in rhythm while lifting the picks up in unison as they worked on the road. I watched them and remembered how my friend Anita's father said that they were not quite human. I felt so uncomfortable when the people in Reitz spoke like that. How could he even think that way? I shook my head as if to erase that memory from my mind, and continued to wait for the light to turn green so we could find the school.

We followed the directions and when we approached the address we saw a sign on one of the posts that flanked the entrance. It read: Eunice High School. A 10-foot-high red brick wall ran all along the front of the school. The clinging, dense ivy that attached itself to the wall made it look as if there was history in every leaf. As we turned into the long driveway, my eyes moved to the red brick buildings ahead, which looked cold, mysterious and unwelcoming.

The head mistress of the boarding house, Mrs. Tennant, greeted us when we arrived. As she pressed her thin lips together, her smile seemed fake and mechanical to me. "Welcome to Eunice," she said as she stretched out her hand to my parents and finally to me. I noticed the large protruding blue veins on the back of her hand, and hesitatingly extended mine as I managed a faint shy smile. Two hairy legs emerged from the bottom of her skirt; she wore clunky black shoes. I tried hard to focus on her face as she spoke, but my eyes kept drifting to those legs. Suddenly, she clamped her bony hand on my shoulder and said, "I'll show you to your cubicle." The place she led us to, couldn't be called a room because the walls only went three-quarters of the way up to the ceiling; a partition that separated one cubicle from the other. It had a bed, a dressing table and a small closet. That was all. My father, who was never Mr. Diplomatic, blurted out, "Look at the size of this room. I couldn't even swing a cat in here." Fortunately, Mrs. Tennant had already left so I don't think she heard him. "Look." He extended his arms out sideways. "I can almost touch the walls on either side."

"Ag, Cookie, stop that," my mother said emphatically. "She'll be fine. Where there's a will there's a way." "It's not *that* bad, Daddy. It's small but it's mine." My mother helped me unpack. We hung the pink curtains she had made, and put the matching bedspread over the blanket. I carefully placed our family photo on the dressing table.

Soon it was time to say good-bye. I watched from my upstairs window as my parents walked back to the car. Even though they had their backs to me, I noticed that my father's shoulders seemed to droop; he reached into his pocket and pulled out a white handkerchief, and brought it up to his face. A tear trickled down my cheek, but when I looked in the mirror, the wave of sadness and apprehension in my belly was replaced by a feeling of excitement, as a sudden sense of independence and possibility emerged. I felt very grown up. I thought, "Hmm, this is not so bad. I can make my own decisions, and do whatever I want." Little did I know that my every move would be monitored and scheduled.

———◆———

CLANG! CLANG! CLANG!

It was 6.30 a.m., and the shrill sound of the bell startled me out of my sleep. It was time to drag my body out of my narrow single bed, with a mattress so hard that I could bounce a ball on it. In one hour's time I had to be standing in the hallway outside the tiny cubicle, which they called my room, fully dressed in my uniform, bed made, waiting in silence along with all the other girls. We were ready for the inspection of our rooms and uniforms by the dorm's girl-in-charge, also known as the dorm captain or the prefect. The prefects were a few selected girls from the matric (senior) year. It may have felt like the wake-up call at a correctional facility, but it was just the start of a typical day at Eunice Girls' Boarding school. It was the end of January 1959, the beginning of the new school year. In South Africa the school year began in January and ended in December. I was almost thirteen.

After washing my face and brushing my teeth, I had hurried back to my cubicle to put on my uniform. I made sure that there were no runs in my opaque black stockings. I glanced in the mirror to see that my green tie was straight, and then buttoned the sleeves of my crisp white shirt with its starched collar. I turned my head, glancing over my shoulder in the mirror to see if my hair might have grown enough to touch the back of the collar. If it had, I would have to pull it back in a ponytail. Our hair was not allowed to touch the back of our collars; I have no idea why. I quickly made my bed, and cleared the top of my dressing table by opening the top drawer and shoving everything into it. I was relieved that the prefect wouldn't be looking inside the chaotic drawers of my dresser during her inspection. Then I tied the laces of my black shoes, which I had polished to a high sheen the night before. I stood up the moment the second bell clanged. It was 7.30 a.m. and time to step into the hallway. I smoothed my navy pinafore tunic with the palms of my hands as I walked out my door. I had made it. I was ready.

There seemed to be a slight delay at the other end of the hall. The prefect was talking to my friend Susan, who was sent back into her cubicle to change her tunic. It was shorter than the regulation of six inches above the knee. I breathed a soft sigh of relief as the prefect glanced at me, peeked into my room and gave me a slight nod, with a smile that looked slippery, as if she couldn't quite hold on to it. My eyes scanned *her* uniform to see if it met the strict dress code. It did. The uniform eliminated any decisions about what to wear each day. We all dressed alike, with no jewelry or make-up. If we wanted to stand out above the rest, we had to do it by achievements: excellence in studies, music or athletics. I liked that concept.

———≫•≪———

WE LIVED OUR lives in accordance with the strict rules, and the clang of the bell, of the boarding school and day school. Clang! Time for meals. Clang! Time for class. Clang! Time for study. Clang! Time for bed. Bells, bells, bells. My head was filled with bings and bongs. After the morning inspection by the prefect, we walked to the huge dining room. Breakfast consisted of porridge — either Tiger Oats, Jungle Oats, Maltebella or Mielie Meal Porridge. I sprinkled on some sugar and hoped that this would be my lucky day, and that there would be no lumps in my porridge. Clang! Breakfast was over, and it was time to walk the short distance to the classrooms.

Red brick arches surrounded the quadrangle; green ivy crept over them. This was where the whole student body gathered each morning at the start of the school day, to hear Mrs. De Jager, the school principal, make the announcements for the day. But first we all lifted our voices as we sang the school song. *"The Wall around has changed since the corner stone was laid..."*

I wondered how the wall had changed since the corner stone was laid? Maybe there was more ivy? Then it was time for prayers, and I was reminded once again that this was not a Jewish school, but a school that made accommodations for Jewish girls — in contrast to Reitz, where I was expected to participate in all the Christian prayers. Mrs. De Jager would, as a courtesy, excuse the Jewish girls by saying "The Jewesses may now leave."

"It's very nice and respectful the way Mrs. De Jager allows us to leave before she starts the daily Christian prayers," I said to my friend Sheryl, "In Reitz I had to participate in all the prayers and Bible studies."

"Me too," she said about her little town. "That's one of the reasons we're here, Lorraine," she reminded me. As we congregated in the nearby classroom, the Jewish prefect led us in our own prayer. I still remember every word, having recited this prayer every day for five years:

Hear O Israel the Lord our God the Lord is one
Blessed be His glorious kingdom forever and ever
And you shall love the Lord your God with all your heart,
with all your soul and with all your might
And these words which I command you this day

Shall be upon your heart, and you shall teach them diligently unto
your children, and speak of them when you lie down
and when you rise up
And you shall bind them as a sign upon your hand
and they shall be a symbol between your eyes
And you shall write them upon the doorposts of your house
and upon your gates. Amen

I embraced this prayer because of my strong belief in God. Although I struggled with the literal translations of the Bible and the ways in which it was interpreted (or misinterpreted), I never had any doubts about the existence of God. I've always believed, and still do, that there is a God. But reciting the prayer had an additional special meaning for me. Standing there with forty other Jewish girls gave me a sense of belonging that I had never had in Reitz, where I was the only Jewish child in the entire school. I felt comfortable and proud of my heritage.

As I spread my wings beyond the borders of Reitz, I met friends of faiths other than the Afrikaans Dutch Reformed Church. I met girls who were Catholic, Anglican, Methodist and Protestant. They were all absolutely passionate about their own religions.

"But you're all Christians," I said to my friend Cathy, who was Protestant.

"Well, we don't believe in all the statues and opulence of the Catholic Cathedrals. We like to simplify our church and concentrate on the Bible, instead of all the gold and statues," she said. My friend Margaret, who was Catholic, believed strongly in kneeling before the statue of Jesus and Mary, and accepted the Pope as God's representative here on earth.

Everyone is so convinced that his or her way of praying is correct. We can't all be right! Maybe none of us is right. Maybe God created all of humanity, while the Bible is just a man-made document to justify people's actions here on earth.

I've struggled with these thoughts throughout my life. I believe in God, the almighty, but my first exposure to the Bible in Reitz, by my teachers, was so twisted and convoluted that my skepticism has remained ever since.

After the prayer, the school day began. With the English-speaking teachers at Eunice High School, there was no discussion about religion or politics in the classroom. Apartheid was neither lauded nor condemned. This, of course, was a major change from what I had experienced from the Afrikaans-speaking teachers in Reitz. The focus at Eunice was on academics. The curriculum was intense. We were expected to study hard and get good grades, for ourselves and for the reputation of the school. For my part, I wanted — and got — good grades because it was important to my parents.

Silence was strictly observed at the end of each period, as we marched in single file from one classroom to the next. Stephne, my new friend, was walking in front of me to our next classroom. I wanted to ask her something, but we weren't allowed to speak as we were moving from class to class, so I had to wait till lunch break. I walked quietly, carrying my armful of books, feeling the rules tighten around me like the starch in my stiff white collar.

We were on our way to biology. We waited for Miss Van Rensburg, our bio teacher, to arrive. She was a kind and sweet person, but not quite as sweet as the heavy perfume she wore, which always greeted us about a minute before she entered the classroom. In five years, she never changed her perfume. One of the girls was carrying her briefcase. It was not unusual to see a student carrying a teacher's case. This was done as a gesture of respect. We all stood up as she walked into the room, just the way we did whenever any teacher entered the classroom.

"Good morning, girls."

"Good morning, Miss Van Rensburg."

"Girls, today we are going to dissect a rabbit. Watch carefully, because you will be graded on your observations."

I steeled myself. I knew this would not be easy for me.

Miss Van Rensburg was an attractive woman with perfectly coiffed strawberry blonde hair. It was short, curly and sprayed with lots of lacquer, so that not a hair could move. Her lips were a shiny electric red. It was a struggle to concentrate on her words: those shiny lips distracted me.

We all gathered around the table where the dead rabbit lay. I had a sudden flashback of the chickens on my mother's kitchen table in Reitz. My stomach did a somersault once again. Now I *had* to watch: I was going to be graded! I positioned myself near the back of the group because I was tall enough to see over their heads. I stood with my hand over my nose to shield me from the smell of the formaldehyde.

Miss Van Rensburg said, "Okay, girls, I'm now going to cut open the stomach. Please watch closely."

The sharp scalpel slid smoothly across the rabbit's stomach. I felt myself sway slightly, but thank God, I was still standing. Then there was a loud gasp from every girl in the room. I craned my neck to see what had provoked the reaction. The rabbit was pregnant! Three baby rabbits, all dead. I had to hold on to the desk with both hands to keep from passing out.

"Oh no," Miss Van Rensburg said, as her hand flew up to her mouth. I could tell it was almost as traumatic for her as it was for us. I deserved an A just for surviving that class.

I hoped I would eventually forget that day, but the image stayed with me forever, just as the image of the dead animals I saw hanging from hooks at the slaughter house had stayed with me, along with the dead chicken on our kitchen table, waiting for my mother to remove all its organs, and the tongue in the cow's mouth. I wished I could shrug these things off like everyone else seemed to be able to do, but those memories were seared in my mind forever. I now had another dead animal to think of when I was served meat at dinner. Again I wished I never had to eat meat again. But my father had told me not to be silly, because I needed my protein.

———◆◆◆———

WHEN THE BELL clanged for "lunch-break," my friends Stephne, Shirley, Sybil, Grace and I, sat in our usual place — the steps in front of the dorm — to soak up some warm sun. We discussed the rabbit incident and I struggled to eat my snack. The others ate without any trouble. How did they do it? Why was I the one blessed with such a squeamish stomach?

Half the students lived in Bloemfontein and went home from school at night. They were called daygirls; Stephne was a daygirl. The other half were called boarders and lived at the school. The boarders were never allowed to leave the school grounds without permission. My friends who were day-girls often brought me my favorite sweets, like toffees, flat black licorice, pink and white coconut-ice, or Turkish delight, with its sweet smell and powdered sugar coating. They also brought me my favorite chewing and bubble gum, Chicklets, Chappies or Wicks. We weren't allowed to have gum. If anyone was caught chewing gum, it was an automatic "record mark". This meant that some sort of punishment was about to be dealt out, like writing out lines or memorizing prose. I always kept my gum hidden in my room, tucked in my socks.

Snack break at Eunice High School

CHAPTER
Six

The Republic Is Born

Esther Brandt was a high jump gold medalist from the 1952 Olympics in Helsinki. She was the track coach for Eunice High School. I couldn't believe my luck: not only would I be coached for the first time by a real track coach, but I would be working with an Olympian — a gold medal winner!

Mrs. Brandt was six-feet tall with a heart just as big. Kindness blossomed in her eyes when she spoke to me; she became my mother figure. I learned about real workouts from her. I also learned to run with the latest lightweight white leather spikes. Barefoot running was now a thing of the past.

There was another huge benefit to being on the track team. The workouts were next door to the school, on a public track. The Eunice track team got special permission to leave the school grounds. I walked out of the gates each afternoon and breathed the fresh air of freedom for a few hours. I saw cars rushing by, mothers pushing baby prams, dogs running next to their owners, and children getting off a school bus. It was

ABOVE: Lorraine Lotzof breaks the tape for Eunice in their under-19 girls' relay victory at the inter-high schools athletic meeting at the Stadium on Saturday.

Winning relay race in Bloemfontein at age seventeen

just a normal day outside the walls. Running provided me the sensation of freedom, both physically and spiritually. Every day I had to live my life by following the strict laws of apartheid and the strict rules of my boarding school, but when I was running, I was in my own world. It allowed me to tune into myself, and I was free and in control. It was exhilarating and it fueled my psyche. I was temporarily transported to another world. And there was yet another benefit. Our brother school also used the track, so there were *boys!* In my all-female world, this was a very big deal. It was refreshing to have some male company for a few hours each day. The guys — Michael, Tom, Peter and others — became my track buddies. No wonder so many girls tried out for the track team! Unfortunately, only a handful made it. My friend Stephne was a tall, strong discus thrower, and she and

I made the team every year. I swear those workouts kept me sane. I was in touch with the outside world every afternoon, but after the workout was over, I disappeared again behind the high ivy covered walls.

———◆———

"WE ALL LIVE in a yellow submarine, yellow sub…"

I was walking back to school after my workout, humming the latest Beatles song.

Suddenly I heard a blood-curdling yell from across the street. Like a pin to a magnet, I was drawn to the gathering crowd.

He was lying face down on the dirty sidewalk, with his arms stretched out in front of him and his wrists held together by handcuffs. The silver metal of the cuffs looked shiny against his black skin. A young white policeman in a khaki uniform was standing over him, with one foot on the three-inch piece of chain that connected the two cuffs. I assumed he was waiting for backup. In the meantime, with a smirk on his face, he was amusing himself, and holding the attention of a crowd of about twenty people, by stepping on the chain with all his weight. The cuffs dug deep into the man's wrists, resulting in more of the ghastly screams I had heard. I gasped softly at the sound of these cries; my eyes scanned the faces of the people in the crowd. There were no expressions at all. They were all just standing there and watching, a human ring of gawkers with blank faces surrounding a black man in agony.

That foot on the chain gave the policeman the look of a hunter showing off his prey, which was now completely at his mercy. Even though I had witnessed similar incidents of whites against blacks many times before, I still got that nauseous feeling in the pit of my gut. I knew that if I spoke up at all, I'd be putting myself on the other side of the fence; showing sympathy, and siding with a black person against a white person, I'd be labeled as a threat to the regime. I wanted to tell Mrs. Tennant to report the policeman to the authorities, until I reminded myself that he *was* the authority. I had to suppress my natural instincts to jump in and go to the aid of a helpless person in trouble. I knew that if I confronted the policeman, I'd be lying next to the man, with cuffs on my own wrists! So all I could do was walk away, just like I had done many times before after seeing incidents of whites against blacks. We lived in a police state and the police answered to no one. I felt frustrated, stifled and muzzled like a dog. It would be years in another place and time before I'd have the opportunity to help those whom I knew to be oppressed and less fortunate.

As I walked away, I wondered about the policeman, who got such enjoyment from inflicting cruelty and humiliation on someone who was already subdued and in his custody. How could the crowd just stand there and watch, as though this was some sort of entertainment? How could people become numb to such casual violence?

That night I couldn't eat.

I kept seeing that man lying on the sidewalk. I told the other girls at the dinner table what I had seen. The reactions were mixed. The English-speaking girls thought it was despicable behavior by the policeman, but agreed that there was nothing we could do. If we protested, we'd be thrown in jail with no trial. Helena, whose parents were Afrikaans, said, "You don't know what the African did. He might have attacked someone."

"But he was already in police custody," I protested.

Helena said, "Lorraine, you have to show them who's the boss, or they'll take advantage of you. Remember, they outnumber us twenty to one, so we have to keep a tight control."

I heard my father's voice in my head again: they outnumber us. But did we have to inflict such cruelty to maintain control? I say "we" because I was part of the system and I did nothing. I wasn't proud of myself. Yet what could I do? The conflicting thoughts played around in my head, until Mrs. Tennant brought me back to the present.

"Lorraine, please take your elbows off the table and sit up straight."

"Sorry, Mrs. Tennant."

At mealtimes we sat like little soldiers. Correct table manners were imperative. We had to take small bites, and put the knife and fork down while chewing. We also had to take small sips of water. No gulping was allowed, and "making cement" (taking a drink before swallowing your food) was strictly forbidden. We sat at long tables with a prefect sitting at the head of each table. The meal began with Mrs. Tennant ringing a little bell to get everyone's attention. Then she would bow her head and say "For what we are about to receive, may the Lord make us truly grateful."

The African staff brought bowls of mostly unrecognizable food to the table. I remember a particularly mysterious dish called samp. I had never heard of it before. It's a white grain-like sticky mush, something like rice, except that it had no taste at all. I tried to drown the samp with gravy. It was always served with chicken or some other meat. When we were finished eating, we had to place our knife and fork neatly next to each other in the center of the plate. Dessert was custard, fruit or Jell-O.

Mealtimes offered us two choices: take it or leave it. I was always starving after my workouts, so I ate everything and didn't care about the taste. The truth is though, that I was *not* truly grateful for some of that food.

I knew I'd have difficulty concentrating on my homework. I was still thinking about the man on the sidewalk.

———◦◦◦———

AFTER DINNER WE were back in the classrooms, which doubled as study halls at night. There were assigned times for each of us to leave the study hall to take a bath. If you took a bath or washed your hair at any other time without permission, it was a punishable offense. I always thought it was the girls who *didn't* bathe and wash their hair who should be punished. At bedtime, after the lights were turned off in the dorm, the only light that remained on for the whole night was the one in the bathroom area.

We were dismissed from the evening study hall, but I still had more work to do for a big test. So I put on my pajamas and pulled my eiderdown off the top of my bed. With my pillow and eiderdown tucked under one arm and Shakespeare's *Macbeth* under my other arm, I walked to the bathroom. I found a spot on the large floor along with the other last minute crammers, who were already sitting on the floor with their books open. I spent many hours on that cold cement bathroom floor studying for exams. "*Pass, damned exams! Pass I say!*" Those were my thoughts, and apologies to Lady Macbeth.

The "no talking after lights out" rules were strictly enforced. The next night, Sheryl, who was in the cubicle next to mine climbed on her bed and tried to look over the wall into my cubicle. "Lorraine, I have a question about our geography test tomorrow." While we were whispering we heard, "Who's talking?" We had to own up or the whole dorm would be punished. "We are," we answered in unison. The prefect called us into the hall. I want you both to memorize page thirty five in your history book and recite it to me ten minutes before dinner next week."

As we each walked back into our cubicles, Sheryl whispered, "I'm sorry Lorraine."

"Don't worry about it," I told her.

Page thirty-five in our history books was about the Anglo/Boer war. I had to memorize the part about how the Dutch established a half-way station at the Cape of Good Hope, serving the ships with fresh fruit and vegetables, and medical attention, as they rounded the tip of Africa. I read how they brought in people from East and West Africa to work the lands, and many were kept as slaves. From 1795 to 1803, the British replaced the Dutch at the Cape. They angered the Dutch/Boers by calling for better treatment for the blacks and coloreds, and in 1833 the British abolished slavery. To escape the restrictions of British rule, the Boers left Cape Town and moved inland. This was known as the Great Trek. Eventually war broke out on October 11, 1899, and after fierce fighting between the British and the Afrikaner Boers, a peace contract was signed in May of 1902, and South Africa became a British Colony. In 1910 the Union of South Africa was established by Britain, and our country became part of the British Commonwealth. It was a lot of information to memorize, but I already knew much of the history. I remembered how my mother told me that even though we had been a British

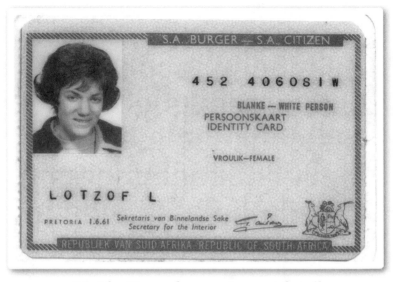

My identity card; a requirement for all
South Africans indicating their race!

Colony, and were still part of the Commonwealth, the Afrikaners had won the election in 1948, establishing apartheid as an official policy, and further restricting the rights of the Africans and curbing their free movement. They had to carry passes, and weren't allowed to travel around the country without permission — which was almost never granted.

The following week Sheryl and I stood outside the prefect's door. I had studied hard to memorize the page she assigned us. With clammy palms and a dry mouth I knocked softly on the prefect's door.

"Come in."

She barely looked up from her desk.

"Okay, start," she said in her gravely voice.

I went first. She stopped me after three lines saying, "That'll do. Now make sure you don't break the rules again." She wasn't even interested in hearing anything from Sheryl.

Letters from my mom

EVEN THE LETTERS we wrote to our parents and friends were regimented.

"Mommy, please can you send me a signed letter listing all the names of the people I'm allowed to write to? If I address a letter to someone who is not on your signed list, they won't mail it." I included a long list of my friends and family. We needed written invitations from people we wanted to visit on "the outside", even our own parents. One letter looked like this:

"Dear Mrs. Tennant,

Please may our daughter, Lorraine, come home for the vacation?

Thank you.

Sincerely,

Mrs. Sadie Lotzof."

It seemed perfectly absurd. "Lorraine, they need to make sure they know where each girl is going when she leaves the school grounds," my mother said. "I like that," she added.

That's ridiculous, I thought. *Even to go home to our own parents?* But the rules were the rules.

⇒◦⇐

"GOOD SHOT," SAID Mrs. Brandt giving me a big hug. "You've been chosen to represent Eunice at the inter-high sports day." I was excited to compete against the best runners from all the towns in the Free State. That honor earned me my "colors"; a special crescent-shaped patch with the words "athletics" sewn under the pocket of my green school blazer. The year was 1962, and the Free State championships were held in Sasolburg,

Winning the South African Junior
Championships, 1963

the petrol-producing city in the country. This was the year after South Africa became a Republic and severed all ties with Great Britain. The Commonwealth countries had been trying to put pressure on South Africa to change its race policies; our government had responded by holding a nation-wide election to determine whether we should stay in the Commonwealth and be subjected to outside pressure, or break away and become a Republic. Being that we were a self-sufficient country, with great wealth in natural resourses like gold, diamonds, coal, minerals, rich soil

Map of South Africa indicating Reitz
in the Free State

The South African Coat of Arms

The flag of the Republic of
South Africa

The flag of apartheid South Africa

and perfect weather, the government felt that it could survive just fine on its own. The people, however, were sharply divided on the issue, and there were fierce debates. The Afrikaners wanted to break away so that they wouldn't have to account for their racist actions to anyone, while the other half of the white population was concerned about being isolated from the rest of the world. My mother, of course, had been on the opposite side of the Afrikaners. The Africans had had no voice at all.

"It's crazy," my mother had said. "We'd be cutting ourselves off from the world. If a foreign country attacked us, the other Commonwealth countries would have to come to our aid, but if we became an independent Republic, we'd be all alone. Also if we became a Republic, the government could continue their evil apartheid policies without accounting to anyone."

"But that's exactly what they want," I had replied. Even at the age of

The South African Maccabi Games patch

fifteen, I knew that the apartheid government was happy to be isolated and free to do as they pleased, and to practice their oppressive policies without outside interference. So in 1961, with Hendrik Verwoerd as Prime Minister, and amid huge celebrations, the country had changed from The Union of South Africa to The Republic of South Africa.

———◆———

IN THAT SAME year, I represented South Africa at the Maccabi Games in Israel. I had sent in an application a few months before; after that, the selectors had followed my progress at track meets. The exciting news arrived via a letter from the Maccabi Association. "Congratulations, Lor-

Lorraine Lotzof

achieved the distinction of being the only girl selected for the South African athletics team that competed at the 1961 Maccabi Games in Israel. In the Junior(under 18) section, Lorraine won two Gold Medals for first place in the 100 metres and 60 metres events. In the latter she established a new Maccabi world record.In the senior (open) events, she came second in the100 metres, winning a Silver Medal, and third in the 200 metres (Bronze Medal).

Maccabi Games blazer, 1961

raine, you've been selected to be part of the South African Maccabi Team in Israel in August 1961." We were one of thirty-seven countries competing in this international event, which featured the best Jewish athletes from their respective countries. These games were held every four years, in the year after the Olympics.

I was so elated when I got the news that I could hardly concentrate on my studies. It would be the first time I had ever left the country.

WHEN I SAW it for the first time, Israel was still a fledgling country, barely thirteen years old and surrounded by hostile neighbors who were calling every day for its destruction. Yet despite this, we saw how Israel had turned the desert green as we passed agricultural lands on the way to Tel

Aviv. When we entered the Maccabi village, in the suburb of Ramat Gan, athletes with different colored team uniforms were milling around, talking in so many different languages that it reminded me of the Tower of Babel. But they all smiled in the same language.

Once we got off the bus, I was aware of a remarkable buzz of energy. I saw that Jews came in an enormous variety, with each group taking on the characteristics and languages of their countries of birth. The Indian Jews wore turbans and spoke English with an Indian accent, while the Americans looked and dressed just like the stars we saw in the movies, with the same lilting accent and the strange sounding "a." Americans would pronounce the word "can't" rhyming with ant. While we pronounce "can't" with the "a" as in "dark." Soon I learned to say "hello," "good-bye" and "good luck" in at least a dozen languages.

On our first evening there, I saw a few members of the Indian team sitting on the grass, chatting with some Canadians. As I walked past, they greeted me. I joined them and we had an interesting discussion about our different sporting events. I was sitting next to a girl who was a gymnast. I smiled when she introduced herself.

"My name is Rifka," she said extending her hand.

"I wouldn't normally associate an Indian with a Hebrew name," I said.

Ever so gently and tactfully, she corrected my ignorance, explaining that the Indian Jews are amongst the oldest Jewish tribes in the world; then she continued to tell me about the Jewish community in Bombay. I was fascinated. Who knew?

'n Jood in die span

DAAR is 'n vaste geloof dat 'n Springbokspan sonder 'n Jood in sy geledere nie veel kans tot sukses het nie. Dié geloof is nooit kragtiger beklemtoon as in die eerste toets teen die All Blacks op Nuweland in 1949 nie, toe die Springbokke met rustyd 3—11 agter was en eindelik 15—11 gewen het, danksy die skopskoen van 'n Johannesburgse Jood, Okey Geffin. Ook die derde toets het Geffin se skopskoen die Springbokke gehelp om te wen.

Op minder dramatiese wyse, maar met gelyke goeie bedoeling het ander Jode ook 'n bydrae tot die Suid-Afrikaanse sport gemaak. Ali Bacher se rol in die afgelope kriekettoets teen die Australiërs is 'n goeie voorbeeld. Met Goddard en Barlow se onvermoë in byna elke beurt om 'n stewige begin te maak, moes die 24-jarige mediese student van Wits op nommer drie 'n groot verantwoordelikheid dra. Sy vasberade kolfwerk en uitstekende veldwerk was 'n kenmerk van die reeks.

'n Dekade nadat Wilf Rosenberg in die Springbok-agterlyn uitgeblink het, is Syd Nomis een van die vernaamste aanspraakmakers as senter teen die besoekende Franse. As hy nie so baie las het van spiermoeilikheid nie, was hy dalk lankal ons nommer-een.

Morrie Jacobson (sokker), Robbie Schwartz en Leon Nahon (waterpolo), Alan Hofmann (gholf), die broers Kaminer (rugby), Julie Mayers en Esmé Emanuel (tennis), Ruby Eilim (tafeltennis), Maxie Ordman (stoei), Lorraine Lotzoff (atletiek), Meyer Feldberg (swem) en Leon Kessel (rolbal) is enkele ander Johannesburgse Jode wat baie tot sport bygedra het.

Translation of Afrikaans text:

A Jew On The Team

There is a strong belief that a Springbok team without a Jew amongst its members, does not stand much of a chance of success. This belief has never been more evident than in the first test against the All Blacks in Newlands in 1949, when the Springboks were behind 3-11 at rest-time and ended with a 15-11 victory, thanks to the kicking shoe of a Johannesburg Jew, Okey Geffin. Also in the third test did Geffins's kicking shoe help the Springboks to win. On a less dramatic way, but with the same luck other Jews also contributed to South African sport. Ali Bacher's role in the playoffs of the cricket tests against Australia is a good example.

(The article goes on to mention the names of other athletes who helped bring victory to their teams because they honestly believed that having a Jew on the team would bring them good luck!)

"Maybe you'll come and visit me someday in Bombay." Her smile was radiant and her shiny black hair cascaded like a waterfall all the way down her back. As I talked to her, my mind transcended our conversation, to my country where an innocent, friendly conversation like this would be a criminal offense. I knew that I could never extend an invitation for her to visit me. If Rifka came to South Africa, she wouldn't be allowed into my home in Reitz, in accordance with the laws of apartheid. In fact, she wouldn't even be allowed to stop for a drink in a café, because in that part of the country, Indians were only allowed to drive through. I felt saddened and embarrassed. We were two young people connected by our faith, yet we were kept worlds apart by our cultures.

———◆———

I WAS IN my fifteenth year, and the youngest member on the South African team. To my surprise, I won a silver medal in the 100 meters and a bronze in the 200 meters, and in the junior competition I brought home two golds in the 100 and 200 meters. I felt so honored to stand on the winning dais to receive my medals.

There was a support group of parents and family that joined the team in Israel and my mother was part of that group. My father had stayed home with Selwyn. It was comforting to know that my mom was there. She had always been such a great support to me. She would save each and every newspaper clipping that mentioned my name and she created a scrapbook that I still have to this day.

The trip to the Maccabi games was my mom's first visit overseas. She

ZIONIST RECORD AND S.A. JEWISH CHRONICLE, FRIDAY, JUNE 23, 1961

Reitz Hails Own Games Star

Lorraine Lotzo. (...... J), one of Maccabi's athletes for the 1961 Games, was the guest of honour at a reception given by the Mayor of Reitz, Clr. A. J. Papenfus, and Mrs. Papenfus. The Mayor paid tribute to the outstanding achievements of Lorraine and thanked her for bringing honour to the town.

The Mayor has sent a letter to the Lotzof family, congratulating Israel on its Barmitz-

vah. He expressed the hope that Israel would grow from strength to strength and would play its part in bringing peace and harmony to all mankind.

Newspaper article

had two goals in mind. One was to watch me run, and the other was to take advantage of the opportunity to get some money out of South Africa and open a bank account in Israel. This was strictly forbidden. No citizen was allowed to have money outside of South Africa. The government was concerned that there would be an exodus of money if it allowed people to open foreign bank accounts. But my mother, who still had her dream of leaving South Africa someday, was determined to do this. She had asked my dad to give her some cash from the sales of the cattle. If the

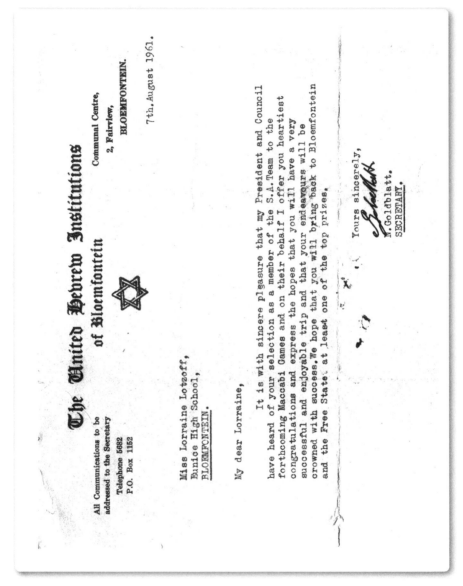

The United Hebrew Institution
of Bloemfontein

money had been deposited in the bank, the government could question a sizable withdrawal, so she had asked that the sum be kept in cash so she could bring it with her to Israel. My father had been dubious about the enterprise.

"Cookie," he had said, "are you sure you want to take a chance like this? What if they find the money on you at the airport? You're crazy. And besides, what could you do with a few hundred Rand?"

"It's a start," she had replied. "David, I have to do this. If we ever need to leave here in a hurry, we'd better have some money overseas." The same insecurity extended to passports. South Africans never allowed a passport to expire; never ever. The passport was the means of getting out of the country fast, if that ever became necessary.

So it was that my strait-laced, highly principled mother had walked through customs with four one-hundred Rand notes stashed in her corset and only a slight sheen of sweat on her upper lip. I had watched her squirm and struggle into her corset many times, and as she pulled it up, it looked so tight; I wondered how she could breathe. I remember thinking that she was going to have to sit on a plane for hours in this corset, with the Rands stuck in it.

When the group got to Tel Aviv, the first thing she had done was to get directions to the nearest Bank Leumi, hail a taxi, and make her way over to deposit the cash. Her main concern had been that she might meet someone she knew in the bank. She had disguised herself with a large straw sunhat and dark glasses; neither had seemed out of the ordinary in the blazing Israeli sun. She had pushed open the big glass door of the bank and had seen, to her surprise and shock, the entire group with

A telegram from the Mayor of Reitz

whom she'd just traveled from South Africa. All of them had parted, supposedly meeting family, and all had quickly found their way to the bank, and intent on doing exactly the same thing my mother had in mind: opening an Israeli bank account. They had all laughed hysterically when they saw each other, but none of them ever spoke about the incident to each other after that.

MY PRINCIPAL, MRS. De Jager, made me feel very special upon my return from the Games. One morning during assembly she announced my name to all the students, saying that I had brought honor to the school. When I went back to Reitz for the school vacation, there was a printed invitation in the mail from the mayor of Reitz, Dolf Papenfus, inviting us to a special tea in my honor at his home. I was so excited. After all, he was the mayor, even if it was only the mayor of Reitz.

That first Maccabi competition was special, but the race that I'll never forget was the one the following year in 1962 in Sasolburg, at the Free State Championships. It was one of the most embarrassing moments of my life.

My great rival was Theresa Van Rensburg. We'd been running against each other for years. She lived in a nearby town called Kroonstad. On that day, Theresa and I won our respective 100 meters heats in the exact same time, setting up an exciting race in the finals. On the track we were big rivals, but off the track we were friends.

Theresa had a new radio, and we decided to relax under a tree in the shade on the other side of the track while we waited to be called for the finals. We were listening to the music and chatting. After a while we heard a gun being fired. We both instinctively sat up and our eyes shot in the direction of the sound. To our horror, we saw that it was *our* race. We were so engrossed in our conversation and the music that neither of us had heard the repeated calls to report to the starter for our race.

I didn't know how to face Mrs. Brandt, or my parents and family, who had come specially to watch me run. The next day in the newspaper, there was a photo of Theresa and me with a story about how the hares fell

An Afrikaans news clipping

asleep along the side of the track, and the tortoise won the race. Being referred to as a tortoise did not amuse the girl who had won the race.

The opportunity to redeem myself came the following year, in the same competition. The first and second place winners would represent the Free State in the South African championships. I was humbled, honored and very nervous when I was selected to compete in the 100 and 200 meters in the South African Championships, against the best athletes in the country. My father arrived at each track meet, lugging his heavy, large 16-millimeter movie camera on his shoulder. Each film canister was only 100 feet long, so he had to be very careful to film at just the right moment. Threading the film and showing it on the large projector was a complicated procedure. Often when the lights were turned back on, there'd be a collective gasp as we saw the entire black shiny film, in a pile of tangled mess on the floor. But I was deeply grateful to my dad for taking these films, which allowed me to watch the races again at home during school vacations.

———◆———

WE MARCHED TO synagogue three abreast.

At Eunice, mercifully, the bell rang a little later on the weekends. I got to sleep an extra hour. There were about 40 Jewish girls in the boarding school. Every Saturday morning we lined up for inspection by Mrs. Tennant before leaving the school grounds for the synagogue. The Christian girls went through the same routine on Sunday before going to church. Our uniform on Saturdays was a white dress and a white Panama hat with a green band around it. A garter belt held up our sheer black stockings, and we had to make sure the seams in the back of the stockings were straight. Mrs. Tennant walked; hands clasped behind her back, shoulders slightly rounded, giving us a careful once-over with her beady, pale blue watery eyes. Her heavy black lace-up shoes clunked with every deliberate step she took. Her gray hair was short and curly, and the wrinkles on her face branched out into different directions. As we stepped forward one by one for her close inspection, her cheap rosewater cologne assaulted me. I exhaled with relief as she gave me a slight nod of approval, followed by "Next," as she waited for the next girl to step forward.

"Girls, be proud of your uniform when you walk on the streets of Bloemfontein, and behave accordingly," she said.

The year was drawing to an end, and I was looking forward to the long, six week Christmas break. A few nights before school closed for the holidays, the African staff, consisting of about twenty men and women who worked in the kitchen, put on a show for us in the dining room after dinner. With beads and bells around their ankles and colorful skirts and headscarves, they sang in perfect and effortless harmony. They swayed from side to side, clapping hands and stomping their feet in rhythm with their singing and dancing, sending tremors through the floor. As I watched them, I wondered if they were all from the same tribe. We learned in school that with the migration down to South Africa, people came from many different African countries, each speaking a different language, with different cultures and customs. Even though the blacks were often referred to as the natives, this was incorrect. They weren't native to South Africa. The only people native to the country were the Hottentots and Bushmen, who were all but extinct. The black Africans all came from different African countries north of South Africa. The apartheid regime fostered and promoted these differences, and encouraged the blacks to remain with their own tribe. For example, all the workers in the gold mines and coal mines lived in hostels near the mines. They were housed separately according to their tribe: Zulus together, Sothos together, Xhosas together, and so on. This policy could have been construed as a kind and compassionate gesture by the government, as an effort to have them maintain their identities and culture. But it wasn't. We all knew better. The separation was to prevent all the groups from getting together and uniting against the whites. This was why the government promoted and encouraged tribalism, and pitted groups against each other. This was the way they prevented the drumbeat of unity amongst the blacks. For the same reason, it was forbidden for Africans to meet in groups larger than ten. The police could come in and break up larger gatherings. The Afrikaners feared that the Africans might unite, and took every step to prevent it.

All of this ran through my head as I was enjoying the performance of the dancers in our dining room. We applauded wildly, shouting "more, more". When their performance was over, Mrs.Tennant gave each of them a small wrapped present for Christmas. I never knew what was in the wrapped package, but the dancers seemed thrilled to get a present. Their broad smiles appeared to show how much they enjoyed performing for us. Were those broad smiles genuine expressions of pleasure — or a cover up? We'd never know. We could never ask.

CHAPTER
Seven

The Magnificent Cape

"Lorraine, what on earth are you doing?"

"I'm making my bed."

I was surprised at my mother's question. Even though I was back home for the school vacation, I became so used to making my bed when I got up in the morning at Eunice that I automatically did it when I got home.

"You shouldn't do that. That's Amina's job. You'll spoil her."

Amina was Gracie's younger sister, and next in line to come and work for us after Gracie left.

"Sorry, I just got used to doing it myself at boarding school."

"Well, you're home now."

I walked to the kitchen and started to scramble an egg for breakfast. Again, my mother was over my shoulder.

"What's got into you? You know we pay Amina to do that. If you make your breakfast once, she'll expect you to do it every time."

I sat down at the table and allowed Amina to finish scrambling the

Table Mountain, Cape Town

eggs. I had to adjust to being home and having servants wait on me again. I smiled to myself as I thought about how much my mother voiced her disapproval of the apartheid policies, yet somehow had no problem having servants herself. Was she being hypocritical? Was she simply a product of her environment? Was I? She wasn't a bad person; I loved her. At the same time, I was old enough now to know that she was not so eager to walk away from the system she criticized. She would justify having servants by speaking constantly of how she treated them with respect and paid them well. (By South African standards, of course.) So as long as you treated them well, was it okay to have servants? I never asked her that question, but if I had, she would surely have looked at me in puzzlement and asked, "But how else? Everyone has servants. We're providing them with employment." I wondered: Would I have servants when I got married and had my own home? We were all a product of the culture, and I was no different from anyone else. Why wouldn't I?

118

It would be decades later, in another time and place, that I'd look back and realize how complicit we all were in the system that made apartheid possible.

AFTER BEING IN Bloemfontein for a whole year, Reitz seemed even smaller and the pace of life even slower. There was a new boy who had just moved there. I was with my friends at the public swimming pool when he came up to me and introduced himself. In Afrikaans he told me that he had heard that I was Jewish.

"Yes, I am," I answered, wondering what was behind that question.

He said, "Someone told me that if a person sleeps with a Jewish girl, they'll have seven years of good luck. Something about the seven lean, and seven good years in the Bible." He said that things had been pretty bad for him lately and he needed some good luck.

"Go and find your luck elsewhere," I said, and walked away.

Yet another reminder that in Reitz I was different, and always would be. I looked forward to getting away from the town for our end of the year vacation.

THE SEA DREW my parents, Selwyn, and me like a powerful magnet. Every December, we'd go for a two-week summer vacation to either Cape Town or Durban. Cape Town was my favorite. It was a long drive, one thousand miles.

We started out before daybreak, in our black Pontiac. My dad had a comment for every car that passed us. The cars going in the direction of Cape Town were called "full pockets." The cars going in the opposite direction, back home away from the ocean, were called "empty pockets." The time passed with our singing, and with Selwyn and me counting the telephone polls and playing the "keeping quiet" game. This was a game that my mother invented. Selwyn and I had to see who could keep quiet the longest without making a sound.

We arrived in Cape Town late at night, but we could still see the outline of the majestic Table Mountain, so named for its flat top, which looks like a table. When clouds drape themselves over the mountain, it's called the tablecloth. The next day we took a drive to Cape Point, the southern tip of the continent, where the Indian and Atlantic oceans meet. My dad had to carefully navigate the curvy road, with its twists and turns, on the side of Table Mountain called Sir Lowry's Pass. Having lived on a dry, dusty farm, and then in the small drought-stricken village of Reitz, I found that these vacations to the coast engulfed and ignited all my senses. They brought me back to life.

I pressed my forehead against the car window until I could see my breath on the glass, and watched the white foamy waves of the ocean crashing, unstoppable, to the shore. I opened the window and stuck my head out, closed my eyes as the wind blew my hair in all directions, and inhaled the salty air of the ocean until it filled my lungs and my soul.

As we stood at Cape Point, my memory drifted back to my classroom, when my teacher told us: "It was at this spot in 1652, two centuries after Vasco De Gama first discovered the Cape in 1494," she tapped the wooden ruler on the large map, pointing to the southern-most tip of the African continent, "that the Dutch East India Company sent Jan Van Riebeek to set up a half-way station to supply fresh fruit, vegetables and other services to the ships coming around the tip of Africa on their way to trade with the East Indies. They called it The Cape of Good Hope. These Dutch settlers were known as the Boers or Afrikaners." She went on to explain that these sailors were there without their women, and that many of them took up with the Hottentot and Bushmen women. The children resulting from these "unions" were neither white nor black. They became known as the Coloreds or Cape Coloreds.

"When the Malays were introduced to the Cape to increase the work force, there was further intermarriage of the races," she said while shaking her head from side to side in clear disapproval. One of the girls asked her when the Africans came to South Africa. "The influx of Bantu-speaking tribes from the North down to South Africa started around the same time. There were the Zulus, Xhosas, and Sothu to name a few."

She said that many years later the British landed at the Cape, but they decided against establishing a colony. "It was the Dutch," she proclaimed proudly, "who recognized the strategic and economic importance of the Cape." The racial caste system they established set the whites and blacks in worlds apart — and left the coloreds in a no man's land. Both groups shunned them. The coloreds developed their own culture and spoke their own brand of Afrikaans, known as kitchen Afrikaans. Thus we were all divided neatly into compartments depending on the pigmentation of our skins. Sometimes the whites were referred to as the Europeans because of their European ancestry, and the Africans were known as the Non-

Europeans because they hailed from other African countries north of the border. It was quite common to see one of two signs on benches or entrances to buildings: "Europeans Only" or "Non-Europeans Only." These signs were a constant reminder that if anyone protested the race policies of the government, they'd be immediately arrested and jailed. We lived in a police state, followed the laws of the land, sat on the appropriate benches, and went through the appropriate entrances.

As we stood at the Cape Point, my mom said, "I can just imagine how the sea-weary sailors felt when they first set eyes on the magnificent Cape." As she spoke, I thought of how they must have held their breath for a moment to take it all in. The city must have flowered before their eyes.

Now seagulls squawked above us while baboons ran along the road, occasionally jumping on our car looking for food. My eyes scaled upwards to the flat tabletop mountain, and then I looked down toward the ocean where the waves crashed on the beautiful Clifton and Muizenberg beaches.

"Tomorrow we're going up the mountain in the cable car," my father announced. The next day, my heart pounded with excitement as we stood in line, ready to take the cable car up to the top of the beautiful Table Mountain. When we finally entered the small cable car, I saw a kaleidoscope of color. Wild flowers of creamy white, butter yellow, salmon pink and brilliant reds all cascaded along the side of the mountain. There were poppies, daisies, proteas, (the national flower of South Africa), and many more growing wild. I was filled with the aroma of the flowers. From the top of the mountain we had breathtaking views of the city and the ocean below. In the afternoon we drove to the wine lands of Stellenbosch, just out of the city, and my parents tasted all the samples of South African wines.

Soon our pockets were empty and we were making our way back home to our dusty little town. I had just a few days to get my uniform ready before returning to Eunice and the start of my second year in high school.

——⊰◆⊱——

THE FIVE YEARS at Eunice went by swiftly. I was now in my final year, preparing for my senior matric exams.

A few weeks before graduation we had to each meet privately with Mrs. De Jager, to discuss our post high school plans. When it was my turn, I carefully pushed open the door with the sign "Principal" on the outside. This office always represented punishment to me. Usually, a student went to the principal's office only when she did something wrong. This time it was different, but the butterflies still flapped around in my stomach as I sat down in the chair opposite Mrs. De Jager, shifting around nervously.

"Tell me about your plans for next year."

I told her that I was going to go to the Nursery School Teachers' Training College in Johannesburg. I told her that my parents and brother had moved from Reitz to Johannesburg and that I would be living at home with them and attending college.

"I've always loved little children and it's been my goal for many years."

"Are you planning to keep up your athletics?" she asked, taking off her glasses, leaning forward and looking straight at me. I told her that I hoped to. Then she stood up, and from across the desk, shook my hand and smilingly said, "Lorraine, you should definitely keep up your running. I want to thank you for the honor you brought to our school."

"Mrs. De Jager, the honor was all mine."

I walked out of her office thinking, *she's a real lady.*

When the day of graduation arrived, December 1963, there were lots of hugs and tears. As we all set out for different parts of the country, we knew that there were some of our friends we might never see again. So at the age of 17, when the time came to sing our school song for the last time at graduation, I got ready to belt out the first line as I had done a hundred times before.

"The wall around has changed since the corner stone was laid."

We were handed a sheet of paper with the words of our school song. This was the first time I had actually seen the words in print. I discovered that for five years I had sung the wrong words! The first line was not;

"The *wall* around has changed..." but in fact: "*Though all* around has changed since the corner stone was laid.... "

I wondered if I would have been allowed to graduate if anyone knew that I'd been singing the wrong words all those years. In that ultra-strict educational environment, maybe I would have been forced to repeat a year!

<hr />

MY PARENTS CAME to fetch me, and as we drove out of the gates I took one last look back at the ivy-covered walls. Then I turned around, laid my head back on the car seat, closed my eyes and reflected back on my strict years at Eunice. I contemplated what I had gained and what I had lost there. We had all been completely intimidated by our teachers. We had cultivated, first and foremost, the habit of unquestioning obedience. We were never encouraged to challenge a teacher if we disagreed or to debate an issue. Never. It was a stifling environment in the classroom. On the other hand, despite the strict environment, there were definite advantages to being in an all girls' school. We went to school to *study*. There were no boys in class to be a distraction, and I was less concerned about asking questions for fear of sounding dumb in front of the boys. The strict rules I had had to live by gave me an order and discipline in my life that is with me still to this day. Living in such close quarters with others, I had learned to be respectful toward my friends and to be considerate toward my fellow students. I learned that rules and laws were there to be kept and not broken, and I learned that if they were broken, there were consequences. It was a character-building experience. Leaving home at such a young age, I had had to become independent. I had made my own decisions, chosen my own courses, found ways to finish my projects on time, and booked my own trips to go home. I had learned to trust my own judgment.

The independence I had earned there prepared me well for a later stage in my life, when I would once again leave home for a far more distant destination. I'm grateful to my parents for their foresight in sending me to Eunice. The pluses far outweighed the minuses.

Johannesburg

It was late afternoon in April 1964, a beautiful autumn day in Johannesburg. I was eighteen and in my first year of college. I loved living in Jo'burg, as it was known colloquially; another name was The City of Gold.

The discovery of gold around Johannesburg in 1886 set off a population explosion and mass migration from all around the world. Johannesburg quickly became the largest and most cosmopolitan city in South Africa, a status it retained even after the gold was stripped clean. For me, coming from the somewhat less glamorous outposts of Reitz and Bloemfontein, it was the most exciting place imaginable to live.

I stopped to do some shopping on my way home from college. As I walked out of the OK Bazaars Department Store, I gazed up at the cloudless expanse of blue sky. Yet another typically gorgeous day. My teased, sleeked-over beehive hairdo was kept neatly in place with tons of lacquer spray. It would have taken a number six eruption on the Richter scale to move a single dark hair on my head. The British model Twiggy had spread her influence all over South Africa. We now wore miniskirts and big plastic earrings. My platform sandals added four inches to my height. My mascara was thick as tar, just like Twiggy's, and my fingernails were long and tapered. I had just bought a new black eyeliner pencil to complete the "hard" look of the middle 1960's.

I arranged to meet my friend Sybil for coffee. I walked to the nearby tram stop for the short ride to the café in the cosmopolitan part of Jo'burg, called Hillbrow, where we had agreed to meet. I sat and waited for the tram on the green bench where the words "Whites Only" were painted in white. Both Africans and whites knew better than to ignore these signs. If a white person sat on a Non-Whites Only bench or walked through a Non-Whites Only entrance, he or she would be viewed as a militant who was defying the apartheid laws, and thus represented a threat to the regime.

Soon I heard the rumbling of the double-decker tram, and saw its long cable arm clinging to the electric wiring that ran above the street. It was red, the color of the "Whites Only" trams; I could get on. The green trams were for the "Non-Whites."

The strict laws of separation were everywhere in Johannesburg. I walked through "Whites Only" doors, sat on "Whites Only" benches in the parks, "Whites Only" buses, trains, schools, swimming pools and hospitals. The state's racist ideology simply became part of the landscape. Occasionally, I thought about my grandparents and great-grandparents, who had lived in countries where, as Jews, they had been discriminated against, in much the way the Africans were in South Africa. Was I complicit by living here and abiding by these laws? Yet what else could one do in the police state into which I had been born? I put the thought out of my head, followed the laws, and tried not to pursue the matter.

Right before the tram stopped near the café however, I saw something I had never seen before: an organized protest.

About fifty students from the Witwatersrand University, known as Wits, were staging a peaceful march down the street in front of the university. They were protesting the government's censorship of newspapers, magazines, movies and books. The homemade signs were crudely painted in different colors. The signs read: "No More Censorship" and "Down With Censorship." No one uttered a sound. They just held the signs above their heads as they marched and let the signs do the talking. I scanned the students' faces for people I knew. There wasn't anyone. The street was lined with policemen on either side taking photos of the students. As their cameras were clicking, I wondered how long it would be before the police used those photos against them. Any anti-government activity was punishable with indefinite detainment. I couldn't imagine myself being brave enough to protest openly like that. I admired them for standing up, yet I wondered if they were brave or foolish. I'd ask Sybil what she thought.

As I got off the tram, my mind went back to my early days in Reitz; I remembered the old bioscope where we saw American movies. We kids used to like to sit upstairs. To get to the upstairs, we had to use a wooden ladder. I always made sure that no boys were behind me, so that they wouldn't be able to look up my dress as I climbed.

The biggest frustration about going to the movies was not the climb up the ladder, or the constant interruption whenever the film broke; it was the censorship. Any scene that had a mixed racial couple or a scene showing a black person in a position of authority would be cut out. The cuts in the film were glaringly obvious; sometimes they fell in mid-sentence. The butchering inevitably interrupted the flow of the story and left us all wondering what, exactly, we were missing and what was so terrible that we couldn't see it. I often heard my parents joking about this; my mom would say, "We're like children whose parents need to censor what we see."

I entered the café and saw that Sybil had arrived just a few minutes before me, and was sitting at the table by the window. I sat down opposite her, pulling at my miniskirt. It was always a challenge to sit in a miniskirt without it riding up to one's waist. Sybil wore her blonde hair piled up high on top of her head, and her black eyeliner was even more severe than mine. She liked to extend the eyeliner out to make her eyes look like cat's eyes. We each ordered coffee and a rusk. The café was known for its buttermilk rusks; when they arrived, we dunked them into our coffee.

"You won't believe what I just saw." I told her. "About fifty students from Wits were in a protest march."

"A protest march?" Sybil was shocked.

"We *never* see a protest march in South Africa. Do you think those students were brave or foolish to do that?"

Without a moment's hesitation Sybil said, "I think they're pretty stupid. Now their photos are on file with the police, and their march won't accomplish anything. It will be headlines tomorrow and then we won't hear another word about it again. We all know why the government has such a strong censorship on all materials."

She meant, of course, that the government didn't want us to see how black people lived in other countries or to see blacks operating on an equal basis with whites in the workplace or socially. We had all heard stories from people who had returned from overseas, from countries where a system of racially segregated streetcars was unthinkable. Sybil said that the government was protecting us from having to see, or think of, such ways of living. They didn't want us to get ideas. We all learned from a very young age that there were certain laws that had to be strictly obeyed. The government was our "father" and we did as we were told with unquestioning obedience, or there'd be severe consequences. Even if someone called for *more* rights, not necessarily *equal* rights for the Africans, that person was branded as a "Kaffir boetie." Being a "Kaffir brother" was tantamount to being a threat to the country, and was very likely to attract the attention of the police. Something called the Suppression of Communism Act, which dated back to 1950, saw to that. The wording was so broad that any person calling for racial change, even a minor change, or expressing opposition to the government in any way, could be branded a Communist, and was subject to house arrest indefinitely without a trial.

When the waitress brought our order, we automatically stopped talking until she had left. We instinctively knew to be careful about who might overhear this type of conversation. If someone heard us and thought we were being critical of the government, we could be reported to the police. When the waitress was gone, Sybil continued, "Lorraine, as you know, anyone who opposes this government has three choices…"

"Yes" I interrupted her, "I know what the choices are."

The three choices Sybil alluded to were:

First: speaking out against the government and going to jail.

Second: keeping quiet and just living our lives.

Third: leaving the country.

There was a silence. Then I said, "My cousin Marcelle has an aunt on her father's side that had to leave the country, because she was found in Soweto conspiring with the Africans. Now she lives in London and can never come back. "

Sybil nodded. "Remember that guy who quickly and quietly left last year?" she asked. "Apparently he was seeing an Indian girl and they wanted to get married. They're also living in London," Sybil added.

I shifted in my seat. "Have you noticed," I asked, "how many of those who have had to leave the country are Jewish?"

This was because the Jews made up a large part of the liberal population, who were considered traitors to the regime. The Progressive Party, headed by Helen Suzman and even the United Party, had a disproportionate number of Jews, people like Joe Slovo and Albie Sachs, who were accused of working with the African National Congress, a radical group that aimed to overthrow the apartheid regime.

"Of course," she said. "I think it's because Jews have fled oppression throughout their history and don't want to be part of oppression in this country. That's what I think."

"And yet," I said, "many Jews, like us, still stay. It's a wonderful life ... if you're white."

"Where else in the world could we live in big homes with pools and tennis courts and have two or three servants?" Sybil asked. "Overseas, this lifestyle would be reserved for the ultra wealthy."

"People overseas say that we're living off the backs of the Africans. They do the hard work and we enjoy the benefits and privileges," I said with unease.

"Well," Sybil said, "they shouldn't be too quick to sit in judgment. If they were born into this society on the "right side of the fence" what would they do? Remember, if you choose to leave this country, you have to leave all your money behind! No one should sit in judgment until they've walked in our shoes."

My thoughts drifted again to my grandparents, who fled oppression in Eastern Europe. They weren't born into this society, and yet they put down roots in South Africa and chose to live under this apartheid regime. I wondered how they felt about it. Maybe it bothered them and maybe it didn't. Or maybe they just wanted to make a living, practice their religion freely and put food on the table for their families. Maybe they weren't political at all.

While I was talking to Sybil, a young African boy of about twelve wandered into the café and went to the counter. His pants were ripped at the knees and his shoes didn't match. He wanted to buy a Coca-Cola. His outstretched hand with its palm facing upwards revealed a few shillings. The woman behind the counter took the coins and then quietly escorted him back to the entrance and asked him to wait there. Then she brought him the Coke and the puzzled child stood drinking his soda at the door. The woman, like me, was a product of the culture. If she had allowed the boy to stay *in* the café she would have been fired or arrested. Sybil and I looked at each other.

"I hope he doesn't grow up to be an angry man who will come after us someday." I said softly. "If an uprising ever occurs, they'll come for *all* of us regardless of whether we supported apartheid or not. My dad says they'll paint us all with one brush." I squirmed uncomfortably in my seat at the thought.

"Oh, don't be so dramatic," she said. "This is our life. You know as well as I do that there are twenty five million Africans and three million whites. If we gave them equality and the vote or allowed them to organize, it would be the end of us." Now she sounded like my father.

I stared into my cup of coffee. I didn't like to think about any of that "end of us" business. The thought frightened me, just like my mother's talk about a bloody uprising.

———※◆※———

AFTER MY COFFEE date with Sybil, I walked home thinking about our conversation.

It was the month of April, and for a very short time the air was filled with the mixture of summer and autumn. The sunset before me glowed, magnificent. It felt good to be able to think after all that talking.

The wail of a siren suddenly shattered the moment's beauty. I recognized the sound immediately: It was one of the vans we called "The Black

Mariah." The policemen who drove those vans were getting ready to look for any Africans still on the streets after dark without a pass. They did this every day. If they found anyone after curfew, they rounded them up and then put them into the Black Mariah. We all knew that bad things, like beatings by the police, happened in the back of these vans.

The worst crime of a totalitarian state is that it forces its citizens into complicity. Even though my parents and I never voted to support the apartheid regime, its policies invaded our private spaces and forced us to become accomplices of sorts — by forcing us to follow the system, ride special trams, and ignore things like the Black Mariah. Realizing this made me feel helpless and guilty.

We were all victims in a sense ... except we were the privileged victims.

———◆———

UNLIKE MANY AMERICAN college students, I followed the South African custom and lived at home with my parents, who were now living in Johannesburg. My mother had insisted on the move when Selwyn came home from school one day with bruises all over his shoulders, the result of a beating he'd received from some boys who had attacked him and called him a Jew. "We're moving to Jo'burg so that Selwyn can be in a school with other Jewish children," my mother had said. She was emphatic on the point. Even though both my parents agreed on this decision, it was my dad who made the biggest sacrifice. My mother would live in Johannesburg and he would be in the Free State during the week, living in a hotel and attending the cattle sales, and he'd come home on Fridays for the weekend. It was a sacrifice he had made willingly for his family.

By the time I got home after my visit with Sybil, it was dinnertime. The aroma of my mom's sweet and sour cabbage soup engulfed the house. We all sat around the table: my parents, Selwyn and me. My mom started ladling the soup into the cream-colored china soup bowls, each with a gold rim around the edges. The soup was scalding, just the way my dad liked it, and the steam made little curls as it escaped upwards from the bowl. I had to blow on each spoonful before I carefully put it near my lips. Although this was my favorite soup, on this night I barely tasted anything. I was preoccupied with the march.

"I saw something today that I'd never seen before." I told them about the protest march. My mom wiped her mouth with the serviette, looked at me for a moment, and then said, "You were too young to remember, but I recall very clearly the day this right wing Afrikaner Nationalist Party came into power. They swept the 1948 elections, being that the majority of whites in the country were Afrikaners. After their win, they coined the term "apartheid." They said they had found a formula which would ensure the future of the white minority into the next century."

"But there was always segregation in South Africa," I noted.

"Yes, but it was never an official policy with strict punishment for those who didn't comply," she said. "Their plan was to fabricate a permanent white political majority by not allowing any non-whites to vote. Daddy and I always voted for the opposing party, and we were plenty worried when this group took over the government. There's not much we can do now."

Just as Sybil had done, she was referring to the fact that any criticism of the government made that person subject to immediate arrest.

In accordance with the law of the land, a person was guilty until proven innocent. Actually, guilt or innocence didn't even matter, because there were no trials and the jail terms were indefinite.

We were finishing our dinner of soup followed by shepherd's pie. Despite my preoccupation, I carefully ate the top mashed potatoes before digging into the minced meat below. I placed my knife and fork next to each other in the middle of the plate, the way I was taught, to show that I was finished.

My dad weighed in. As usual, he opposed the regime and was ready as always to vote against it, but he was concerned that if the Africans were given the vote or even more freedom, it would be suicide for us. "They outnumber us twenty to one," he reminded me. "I don't think they'd stop and ask which party you voted for." My parents each discussed the protest with their well-worn positions: "We'd all be painted with one broad brush," he said with a sweep of his hand side to side, imitating a paintbrush. "And by the way, how do we know that if the Africans were in power, they wouldn't do the same to us?" he asked. My mother repeated *her* famous line: "We're living in a fool's paradise." This time, however, she added: "My prediction is that someday, when they get organized and rise up against the whites, there'll be the worst bloodbath the world has ever witnessed."

"Mommy, that's a terrible thing to say."

"We're all bloody fools," she said. It sounded like "bladdy fools."

"If they could organize and arrange to put some poison in every white person's afternoon tea, they could wipe us out in one day."

According to my mom, we were constantly poised on the brink of some tsunami-like disaster that we couldn't do anything about. I envisioned all the whites being swept up together in the lashing of a big angry wave and deposited into the hungry sea. Even though I knew she didn't intend it, that kind of talk from my mother created a lot of anxiety in me. The fear started in the base of my spine and worked its way up to the back of my neck: I had visions of thousands of Africans marching into the towns and cities all over the country carrying spears and shields, chanting as they shook their spears, ready to kill all the whites. I could never imagine a peaceful co-existence between the racial groups after all the years of oppression.

———◆———

MY OWN POLITICAL views were now taking shape. They were somewhere between my mother's and my father's. I believed that every human being should be treated with respect regardless of skin color, yet my dad's voice always echoed in my head, reminding me that "they" had much to be vengeful about. I had been born into a culture that seemed to require a "them" and an "us" situation. This fact left both a constant nagging pull at my conscience and a practical sense of alarm.

My mother spoke about an African man who had been jailed for many years for speaking out against the apartheid regime and wanting to overthrow the government. She was convinced that if he ever got out of jail, he would rally his people, filled with revenge and hate, and come after all of us. "I can't blame him, but God help us if he ever gets out of prison."

He was the head of the African National Congress, also known as the ANC, regarded by most whites as a radical black party. I didn't know anything about him other than what I read in the papers. He was described as a terrorist, a trouble-maker who advocated violence. His name was Nelson Mandela.

Time would prove this assessment of Mandela wrong, of course. Even though I had been brought up to associate the name Nelson Mandela with terrorism and violence, history had different ideas.

How was the South African regime able to brainwash sensible people like my parents and me? As my friend Sybil said, you have to live in a place to truly understand it. The government's very real threats of imprisonment for anyone foolish enough to speak out, and the constant scare tactics about the "black takeover," made the most sensible person become complicit. And I was complicit. I believed what I was told by my parents, and they believed what they were told by the regime they opposed.

—————◆—————

THE WORLD WAS now putting pressure on South Africa to change its race policies, and they threatened sanctions. Our government took a stubborn stance, and refused to budge one inch from the apartheid state it had created. We were a self-sufficient country, with a strong military and all the natural resources we needed. The regime didn't have to buckle to anyone. They continued to rule with an iron fist. They did not care what the rest of the world said or did.

As it turned out, however, I did care. I knew for certain that I cared when the International Olympic Committee decided to ban South Africa from the Olympic Games in Tokyo in 1964. I had won the South African championships that year, and my place on the Olympic Team was a real possibility.

My new coach, Dusan, broke the news to our group of runners at our workout. Dusan pulled out the newspapers tucked under his arm and showed them to us. We were all stunned. The IOC said that unless South Africa was prepared to have interracial trials and send a fully integrated team, they'd be barred from sending any team at all. We knew that the government would never send an interracial team. The controversy was effectively over. We would not be going to the Olympics. It was an enormous blow. "The only ones who will suffer from this ban are the athletes," I said to my workout buddies.

"Exactly," Dusan added. "The government won't change its policies just so that a group of athletes can go to the Olympics."

"There's a point to this," one of the guys said. "If you win a gold medal at the Olympics, you're just a gold medalist, but you're not necessarily the best in the world. As long as there's a country that is depriving a segment of its population from competing, how do you know what talent lurks amongst those people. So you're only the best amongst those who were allowed to compete"

"It's not fair," I said, taking off my spikes. "We've all worked out so hard to reach this point. Sports and politics shouldn't mix. Why should we suffer for the policies of the government?" I knew it was a rhetorical question. No one could answer it, but some tried. The pole-vaulter, Danie said, "We can't separate ourselves from the politics. After all, we live in this country and enjoy its bounty, so that makes us accomplices to the policies."

"I disagree," I said. "I didn't choose to live in South Africa. I was born here. This is my home and this is where my parents and brother live." I continued, "The Olympics is a dream of every athlete. Why should a talented athlete be denied that chance?"

"Because the white athletes, just like any other profession, are part of the fabric of the society," Danie added. I was trying hard to see his point of view, and deep down I knew he was right. In fact, as he spoke, an image from the recesses of my mind played out: those little African children chasing after my father's truck on the farm. I remembered how astonished I had been at their ability to run fast, and keep running. Such amazing raw talent! What would their lives have been like if they had had the opportunity to be trained by a good coach? What about those young black boys and girls who never even have a chance to find out whether they have a talent?

Still, the deep hurt in my soul was clouding my rational thinking. Danie might have been right, but the loss didn't hurt any less because of that. This was as close as I would ever get to realize my Olympic dream, and that dream was now shattered.

"I wonder if this will discourage future young athletes from pursuing their talents and dreams," I said to him, taking off my running spikes.

I drove home after my workout with a thousand thoughts mulling around in my head. *It's not my fault. I didn't make the apartheid laws. Why should I be denied my opportunity to try out for the Olympics? But*

Danie says we're all guilty just by living here and enjoying what this country has to offer.

This was yet another price we were paying for living in South Africa. On the one hand, I was living a privileged life, with a large home and servants. Many of my friends had pools and tennis courts too. Yet on the other hand, we were the pariahs of the world.

I wondered if anyone would protest and speak out. But I knew the answer. They wouldn't, because no one wants to spend the rest of his life in jail, and that is exactly what would happen if anyone crossed the authorities. Debates like this went on all over the country, but they took place in the privacy of people's homes. Apartheid came with a steep price, and all the citizens paid the price together.

We lived in a sports-crazy country, and this ban hit us all hard. Our rugby and cricket teams were also banned from international competition. Along with the censorship and other strict laws, it was just another thing we had to learn to live with.

The South African Olympic team was never officially announced, but given my times in the 100 and 200 meters that year, I'm sure I would have had a place on the team. This was my one shot. In four years time, who knew where I'd be in my life?

Eventually, I accepted reality. My Olympic dream was over before it had begun.

Looking back now, I'm able to see the big picture more clearly. I realize that in the grand scheme of things, the Olympic dream was a moment in my life, while the apartheid oppression was an ongoing daily occurrence for part of the South African population.

I remember being disappointed for Dusan too. He had invested so many hours coaching me.

My mind drifted back to the first time I met him.

◆

MY PARENTS HAD moved to Johannesburg, the city of gold, in 1962. I was in my matric (senior) year at Eunice High School, so I stayed there until the end of the year, when I graduated. One afternoon during my school vacation, while visiting my parents in their new home in Johannesburg, I went to the Wits University track to work out. I noticed a few other athletes warming up, but I mainly focused on my own workout schedule, the schedule that Mrs. Brand gave me. While I was resting between my repeats, a man walked up to me. He was of medium height with a stocky build and light brown straight hair. He had piercing blue eyes and an accent that I'd never heard before. He said, "I couldn't help noticing you running. You have a very easy and good running style, and you look as if you've been coached. Do you belong to a track club here in Johannesburg?"

"No, I go to school in Bloemfontein," I answered. I introduced myself and told him that I'd be moving to Johannesburg the following year.

"My name is Dusan."

He said that he'd be interested in coaching me, and he invited me to join the group. When he gestured toward the guys who were warming up on the other side of the track, my mouth dropped open. They were some of the top runners in the country. There was Judge Jeffreys who was the South African record holder in the 100 and 200 meters; Peter Rich, the

400 meters hurdles champion; Donald McDonald, another champion hurdler; Neil McDonald; Stanley Wald; and a few others.

I was overwhelmed that a coach of this caliber would be interested in coaching me, and was thrilled to accept his offer. Dusan told me that he had emigrated from Belgrade in Yugoslavia, where he coached the Yugoslavian Olympic team before leaving to come to South Africa. He said with pride, "I'm a Serb." I couldn't wait to tell my parents about my meeting with Dusan.

"He told me that we'd be doing weight training in the winter and track work in the summer." I was excited to share the news with my parents.

"Weight training?" My father seemed horrified. "I'm telling you, Lolzy, women aren't supposed to lift weights. You'll damage your insides and you won't be able to have children one day. It's not healthy for a girl to run track like that, and it's certainly not healthy for you to lift heavy weights," he said.

The next time I saw Dusan, I told him what my father said.

"You tell your father that you'll be so strong and healthy that when you have children one day, you'll hop on and off the delivery table." My father wasn't convinced, but I eventually won him over. He continued to accompany my mother to all my track meets, with his heavy 16mm movie camera slung over his shoulder.

———⊰◆⊱———

EVEN THOUGH I was devastated about the expulsion from the Olympics, I knew that I'd be able to try out for the Maccabi Games held in Israel the following year, 1965, for Jewish athletes from around the world. The

International Olympic Committee didn't govern the games in Israel, so South Africa could still send a team. My non-Jewish friends weren't so lucky. They now had no opportunity for international competition.

After the 1964 Olympics, the Japanese swimming team made a world tour and asked if they could swim some exhibition races against our swimmers. This was an enormous honor for South Africa, and we all looked forward to it. However, the government had a monumental dilemma. According to its own laws of apartheid, the Japanese were not considered white and therefore weren't allowed to swim in our pools or compete against our white athletes. The government concocted a solution. They decided to declare all Japanese in the country "honorary whites." As my mother always said, "They'll twist things to suit themselves."

From that point forward, the Japanese living in South Africa could enjoy all the privileges that the whites had. This privilege was not extended to the Chinese, only the Japanese. It made about as much sense as the rest of the system did.

It was twenty-five years before South Africa was once again allowed to compete in international sports competitions.

CHAPTER
Nine

Love At The Maccabi Games

The seconds between "Get Set" and "Go" always seemed like an eternity, but when the starter's gun finally sounded, every ounce of adrenalin in my body rushed forth like a raging river propelling me out of my starting blocks and toward the winning tape, which at that moment seemed much further away than just 100 meters. With an exhale on "go" and a quick inhale, I held my breath the whole way like I always did, so as not to exert any extra energy. As I sprinted toward the finish line, my muscles yelled for more blood; my senses were numb. I could feel the wind brushing against my cheeks and I was vaguely aware of a swelling sound coming from the crowd in the stands. I was hoping that my legs would keep up with my willpower.

The year was 1965, I was nineteen, the place was Israel, and the event was the 100 meters final at the the Maccabi Games. South Africa was once again one of thirty-seven countries competing, and I was privileged to participate.

I'd worked hard to get to that point, doing my long road running to

The Maccabi Games poster for 1965

build stamina before classes early in the morning and then doing speed work on the track in the late afternoon. There were months of interval training, running about ten repeats of a certain distance — say, 100 or 200 meters at a specific speed — with a five-minute rest between each one, and then practicing hundreds of "starts." During the "off season" there'd been rigorous weight training, and, of course, all the sweat and strain that had come in the years before. It all came down to this moment.

Split seconds may be tiny slivers of time, but they are also the difference between winning and losing a race. In my head, I could hear my coach's voice saying, "C'mon Lorraine, this is it."

As the finish line rushed towards me at lightning speed, I crossed over ... first. I checked the clock. It was a new Maccabi record. I bent over with my hands resting on my knees, gasping for air. I felt thrilled and honored to have won a gold medal for my country.

I found myself thinking about how this all started seven months earlier.

——◆——

"MAZEL TOV! YOU made the team!" My mom had phoned me at college with the news. I felt a thrill run through my body. My insides swirled. "I have to phone Dusan right now to tell him," I said.

I could hardly contain my euphoria as I told him the great news. Dusan knew this was my dream. I had gone to these games in 1961 and I desperately wanted to go again in 1965, especially after the disappointment of South Africa being expelled from the Olympics the year before.

It was January when I found out, which meant I had seven months to prepare for the Games. Dusan immediately started me on a training program to build endurance and strength, using long distance running and weights. Then, the last month, I'd be reducing the distance and increasing the speed. "Tapering off," was the way he put it. The goal was to peak in August when the team was to leave for Israel.

I sat on the soft green lawn, in the shade cast by the large cricket scoreboard at one end of the field. The grass track at the Wanderers Club circled the cricket field in the center. I was unlacing my spikes after a hard workout, with a sheen of sweat still on my forehead and upper lip. My Yugoslavian coach Dusan sat down next to me and asked, "What is the history of the Maccabi Games? How did it start?"

While massaging my tired, aching feet with my hands, I explained, "These Games were first held in what was then known as Palestine in 1932."

"Really? Before World War II?"

"Yes. There was a lot of anti-Semitism sweeping Europe after the Nazis gained power in Germany, and the British were blocking Jewish entry into Palestine. So, many Jews from European countries attended the Games in 1932 as a means of entry into the country, and of escaping the Nazis — and then they just stayed. An uncle on my mother's side was one of the athletes who escaped the Nazis as a member of the track team from Poland, and then stayed on in what would eventually become Israel. His daughter Aliza and I are still in touch today."

"That's a great story," he said.

I'm sure Dusan also had a great story to tell, but I never heard it. He, too, was an insider and an outsider. As I turn back the pages in my memory, I can't help but wonder what he thought of the apartheid system, and what his life was like in Yugoslavia. At that age and stage of my life, my relationship with Dusan was all about starts, dashes, stretches, and times. If I could, I'd like to spend an hour with him today and ask him more about his own history.

The Maccabi Games became an opportunity for the best Jewish athletes from their respective countries to meet and bond in an atmosphere of sportsmanship, camaraderie, and healthy competition. The whole South African team gathered a few days before our departure for Israel. There

were over 100 athletes from all over the country who were going to participate in various sports. I met the manager of the track team, Lou Abrams.
He had a receding hairline and big warm smile under his dark moustache.

"Nice to meet you Lorraine. I've been watching you run for a long
time, and I look forward to working with you."

"Thank you, Lou."

We were all issued the dress uniforms that we would wear at the
Opening Ceremony, as well as outfits for the competitions; the uniform
displayed the traditional green and gold colors of our country. The green
blazer with the Star of David on the pocket fit me perfectly. I ran my
hands over the soft, light fabric of my running shorts and top, and noticed
that the quality was much improved from the last games four years ago.
I went into the change room and tried the new outfit on, then pumped
my arms back and forth as if I were running, to make sure the armholes
were wide enough to be comfortable. Everything was perfect. I looked at
myself in the mirror in the new uniform. I was beginning to get psyched.

When we boarded the EL AL plane in Johannesburg in August, I
was ready to go. The eleven-hour flight went quickly as I chatted with all
my new teammates. The team consisted of the finest Jewish athletes in
South Africa, and it was good to see the faces that went with the names I
had read so much about in the newspapers.

Sooner than any of us expected, we heard the pilot, with his Israeli
accent say, "We'll be landing in Tel Aviv's Lod airport shortly. Please fasten your seatbelts and bring your seats to an upright position."

"Wow, look how Tel Aviv has grown," I said in amazement. I was
glad I had gotten a window seat. As we descended on Tel Aviv, the plane

cast its shadow over the pale sand-colored buildings, the color of milky tea. We were about to touch down in Israel, the land of my people, the land that I learned so much about in Bible classes back in Reitz. Not only that, but I was there to compete in the Games. I took a deep breath to steady my nerves.

As we touched down and the tires hit the runway, the stewardess said, "Welcome to Israel." Immediately the song "Havenu Shalom" played over the intercom. There was a lump in my throat and I swallowed hard. At the airport we saw the familiar sight of Israeli soldiers in their khaki uniforms with Uzis slung over their shoulders. These dark, good-looking men and women soldiers were part of the Israeli landscape, providing a feeling of comfort in this hostile terrain. I noticed that there were no signs segregating people. Everyone walked through the same doors and sat on the same benches.

As the bus drove us from the airport to the Maccabi Village, I over-heard excited conversations all around me about how much had changed in just four years. It was as if my teammates were reading my mind.

"Look at all the new buildings and roads."

"Can you believe what this little country has achieved here in the desert?"

"Look at all the orange orchards and flower farms."

"It's amazing how Israel has turned the desert into a garden. It really has flourished and made the desert bloom."

Finally we turned into the village. I was immediately struck by the festive mood. Israeli music was blaring from large speakers and the flags of all the countries flanked either side of the entrance. They hung limp in the hot blazing Middle Eastern August weather. Already the torrid air stuck my clothes to my skin.

There were countless new people to meet, but I couldn't get too caught up in socializing until my races were over. I had to stay focused on my reason for being there. I needed to keep the three D's sharply in my mind ... dedication, determination and desire. *Stay focused, stay focused.*

The night before my first race, the 100 meters, I lay in bed, visualizing the race in my mind before falling asleep. I saw myself over and over again sprinting down the lane to the finish. I also recalled Dusan's words.

Standing on podium

"Remember that 100 meters is won or lost at the start. There is no time to make up for a slow start. You *must* be out of those blocks first. You've practiced it a thousand times."

The day of my race I was fighting my own private war of nerves, trying to still the turmoil in my stomach. I made sure, as usual, that none of my opponents knew how nervous I was. I did my warm up by jogging a few laps first and then stretching. I never made eye contact with my opponents. This was the strategy that always worked for me. When the race was over, I was the friendliest girl in the world, but not before.

⇒•⇐

AFTER MY 100 meters race, while I was still savoring my gold medal, Lou, the manager of the track team, came to me with a suggestion that threw me completely off balance.

"There is an opening in the 400 meters tomorrow and I want you to run in that race."

Is he serious? I asked myself.

I laughed and said, "Lou, you've got to be joking. I've never run a 400 meters race before. I'd have no idea how to pace myself. Besides, my 200 meters race is the day after. I'm not going to drain my energy on something I've never done before and risk jeopardizing my chances in the two hundred." That was my best event.

"No," I said emphatically, shaking my head. "How can I run a race like that for the first time in an international competition?"

"Lorraine, listen carefully," he said, putting his hand on my shoulder, and I noticed the intense look on his face. "During workouts, you run 400's five or six times, so you know how to do this. Think of it as a practice. This won't hurt your 200 race. You're in great enough shape to run it and then come back the next day with no problem at all." I could feel his penetrating gaze as he waited for my response. After much deliberation, but still with enormous doubts, I overrode my own instincts and agreed.

"Great, here's how you run it. Just get out in front and then try to hold the lead for as long as you can."

I remembered feeling the same bewilderment a few years earlier when Dusan had approached me with a suggestion that seemed just as crazy.

"Lorraine, I want you to try running hurdles."

"What? Why?"

"Because you're tall, you have the speed, and you've got a nice long stride. You could be an excellent hurdler. Just try it."

So I tried it. At the next few workouts I learned how to count my strides between the hurdles, "one, two, three, up." I'd shoot out my front leg, arms out to the side for balance, and then snap my leg down on the other side of the hurdle.

The day of the track meet where I would be making my hurdles debut, I stood behind my starting blocks. I tried to scan my lane to the finish like I always did. I couldn't because the hurdles were in the way. I panicked.

What if I don't get my rhythm right? What if I fall on a hurdle?

Mentally, I was in no shape to run. Then I did something I'd never done before and have never done since. In fact I've never told this to anyone; writing it down in this book is the first time I've admitted it. I *inten-*

tionally got myself disqualified by making two false starts. I told Dusan flatly that I would never run hurdles again. My career as a hurdler ended before it began.

Now I was hoping Lou's crazy idea wouldn't end the same way. The next day, after my usual warm-up, we lined up for the 400 meters. Could the other girls hear my pounding heart? My nerves were shaking like the needle on a bad compass. Usually my nervousness before a race was adrenalin; I welcomed that jolt, and actually relied on it to push me beyond what I thought I could do. But this was different. I was panicked and I was way out of my comfort zone.

I had the inside lane and stood waiting for the starter to call us to our marks. I zeroed in and again scanned my lane to the finish, but this time it felt awkward as my eyes traveled along the lane, around the track with the final stretch behind me, to complete the full lap. I realized I was looking backwards approaching the finish line. I couldn't believe I agreed to do this.

Then I heard in Hebrew, "La'mekomot." I crouched down on my marks, took a deep breath and made sure each foot was securely planted against the blocks. "Hi'kon." I raised my hips to the set position with every muscle fiber taut and waiting.

When the gun sounded, I pumped my arms and blasted out of my starting blocks like a bullet. I was immediately out in front. I was a sprinter, after all, and that was the only way I knew how to start. I reminded myself to breathe; the distance was too long for me to complete it in a single breath, as I routinely did when running the hundred.

When I approached the final turn in the track I started to feel the effects of going out too fast and not pacing myself. Suddenly my legs started to feel weighty, as if I had cement in my shoes. I didn't know that lungs could sting so much; I was struggling to get air. In the final stretch, I had slowed down to what felt like a jog. I felt like a fly in Vaseline. I was laboring and gasping for air and my lungs were burning with every breath. Usually, running competitively was exhilarating for me. Flying down the track during a race I had trained for, with every cell filled with life — this was what I truly loved to do. But this race was different. It was torture. I was completely out of control. I just wanted it to end.

What was I thinking, running this race with no preparation or experience? Why did I let him talk me into it? Why isn't the winning tape getting any closer? Where are the other runners? How come they haven't all passed me by now?

Like a lighthouse in the fog, the finish line finally came into focus, and slowly but surely it crept closer and closer. Then, to my own shock and disbelief, I stumbled across the winning tape...first.

I flopped on the grass like a collapsed soufflé and thanked God, not for the victory, but for the fact that I was still alive. I had gone out way too fast, and then nearly fallen apart in the second half. I'd gained such a big lead, however, that the other runners weren't able to close the gap in time. It was clearly not the way to run a race, but it did get me another medal.

Two gold medals. I couldn't believe it. I wanted to kiss and kill Lou at the same time. I walked back into the village with my medal around my neck. Congratulations were coming at me in every language, but I could barely acknowledge them. I was exhausted and all too happy to get to my room for a well-earned shower.

400 meters race Israel 1965

—⟹◆⟸—

THE HOUSING FOR the athletes consisted of a few square shaped buildings, each about four or five stories high. They were built around a central courtyard, with all the terraces facing inwards overlooking the garden
below. The American and South African teams were housed in the same
building. The afternoon after my crazy 400 race, back in my room after
my shower, I wanted to look down at the courtyard, so I stepped onto the
terrace. I was vaguely aware of someone standing on the terrace opposite
mine with about fifty feet separating us. He was looking up, and seemed
to be talking to someone on the terrace above me. As I leaned over the

railing to look down I heard, "Hi." I lifted my head and my eyes moved in the direction of the voice. It was the guy on the terrace opposite mine. I noticed the "USA" on the front of his T-shirt.

"Hello" I said to the handsome stranger.

"Don't you remember me?" he asked. His accent was distinctly American; his voice trailed up at the end of the sentence, in the way of asking a question that all Americans seemed to have. I focused more closely on his face. I'm not always good with names but I never forget a face, especially one as friendly as his, with appealing boyish good looks. I was quite convinced that I had never seen him before.

"Should I? Have we met?" I asked. I felt certain he was giving me a line.

"Sure, at the last games. Don't you remember?"

"No. If we've met before," I said, "what do you know about me?" I looked him straight in the eye, challenging him.

"You're from South Africa and you're on the track team," he said with a disarming smile.

With a furrowed brow and a puzzled expression, I peered even harder at him. Now I felt a little embarrassed that I didn't remember him at all. He told me his name was Richard and he was a swimmer on the American team. Nope; it didn't ring a bell.

His sandy colored hair was cut very short in the typical style of a competitive swimmer. His broad shoulders and the muscles in his arms were well defined from what looked like years of workouts. We spoke for a while, and I was amazed at how much he knew about me.

When I reluctantly left to get ready for dinner, I was still puzzled that I had no recollection of him whatsoever. Even though I had only been 15 at the last games, I'm sure I would've remembered him. Was I losing my mind? That night when I got back to my room after dinner, I found a note under my door. I stooped to pick it up and it read:

"Good luck in the 200. Would like to take you out. Please. Rich."

A smile found its way to the corners of my mouth. I walked into my

Note from Richard

room and I tucked the note safely in the drawer next to my bed.

THE NEXT MORNING, while I was enjoying the traditional Israeli breakfast of yogurt with sliced cucumbers, tomatoes, humus, pita and fresh bread, Richard walked up to me and asked whether I had gotten his note. Some of the American swimmers were going to the nearby beach in Tel-Aviv to have a beach party after dinner that night. "Would you like to come with us?" he asked.

A beach party! I had only seen those in the movies. What a great way to celebrate the end of my competition. I would have loved to go with him ... but I knew I couldn't because I had already made a date with another American on the track team. I had been jogging around the track the day before when Bill caught up to me, and we jogged together for a while. He introduced himself and after some casual conversation, asked if I wanted to go out the following night. He was going into Tel Aviv with his coach for an early dinner first; we were planning to meet at the entrance of the village at 8pm when he got back. I had to decline Richard's offer.

I felt bad about that ... but I needed to put all this out of my head. It

Lorraine Lotzoff of South Africa, outstanding women athlete of the Games, who won and set records in the 100, 200 and 400 metre dashes.

200 meters Maccabi Games 1965

was time to stop thinking about dates and beach parties. There was still another race to run today.

Before my 200 meters race, an official held out the small satin pouch that held the plastic discs with the lane numbers, as is done before each race. I reached in and drew lane two. I would be running in my favorite lane in my favorite distance race. I shook my arms and legs to keep my muscles loose and my nerves intact. I stood behind my starting blocks and allowed my eyes to travel down the lane to the finish line.

Visualize. Visualize.

The starter called us to our marks. As I approached my starting blocks, for one milli-second a thought flashed through my head. *I hope the 400 meters didn't take too much out of me.* I quickly dismissed the thought. I crouched down; my fingertips carefully found the edge of the white line.

"Get set," he said in Hebrew. I raised my hips, weight on my arms and with every muscle taut like an arrow in a bow. I sucked in as much air as I could and held it for as long as possible.

"Go!"

I took the lead immediately and held it all the way. With the roar of the crowd I felt as if I was running into the mouth of a lion. Three gold medals and another Maccabi record.

I was standing on the winning dais for the third time, listening to "Die Stem," the anthem of my country. I touched the gold medal around my neck and watched as the South African flag was raised. *What an honor to be experiencing this.* In that moment I was proud to represent my country. For a few minutes all the injustices and ugliness of apartheid

ZIONIST RECORD AND S.A. JEWISH CHRONICLE, FRIDAY, SEPTEMBER 10, 196?

Lorraine is heroine of S.A. team at Maccabi Games

TEL AVIV: Nineteen-year-old Lorraine Lotzoff of Johannesburg is the heroine of the S.A. Maccabi team. She won three gold medals at the Maccabi Games.

Giving one of the best performances at the Maccabiah, she came first in the 100, 200 and 400 metres.

South Africa finished fourth in the Games. It won 11 gold medals, 11 silver and five bronze.

As expected, the Americans dominated most of the events and collected more medals than any other country.

Their enormous haul of 163 medals — including 75 gold — bettered even their magnificent performance at the Games four years ago, when they won 114 medals.

Their overwhelming superiority was challenged only by Israel, who finished second with 35 gold medals. Britain came third with 15 gold medals.

Although South Africa only came fourth, it can, in view of the size of its contingent, compared with the far larger teams, from America, Israel and Britain, be proud of its achievements at the Maccabi Games.

Jewish news papers

LORRAINE LOTZHOFF

By ERNST KLEYNHANS (Springbok Athlete.)

Fabulous Lorraine Lotzhoff — Three Gold Medals

The athletic contingent that represented South Africa at the Maccabi Games on the 3rd August, 1965, in Israel, consisted of five members: Ralph Youngworth, Steve Wald, Alan Sherman, Lorraine Lotzhoff and Neville Soll.

Lorraine Lotzhoff achieved the fantastic distinction of gaining three gold medals — an incredible performance! The Gold Medals were awarded for the 100 metres, 11.9 secs.; 200 metres, 25 secs.; and 400 metres, 59.4 seconds.

South Africa can indeed be proud of such a record.

SPRINGBOKS OVERSEAS, 1965 — 23

Woman athlete of the year

vanished, and I thought about my country's good people, natural beauty, and gorgeous weather. I enjoyed the moment. As I inhaled the cheers, with my body and my clothes still wet with sweat, my mind drifted to my family, friends, and coach back in Johannesburg. I couldn't wait to tell them. I could just hear my father asking, "How can you win three golds when you were only selected for two races?"

I would answer, "It's a long story."

⟨⸻◈⸻⟩

"So where's your date?"

At 8 pm, as arranged, I was waiting at the entrance for Bill, my date for the night. Richard had shown up with a group of Americans, a blanket rolled up under his arm on their way to the beach. I noticed there was a slight weakness in my knees just from seeing him again.

"I don't know. He must have been delayed in Tel-Aviv." I answered.

"Well, let's give him till 8:15, and then why don't you come with us to the beach?" There was a pleading look in his eyes. At 8:15 pm there was still no Bill, and I realized I felt glad about that. I was off with Richard to my first beach party, with a skip in my step.

A delicate spray of stars started to flicker high in the Middle Eastern sky as we sat down on the pink fuzzy blanket Richard had carefully laid out on the sand. I was vaguely aware of laughing and singing. The space between us filled quickly with words, and our conversation flowed easily and effortlessly. His casual American drawl was easy on my ears as he started to tell me about his family, his hobbies, how and why he became a swimmer. His maternal grandmother, whom he referred to as "Bubbie," had played an important role in his life, and he spoke of her with great affection.

"Where does your grandmother live?" I asked.

"She lives near a beach on Long Island called Long Beach. I love to go visit her there." A smile crept over his face as he added, "Even though I'm an All American swimmer, whenever I go into the ocean for a swim, my eighty-two-year-old grandmother stands at the edge of the water watching me to make sure I don't drown."

"If you got into trouble in the ocean, would she swim out to save you?" I asked.

"I don't think so."

We both laughed.

I was impressed that his family was so important to him. He spoke of his two older brothers with great love and admiration. There was a seriousness to him that I found appealing.

"How did your parents come to be in South Africa?" he asked me with genuine interest.

I told him how my grandparents left Latvia when my dad was six years old, and that my mother was born in South Africa. I told him about my brother, my favorite food, college and about my eighty-year-old grandmother. I told him everything that seemed worth telling.

"I lived on a farm for the first three years of my life, and then in a tiny neighboring town."

"You rode on tractors and horses, while I rode subways and buses in New York," he said.

"How much more opposite can it get?" he said. We both laughed again.

The moon began to wrap itself around us with its silvery glow. The night air was still and warm and the blanket felt soft against my legs. There was a definite connection with this stranger I had only known for two days.

"I can't believe I don't remember you from the 1961 games," I said. Then he confessed that we had, in fact, not met before. He had been standing on the terrace talking to some of the guys on the South African water polo team who had the room right above me. When I walked onto the terrace, they had helped him by feeding information about me to him; they had mouthed my name and pumped their arms to imitate a runner. They were directly above me and I couldn't see them. "That's how I knew so much about you," he said.

"Pretty sneaky ... but clever," I said, and laughed again. I had developed an instinct a long time ago, while living in Reitz, for sizing up a person's character, whether they were genuine or a phony. I remember how some of my friends' parents were genuinely friendly to me, because they liked me and because I was their child's friend. However, others would say things like, "I met someone the other day that was Jewish and he was so nice." I wanted to ask, "Are you surprised that he was Jewish and nice?" But of course I suppressed my feelings and said nothing. People who said things like "some of my best friends are Jewish" carried a red flag for me. But despite the little trick Richard played on me, my instincts told me that this was not a devious person, not a smooth talker who was dishonest. He had just found a creative way to break the ice and start a conversation by pretending to know me. My antennas sent out a green light; it was perfectly okay to be with him.

Without warning, Richard leaned over and placed a soft, gentle kiss on my lips, tentative but lingering. It was as if the moon had dropped a curtain around us. I couldn't see anyone else on the beach anymore. The crowd was reduced to just the two of us. I was afraid to breathe lest I break the spell of the moment.

———≫◦◦≪———

THE NEXT MORNING at breakfast, Bill came up to me to apologize for missing our date. He got stuck in Tel Aviv and couldn't get a cab. I said,

"Don't worry about it. I understand." What I really wanted to say was "Thank you for being late."

When the competition part of the Games was officially over and the closing ceremonies were completed, all the countries took their athletes touring around Israel for a few days before returning home. Richard got special permission to leave the American team and toured around with the South Africans. After the second day of touring, when we got back, we decided to go for a walk outside the village after dinner. First he needed to go back to his room to get his pass, which he had left on the dresser, in order to be able to get back into the village. When we got to his room, it turned out that his roommate was out for the evening. We were alone in his room. He walked up to me. Suddenly, I found myself in the warm circle of his muscular swimmer's arms; he was kissing me. Somehow, I knew we weren't going to go for that walk after all.

His pass remained on his dresser untouched.

——◆——

OUR TIME TOGETHER was quickly coming to an end. We only had one more day. After that, our planes would be taking off for opposite ends of the world. The words of John Denver's song "Leaving on a Jet Plane" took on new significance. There was a dull ache in my heart. The American team was leaving first, and I went to see him off at the airport early the next morning. We clung to each other for a minute, and with a sting in my gut I turned and walked away. I didn't want him to see how my eyes were welling up.

We made all sorts of promises about writing and visiting each other, and we discussed getting married someday. Was I serious? How could I talk about getting married to someone whom I had only known for four days and who lived 10,000 miles away? This was so unlike me. Didn't everyone always tell me how levelheaded and practical I was? But my feet had been swept out from under me, and I must have landed on my head because I wasn't thinking clearly anymore. Or perhaps I was thinking with my heart.

Richard and I in the Maccabi Stadium

Richard's pass for Maccabi Games

CHAPTER
Ten

The American

"I met a great guy at the Maccabi Games and we want to get married. There's only one thing though. He's an American, and we can't get married for three years. He's at the Air Force Academy in Colorado, and he isn't allowed to be married until after he graduates."

I was back home, anxiously awaiting my parents' response to what I was certain was the most important event of my life. The wordless pause seemed to stretch out forever.

I saw my mother raise her eyebrows for emphasis. She lifted the china cup to her lips and took a sip of tea. She didn't even look up as she said, "You really want to marry someone that you've known for only a few weeks?"

I didn't dare tell her that I had only known Richard for *four days*. There was a smile on the corners of my dad's mouth as he said, "Three years is a long time when you're at opposite ends of the earth." He was slicing an apple with his sharp pocketknife and, like my mother, he didn't even look at me. He kept his eyes glued to the apple. They changed the subject. Clearly, they weren't taking this conversation seriously.

Until the blue aerogrammes started arriving once a week.

———◆———

I HURRIED HOME every day from college as fast as my clunky Renault Dauphine could go. I always got out of the car briskly and hurried to the mailbox, in anticipation of opening that blue aerogramme with the USA stamp on the front. My heart would quicken as I pried the envelope open. Once inside the house, I would sit and devour every word. After a few months of those weekly letters, my parents started to take notice, and their amused glances quickly turned into expressions of deep concern.

The letters gave us a platform for a remarkable transcontinental conversation. Richard and I were each nineteen and, through those letters, we decided that it would be unrealistic to expect either of us to stay home waiting for three years.

"I can't expect you not go to on dates for three years," I told him, in a blue aerogramme.

"I can't expect that of you either," he said in reply.

So we agreed, via our letters, that we would continue to live our lives, going to parties and dating, and then when the time came for him to graduate, we'd review the situation and see if we still felt the same way and still wanted to get married.

———◆———

ONE NIGHT AT a party in Johannesburg, I met Andrew. He was every mother's dream for her daughter: a nice guy, Jewish, good looking, studying to be a lawyer. He not only came from a great family, the great family lived around the corner from us.

Andrew and I started dating ... but I still looked forward to Richard's weekly aerogrammes.

"Maybe now she'll forget about the American," I overheard my mother tell her friend on the phone one night. A few months later, she cornered me:

"You have to stop thinking about the American. You have this unrealistic dream. While you have your head up in the clouds, be careful not to miss opportunities down here on earth."

Even Dusan, upon hearing about the "guy from America" had said, "I hope you're not serious about this. You have everything you want here." Then he reminded me about the adjustments he had had to make when he left Yugoslavia to come to South Africa. "It's not that easy to change countries," he added. Dusan didn't want me to go anywhere, and I couldn't blame him. We had developed a very close athlete/coach relationship. He knew almost everything about me; he knew when to push me harder and when to let go; he even knew my bio-rhythms. He had invested many hours coaching me, and he always starting shifting about nervously when I spoke about "the American."

My mother and Dusan assured me that it was a mistake to wait for Richard; so did a number of my friends. Then when my father joined in pressuring me, I started to buckle.

Aerogrammes from Richard in Colorado
to me in Johannesburg

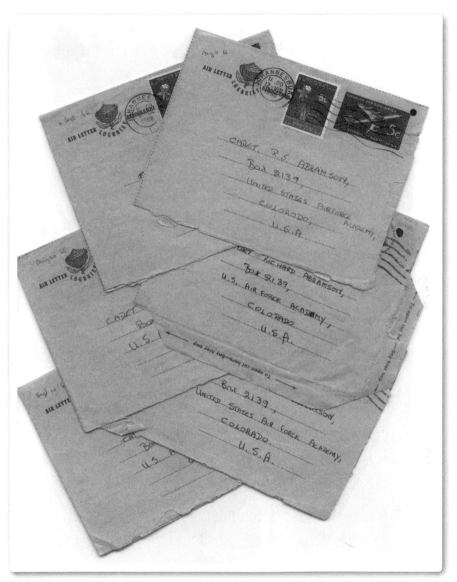

My aerogrammes to Richard

Could they be right?

As I continued to date Andrew our relationship grew stronger, even though our interests were very different. He had no interest in sports of any kind, including my career on the track. "You're a runner?" he asked, surprised, when I told him about what I loved to do most.

As we continued to date, I got the sense that he tolerated my running, but that there would never be real enthusiasm on his part. It was as though he were thinking: "How bizarre to spend hours training to see who can get to a finish line first!"

Andrew was the studious type, and I spent many hours in his room, reading a book while he studied for his law exams. After a few months he started to talk indirectly about getting married. I knew I didn't have sparks and passion for him, as I did with Richard, but I wondered if perhaps that was because Richard was still in the background.

Then one day he proposed to me. "Let's get married," he said. It was at the end of a meal in a lovely restaurant. The moment the words were out of his mouth, I heard my mother's voice in my head: "Be careful not to miss opportunities down here on earth."

I accepted. *Maybe I'll start to forget about Richard, and then things will improve with Andrew. After all, I can't find any fault with him. He's kind and considerate and he loves me.*

My parents were overjoyed when we told them of our engagement.

———♦———

I HAD TO write and tell Richard.

Every word that made it from my pen onto the page seemed agonizingly wrong. I crumpled up the first four attempts and threw the pages into the rubbish bin. Finally, I settled on the letter that I would send, but I was still not completely satisfied. There was no way to write a satisfactory letter about this. There was no way to say what had to be said without hurting him.

"Rich," I wrote, "Maybe this was all too unrealistic. We have too many things going against us. I'm getting pressure from everyone, my parents, some family and even my track coach. They're telling me that I'll be making a big mistake. They're saying that we're young and not thinking clearly. I've met someone here and he wants to marry me. I'm getting heavy pressure from my parents. Maybe it wasn't meant to be after all." I wrote a few more pages and then I felt tears well up in my eyes as I dropped the letter into the mailbox at the post office.

Even though the sun was shining brightly, everything looked as drab as a shoelace to me.

⸺◆⸺

SOMETHING'S NOT RIGHT.

Very soon after Andrew and I got engaged, I realized that something was terribly wrong.

I'd come home from college eyeing the mailbox, knowing that there was no blue aerogramme waiting for me inside it. I started to miss Richard's letters.

How could I be marrying one guy while still thinking about another?

The question wouldn't go away. I couldn't sleep at night. Richard's face kept lurking in the crevices of my dreams. I lay wondering about his reaction to my letter. Would he reply or would I never hear from him again? These thoughts were almost too painful to bear.

I sat in class at college staring out the window. My body was there, but my mind was in Colorado. I glanced at my watch. It was 3:00 pm in Jo'burg, which meant 6:00 am at the Academy. Richard would soon be getting up. I thought about our night on the beach in Israel. I had felt on top of the world. Why wasn't I feeling on top of the world now? Why wasn't I feeling the same electric jolts down my spine with Andrew as I did with Richard? The anguish in my heart was torture. What had I done?

Compounding the difficulty was my own certainty that, as agonizing as all of this was to me, I was not entirely the victim in this situation. Saying yes had not been fair to Andrew. He was a good and kind person who deserved better than this.

This thought came crushing down on me like a giant slab of emotional concrete. With every passing day, it became clearer and clearer to me that I had made a huge mistake. I had succumbed to parental and family pressures that were set on me not marrying someone from another country and not moving away from South Africa. I had been conditioned — or had I conditioned myself — to simply endure that which I was helpless to change. I had been trained to obey the authority around me: to accept the laws of apartheid, to abide by the strict rules of my boarding school, to respect my teachers by never questioning them. It had never occurred to me to disobey my teachers or my parents. Now once again, I had dismissed my better judgment and done as I was told. The only problem was, my instincts were now screaming at me.

This time, I saw that following the wishes of my elders was not in anyone's best interest — not mine, not Richard's and certainly not Andrew's. For all of my life in apartheid South Africa, I had witnessed acts of cruelty perpetrated on other people, seen and heard many situations where people who did not deserve to be hurt had suffered. I had learned to turn away from these situations and suppress my feelings about them. This, however, was the first time I could think of where I was the perpetrator. Even though the circumstances were vastly different, I had made a bad decision under pressure; even though it was not my intent to hurt anyone, I was, one way or the other, about to hurt someone who did not deserve to be hurt. The only question was whether I was going to hurt Andrew by marrying him when I knew the marriage wouldn't work, or hurt him by calling off the engagement. Once I realized that, I couldn't stop thinking about it. I had a hard time getting to sleep that night.

The next day, I woke up, lay in bed for a long time, and listened to my heart. I knew what I had to do. I had to accept the reality that a mistake compounded would only get worse. I had to break my engagement and try again with Richard.

This is my life and my future, I thought. *I can't control the wind now, but I must try to adjust my sails.*

⋙◆⋘

FOR THE VERY first time, I had to stand up to my parents and all those around me, and follow my own instincts — not theirs — about something truly important. I had to break out of the shell of submission, denial, and obedience I had created for myself, and do what I thought was right for me.

I sat down at the breakfast table with my parents, took a very deep breath, and said out loud the words I had been practicing silently for hours: "I'm breaking my engagement with Andrew." Another deep silence fell over us all.

"How long have you been thinking about this?" my mother asked, once she had regained her composure.

"For months. It's been eating me up."

"Why didn't you say anything to us?"

"Because I needed to think it through, and come to this decision all by myself. I didn't want to be influenced by anyone. I won't be happy in this marriage, and ultimately Andrew won't either. I never wanted to hurt another human being, but I know I am about to hurt Andrew, and I'm sick about it. This is something I will regret for the rest of my life. Once I tell him, I will have taken the hearts of two wonderful guys and broken them in half: Richard when he got my letter, and Andrew when he finds out I'm calling this off. Their only fault was that they both loved me. I just want you both to know this has not been a snap decision. It has been gut-wrenching, and I can barely look at myself in the mirror, but it's the only thing I can do now."

My parents didn't say a word. I was on my own.

LOOKING BACK, I realize that, while my memories of my conversations with my parents and with Richard during this period are surprisingly vivid, I have a complete mental block about my conversation with Andrew when I told him I wanted to break off our engagement. I know it took place; I have no memory of what was actually said. Maybe if I were a psychologist I'd have a better understanding of what causes the suppression of a painful memory. I know it's locked somewhere in my subconscious, but so far it's a blur and I simply can't retrieve it. I do, however, remember that I sent my mother to his house to return the ring. I couldn't bring myself to do that. I can only hope that Andrew found his own happiness in life, happiness that I know he's entitled to and deserves.

NOW I HAD to write to Richard and tell him about the terrible mistake I had made, and how I had allowed everyone to put doubts in my head. I spent a long time on that letter; I remember that my hand was shaking as I dropped it into the mailbox.

He's never going to answer this. I'll never hear from him again and I can't blame him.

I had made a complete mess of my life. I couldn't eat and I couldn't concentrate on my studies. But at least I had done the right thing.

Then a week later the phone rang. I heard the familiar American twang: It was Richard. I was stunned and speechless.

"I got your letter. I'm not going to ask what happened. I just want to tell you that I'm trying to make arrangements to take the next military flight down to South Africa."

My heart stopped. I suddenly felt immensely grateful to Richard for being willing to look past my mistake. I wanted to bury my head on his chest and say, "I'm sorry, I'm sorry, I'm so sorry" — but what I said was simply, "We have a lot to talk about."

He agreed.

Happy tears ran down my cheeks. When I hung up the phone, I noticed that the leaves on the palm tree looked greener, the birds were singing more beautifully, and the snapdragons were more vibrant. I noticed, for the first time, how beautiful the snapdragons were that year.

"The American must really love you, Lorraine," my dad said, "for him to fly all the way here to see you."

<hr />

AFTER TWO YEARS apart, Richard and I were finally to be reunited. It was July of 1967 when he arrived at Jan Smuts airport in Johannesburg.

My heart felt like it was about to jump out of my chest; I held my breath every time someone walked through the customs door. When I finally saw him, the world spun. I waved wildly until I got his attention. It was as if no time had passed.

Separation made for a much more intense togetherness, and although his visit was short, my parents could now associate a face to this guy. He was no longer "the American." He now had an identity. Over the next few days, they began to see the qualities that had attracted me to him: his maturity, his kindness, his values, and the importance of family to his life. Of course, they also got to see that ten-thousand-watt smile that had won me over.

Our maid, Anna, and Enoch the gardener, had had no idea where America was, but they had known that my boyfriend was coming from very far away. "He's coming from the other side of the sea," Anna had explained to Enoch. After my parents had met him, I took Richard into the kitchen to introduce him to Anna and Enoch, who had been waiting excitedly to meet someone who they knew was very important to me, but who, for all they knew, might as well have been from Mars. With a big friendly smile, Richard immediately extended his hand to shake theirs.

It was an awkward moment. They didn't know how to respond: white people did not shake hands with black people in South Africa. But Anna wiped her hands on her apron, reached out to grasp Richard's hand, and with a wide smile, pumped his hand wildly. Enoch followed suit; our servants had shaken their first white hand, and the heavens had not collapsed.

They laughed when they heard his accent, and said: "Ooooh Mees Lorraine, he talks so funny."

———⟫◆⟪———

RICHARD AND I sat up late into the night talking. "I like your parents and brother," he said. "You didn't tell me you had such a beautiful dog."

He even likes my dog!

"I noticed a hesitation when I wanted to shake hands with Anna and Enoch", he said. "Why was that?"

"Because in my world Africans and whites aren't allowed to shake hands." I explained, "The government would call that socializing, which is forbidden across the racial lines. This is what happens when two different societies collide; what seems like the most natural gesture to one person is a criminal offense to the other."

"Shaking hands is a criminal offense?" he asked, amused

"In this country it is."

"Doesn't that strike you as ... ridiculous?"

"Oh, you haven't seen the half of it," I said, laughing. "Just please be sure not to talk openly about that in public."

"About what exactly?"

"About what is and isn't ridiculous in this country."

THE NEXT DAY I drove Richard around Jo'burg. We went into a shop. Above one entrance a sign read "Europeans Only." The other sign read "Non-Europeans Only." He got ready to walk through the "Non-European" door. I caught his arm and directed him to the European entrance.

"I'm not a European, I'm an American," he said.

"I know it doesn't make sense. Nothing much does in this country. Trust me; you want to come with me through the European entrance."

"WHY IS ENOCH polishing the floor *under* the rug?" Richard had pulled me aside so he could ask me this question in private.

I shrugged and said, "He does that every morning."

184

"He folds back the carpet, and polishes the floor underneath *every day*?" Richard was smiling as if to say, "This, too, is ridiculous."

I realized how absurd it was, but my mother, like other South African housewives, had to keep the servants busy. Richard made me wonder what Enoch thought about being ordered to do such a meaningless activity; in any event, he had no say in the matter. Enoch would wash the windows four times a day if we told him to do so. We never thought about the indignity.

———————

I TOOK RICHARD traveling a bit around the country; we went to the Game Reserve for a few days. My parents sent Selwyn and his friend with us to act as chaperones. It was unheard of for a couple who were not married to travel alone together.

"I love South Africa," Richard said as we stared at some astonishing scenery. "This country is stunningly beautiful, and the people are so friendly. I'd love to live here after we get married ... but of course we couldn't. This place could blow up at any time. The United States has a much more secure future for our children than South Africa."

By making our lives in America, I wouldn't have to put insecurities and anxieties in the heads of my own children the way my mother did to me. They would be brought up in a country where they could live in security and be embraced as full citizens, with their religious rights and freedoms guaranteed by the law of the land.

I agreed with Richard. We would live in America.

———◆———

A FEW NIGHTS later, after dinner, my father sat us both down. He looked at us and said to me, "If you're really going to go through with this idea of getting married, we'd like you to go to America for a visit first, and meet Richard's family and see some of the country before making such a big commitment." We both agreed that was a good idea. I stood up, walked over to my dad and gave him a kiss on the cheek. I appreciated his support and understanding, knowing full well how hard this was for him and my mom. I tried to focus on what my father was saying ... but what I was really hearing was my father using Richard's name for the very first time. He was no longer "the American."

CHAPTER
Eleven

An Unromantic Proposal

On December 6th 1967, six months after Richard's visit to South Africa, I bade farewell to the warm days of summer and boarded South African Airways for a journey to a country I'd never visited and did not quite know how to imagine.

We were both on our Christmas breaks; I would fly to meet Richard in America. We were going to spend a week with his family in New York, after which I would fly with him to Colorado Springs to the Air Force Academy, where he had arranged for me to stay with a family on the base.

That morning, as I sat on the plane waiting to take off, I put my head back, closed my eyes, and replayed the incident when I had told Dusan that I was going to America.

At first Dusan had been mute as a stone. There had been a long, jaw-clenching silence; then he had said, "So — you're really going to do this? You've worked so hard and now you're going to throw it all away?"

"I'll be coming back in mid-January, I told you."

"Yes — just as the track season gets into high gear, with the South

African championships only two months away."

"Dusan, I'm not going to throw it all away. I promise I'll continue to work out while I'm there. I'll find a track."

He stared at me — unconvinced, betrayed, his mind made up: I was making a mistake.

"You're going to visit this boy, and you're probably not even going to marry him. You're just wasting your time."

He was hurling verbal grenades at me, and his words, curt and sharp, stuck into me like thorns. I'd gotten far more support and understanding about my marriage from my parents than I ever would from him. I was determined to come back in great shape to prove him wrong. No one was going to derail me again.

"Please fasten your seat belts," said the voice over the intercom. "We are next in line for take-off."

<hr />

AFTER SEVENTEEN HOURS, three meals and two movies, it was time to land at New York's John F. Kennedy International Airport. It was night time in New York.

My seat belt was securely fastened but my nerves were not. When I looked out of the plane's window, a blanket of a million lights sparkled like diamonds and signaled that we had arrived. I saw bridges spanning across rivers, with cables draped from one end to the other, elegant and graceful. I saw spires and blocky skyscraper tops, and the Empire State Building and the Statue of Liberty standing in her harbor. I'd read so much about that very harbor, the starting point for millions of immigrants searching for freedom and dreaming of a better life. There was a similar story for the immigrants who came to South Africa.

New York lay below us, waiting, sparkling, enticing, and revealing something new in every instant. I couldn't believe the amount of traffic on the roads; car lights melted into long streams of red ribbon on one side and yellow on the other. It stretched on for as far as I could follow. I was someplace new; I was now on Richard's home turf. The woman next to me was telling me something, but I didn't hear a word she said.

———————⟫◆⟪———————

I WALKED OUT of the customs area with hundreds of people scurrying past me, feeling like a pebble in a creek. Then I heard someone call my name. I saw Richard waving. My heart soared and my nerves relaxed. As utterly foreign as this place was to me, I knew I was in the right place the moment I saw Richard's face.

Outside, the cold December air hit me, and I saw my own breath for the first time. We got into Richard's car and he turned on the heater. *Wow, a heater in a car.* The steering wheel was on the wrong side. I covered my eyes with my hands as he entered the highway on the "wrong" side of the road. He laughed at me and said, "You'll get used to it."

When we got to his house, I saw that there was a mezuzah on the doorpost; I found it comforting and welcoming. My mind flashed back to the prayer I had said every day at my boarding school, the one about "the sign upon the door posts of your house and upon your gates." I took new comfort that these symbols extended to Jewish homes all over the world. When I walked past the mezuzah and into his home, I instantly felt that I belonged. There was a connection; I knew that, in this house, I didn't have to wonder what the occupants thought about Jewish people, the way I had when I met new people growing up. Even though Richard and I had such polar opposite upbringings, he in New York City and I on a farm and then a small rural town in South Africa, being Jewish gave us an enormous amount of common ground.

Richard's parents and brothers were friendly, and I immediately felt at home. The big house was like a mansion. It was the first time I had seen a "center hall colonial." Stairs went below ground level into an area they called a basement. I'd never seen one before.

"WHY WOULD ANYONE want to live anywhere other than New York? It's the greatest city in the world."

Richard's father was holding forth in his loud, booming voice. It seemed like an arrogant thing to say to a visitor, but I let it go. Allan, Richard's oldest brother, showed great interest in South Africa and had a lot of questions. "I'd love to go there someday," he said. Both brothers had swum in previous Maccabi Games; much of our talk was about South African swimmers they had met there. I felt comfortable and relaxed.

There was no way I could have suspected that Richard's parents were just as skeptical about our relationship as mine were. Their questions and concerns were similar to those my parents had been repeating for months.

Before I arrived, they had asked Richard, "What if you marry this girl and she gets homesick?" They had asked their close friend Arthur to try to talk Richard out of this foolish idea of marrying a foreign girl and bringing her to the States. My parents asked me similar questions. "What if you get homesick? He has his family there and you have no one." I'm not sure how we both stood up to all this, but we did.

"Do you have a winter coat?" his mother asked me upon my arrival at the house. I was surprised at her question.

"This *is* my winter coat," I told her, holding up my light camel wool coat. She laughed.

"That, Lorraine, is a spring coat," she said, trying to hide her amusement at my obvious lack of understanding about the realities of winter in New York.

"Let's go shopping tomorrow," she said.

———✦———

THE NEXT DAY we walked into Alexander's coat department, where they were having a big 50% off sale.

"Try on this black Shearling."

As I slipped my arms into the sleeves, I felt the weight of the fur. It was as if I was climbing into a bear.

"That," she said "is a winter coat."

I appreciated this generous gift from her. Now I was actually ready for the winter weather I would be facing in New York and Colorado.

———✦———

IN NEW YORK, I found myself amazed at everything. The city was exotic and exciting, and there was an energy to the place that I had never felt anywhere, ever. The sights and smells of the city — steam gushing out of manhole covers from the subway below; the scent of hot chestnuts, pretzels and candy-coated nuts sold from the carts on the street corners — all of this was profoundly new to me. So were the massive skyscrapers. By the end of the week I had a pain in the back of my neck from constantly tilting my head upward to stare at them. I couldn't believe that the ground could support so much concrete and steel, and I marveled at the fact that there was equipment and brave men that could go up high enough to build those buildings. When we entered an elevator, the thought of cables that length got me a bit jittery.

To hail a taxi, I learned, one simply raised one's forefinger up in the air. Astonishing! Sometimes Richard and I traveled by cab, but most of the time we walked along Central Park South, where the horses and carriages were lined up along the sidewalk waiting to give tourists a magical ride through the Park. The smell of the horses and the clip-clop of their hooves on the road transported me unexpectedly back to the farm for a few moments. But the pace of the pedestrians, and the disconcerting habit they had of avoiding making eye contact with other people on the street, was very different from the world in which I had grown up.

"Where are all these people rushing to?" I asked Richard. "Why doesn't anyone say hello?"

"The pace is just faster than you're used to. They're not unfriendly; you just can't greet millions of people as you walk by."

"I guess not." This was a far cry from Reitz, where I had known everyone.

There was just a dusting of snow on the sidewalks of Fifth Avenue that I found alluring.

"Wait 'til we get to Colorado," Richard said as we walked. "You'll see real snow and plenty of it." As we got to the middle of the next block, I saw something new, something that transfixed me: a white guy and an African-American girl were walking, holding hands. In public. Right there, out in the open.

Discreetly, I pointed them out to Richard. "That is strictly forbidden where I come from," I whispered. I thought of how normal, how routine injustice seemed in my country.

I noticed a policeman standing on the corner. The couple would have to walk right past the policeman. I stood for a moment to watch them and to see how he would react. As the policeman saw them, he nodded his head and mumbled "How ya doin'?"

"I can't believe my eyes," I said.

Richard just laughed. This was a natural scene in his world. I wondered if that couple knew how lucky they were to be living in a country where they were free to live their lives as they wanted. In South Africa, they would have found themselves in the back of a police car with handcuffs slapped on their wrists.

Next, I saw a group of guys walking together and laughing. They were all different races, white, Asian and African American. They seemed completely at ease with each other. This was why my government back home had to censor everything. They didn't want South Africans to see

193

this type of camaraderie amongst the races. After all, we had been taught that it was God's will to keep all racial groups separate. Here, everyone entered the stores through the same doors; everyone sat on the same benches in Central Park.

I was getting my first real taste of a free society.

When I look back now, I realize, of course, that race relations in America were not as smooth as they appeared to me on that day, especially in the South. But I could only go by what I saw in New York, a large cosmopolitan city. The Civil Rights Act had just been signed, in 1964 by Lyndon B. Johnson, and Martin Luther King had given his famous "I have a dream" speech not long before that. However, for me, coming from my police state in South Africa, this *was* a free society — at least by comparison with the society I had just left. The book stores and libraries filled with uncensored books were proof enough of that.

———⟫◆⟪———

WHEN IT WAS time for Richard to return to school in Colorado, I was excited to be going with him and to see the place from which all the blue aerogrammes had originated, with the now — familiar zip code "80840". As our plane descended into Denver, I gasped as I beheld, for the first time, a completely white world below me. Having never seen real snow before, I found it a magical sight. The earth lay protected under a blanket of white.

I couldn't wait to touch the white stuff. The Rocky Mountains were breathtaking — yet they looked cold, desolate and foreboding at the same time.

When we got off the plane, the freezing air literally took my breath away. I inhaled, and the cold air found its way down to my lungs as if to say, "Lungs, welcome to winter in Colorado." I was grateful for my new warm shearling coat.

As we drove from the airport to the Air Force Academy, the trees balanced three inches of snow on each limb like jugglers. The bushes and fingerlike twigs peeked through the snow as though they were desperately reaching upwards for some sunlight.

"Wow," I said, awestruck. "I never thought winter could be so beautiful."

Richard had arranged for me to stay with a wonderful family, Colonel and Mrs. Raful and their two sons Bruce and Larry, who lived on the Academy grounds. When we reached their house, I got out of the car and dipped my hand into the newly fallen snow. I scooped up a big handful to taste. The snow felt soft, cold, and nothing like the white cotton that it looked like from the inside of the warm car. As I brought my hand towards my mouth, I stuck out the tip of my tongue to take a careful and delicate lick. It felt cold on my tongue, but not as cold as my fingers were. I noticed they had turned bright pink. The tingling sensation was turning to numbness; I was losing feeling in my hands. I cupped my hands over my mouth and blew warm air on them.

We started walking. I knew I had had ten toes when I started the journey, but after a few minutes in the subzero (a new word I learned) weather, I felt as if my toes had abandoned my feet. I took one step toward Richard and slipped on the ice, landing ungracefully on my butt.

"You'll need gloves to handle the snow, and it wouldn't hurt to wear thick socks and boots," he said, helping me back onto my feet. He was smiling at my ignorance about the American winter.

I told him, "Not only have I never owned a pair of gloves or boots, but I don't think they even sell them in sunny South Africa." Clearly, I had a lot to learn.

Richard got special permission for me to work out with the Academy track team. The coach, Arnie Arnoldson, allowed me to run with the guys. We worked out indoors, a new experience for me. They didn't have an indoor track, so we ran in the halls of the gym. There were no women allowed at the Academy during those years; I was the first woman to run the halls of the athletic facility. I was amused when the cadets passing by took a double take: "What was that? A woman?"

The guys in Richard's squadron, the 21st, were so welcoming. There was Bob, Bill, Peter and many others. They had never met a South African before, let alone a Jewish one. "A Jewish African," one of them said with genuine fascination. This squadron consisted of a group of guys who had bonded like brothers. (Their bond would endure, and it remains strong to this day.)

One evening after classes, Richard came to take me for a drive. He looked handsome in his blue uniform. We drove past the Red Rocks and took in all the natural beauty of Colorado. While we were enjoying the ride, he told me about the philosophy of the Academy and the strict Honor Code that they lived by: "We will not lie, steal or cheat, nor tolerate anyone amongst us who does," he said.

"So if you catch someone breaking the Honor Code, do you have to turn him in?" I asked.

"Absolutely. When we put our lives in someone's hands, like in a wartime situation or up in the cockpit, you have to be able to trust that person implicitly. A strong moral character is imperative."

I was impressed.

"By the way, on Sunday I'm going to take you skiing," he said.

"Skiing? Are you serious? I just saw real snow for the first time last week."

"No problem. You're an athlete; it'll be a piece of cake for you."

———————

ON SUNDAY MORNING I dressed in my borrowed red parka and borrowed blue gloves and hat, excited for my skiing debut. As Richard and I ascended Loveland Mountain, I felt exhilarated. It was my first time on the heart-stopping ride of a chairlift. Light snowflakes started to gently drift down to earth, and the panorama of the mountains was spectacular. *Can it get more romantic than this?*

Then I heard Richard say, "Uh oh."

"What's the matter?" I asked. I didn't like the sound of his voice or the worried look on his face.

"They've done away with the halfway point," he said, sounding a bit panicked. "We have to go all the way to the top of the mountain."

I glanced back and saw the ski lodge getting smaller and smaller. My heart was pounding harder and harder. I grabbed the edges of my seat, and all thoughts of romance vanished as I contemplated spending the rest of my life at the top of Loveland Mountain.

I thought of my friends in South Africa who were probably enjoying their Sunday afternoon game of tennis, or sitting next to their pools. I could hear the tea-kettles whistling all over my native land, as the maids brought the tea with plates of Lemon Creams and Ginger Snaps cookies. They were probably dangling their toes in the warm blue water; I was on my way to the top of an expert ski slope with no clue how to get down. The freezing air closed in on me; the temperature was getting lower as we were getting higher.

"How much longer?" I tried to keep the panic out of my voice, even though it sounded an octave higher than normal.

"We're almost there."

The time dragged on.

"Okay, get ready to ski off," he instructed.

"*Ski off*? Are you saying it doesn't stop so that I can get off?"

I almost met my maker trying to get off that moving chair. Then I looked at the sheet of ice at the top of the mountain and was terrified all over again.

"We need to get a bit lower, beyond this ice" Richard said.

"How do I do that?"

"Look I'll show you. It's easy. Watch carefully."

He skied a ways down and then stopped and looked up and waited for me to join him. Now I was supposed to know how to ski.

The weather and my own fear held me in an icy grip. I was standing at the summit of Loveland Mountain, and I was terrified. I was being slapped in the face by the frigid air, which even *smelled* cold; I realized I was having trouble breathing. Richard's fellow cadet Mike Thomas was kind enough to stay with me. He was patient, and tried gently to persuade me to try to ski down. A ski patrol man suddenly appeared, noticed my obvious distress, and asked if I needed help. I said, "Yes — please help me to get back on the chairlift to go down." I took the lift back down and ignored all the calls of "chicken" from the skiers going up. I waited for Richard in the lodge, in front of the fireplace, sipping steaming hot chocolate. I couldn't think of a drink that had ever been more welcome. As I circled my hands around the warm cup, I felt myself coming back to life. I sat there quietly, debating whether I should ever speak to Richard again.

He apologized a million times. Eventually his kisses and hugs melted away my anger, but that was the first and last time I ever tried skiing.

———

RICHARD HAD TO be back at the Academy by 11pm. We got back at five past eleven.

"Oh no ... I have to sign myself in late," he said.

"But there's no one here," I noted. "You're only five minutes late."

"I can't lie. That's part of the Honor Code that we live by."

We both knew that by signing himself in late, he would be grounded for one of the days the following weekend, which meant less time for us together. I scratched my head and tried to understand. This strict Honor Code made Eunice, my boarding school, look like a "free for all." Yet I respected his high principles.

———

SOON IT WAS time for me to return to South Africa. Everyone had been amazingly friendly, and the country had been beautiful. I knew I would have no problems living in America as long as I stayed off the slopes!

I got home the first week in January. The South African track championships were only a few weeks away. During my first workout after my return from America, I could feel Dusan's eyes fixed on me, checking to see if I had lost any of my conditioning during my visit abroad. I smiled, knowing that I had kept my promise to him, and to myself, to continue

*Winning the South African Championships
in a very close race*

my workouts at the Air Force Academy. I heard that cadet's astonished voice again in my head, "What was that? A woman?"

When I lined up for the start of the 100 meters race at the South African championship, I felt a heavy load on my shoulders. There was a lot riding on this race. If I did poorly, I'd be accused of giving up my opportunity to be the South African champion, of having given everything up for a boy. My heart pounded as I felt the double pressure: the race, and the ramifications if I lost. I was running this race not just for me, but for Richard too. That gave me inspiration. To my relief and my coach's delight, I won the 100 meters. I was the women's South African 100 meters champion of 1968.

After winning the South African championships, I was surprised, honored, and completely overwhelmed to learn that I had been named South African Woman Athlete of the Year. An even bigger shock came, however, when I got the news that I had been named as one of three nominees for the Helms Award, as the top athlete in the entire continent of Africa! The other nominees were Karen Muir, the great South African swimmer, and Kip Keino, the amazing Kenyan long-distance runner. Keino won, and certainly deserved to. I had never, in my wildest expectations, imagined that such a nomination would come my way. I will always cherish the memory of being placed in the same category with those two remarkable athletes.

A week after I got home, Richard phoned to discuss a wedding date, and asked when we could officially get engaged.

"Since we import diamonds from South Africa, it would make sense to buy the stone down there," he said, with his ever-practical mind.

A few weeks later I got an international bank check in the mail, and my mother and I went shopping for an engagement ring. That night, with my heart racing like a sprinter, I placed the overseas call to Richard.

"Congratulations," I said, "We're engaged. I chose an emerald cut diamond set high in a yellow gold setting." The diamond sparkled into my heart, and all that it represented suddenly struck me.

"Rich," I added with a smile on my face, "I think you win the prize for the most unromantic proposal *ever*."

He laughed and said, "I'll make it up to you."

I told my fiancé I loved him, and hung up the phone.

———◆◆◆———

As my mother and I were putting the finishing touches on the plans for the wedding, the booming voice of the 21st squadron leader was yelling, "Left, left, left right left," as he marched his group of cadets to the graduation ceremony. Across the ocean, the Air Force Academy was about to celebrate the commissioning of its graduating class from this prestigious military establishment. It was June 5, 1968, a warm summer's day in Colorado. This impressive campus, which sits nestled at the foot of the majestic Ramparts of the Rocky Mountains, has as its main feature the multi-faith chapel, with spires that reach up to the heavens like arms in prayer and shine brilliant silver when the sun catches them. The sea of blue uniforms gathered on the football field to hear the long awaited words from the Secretary of the Air Force, Harold Brown, *"Gentlemen, you're dismissed."*

They tossed their white dress hats into the air as tradition dictates, with a thunderous roaring cheer. One of these handsome young cadets was about to board a plane a few days later to fly 13,000 miles to South Africa ... to marry me.

"Every mother dreams of making a wedding for her daughter," my mom told me, "but knowing that you'll be leaving soon after is like a stake in my heart." I noticed tears welling up in her eyes. I was filled with conflicting emotions myself: the excitement of a young bride-to-be, mixed with a touch of sadness.

The day after Richard was commissioned as an officer, Robert F. Kennedy was assassinated. It was a tumultuous time in the world. The Vietnam War was in full swing; President Johnson had signed the Civil Rights Act into law just a few years before, in 1964. Martin Luther King had been gunned down in Memphis two months before Richard's June 12 scheduled arrival in Johannesburg.

Richard arrived just four days before the wedding. Looking back, it seems to me that our scheduling choices were cutting things awfully close, and left us a narrow margin for error, considering all the preparations we still had to make together. But he showed up on time and without incident.

Now here we were, June 16th 1968, after three years and dozens of blue aerogrammes and audiotapes darting back and forth across the Atlantic Ocean, getting ready to walk down the aisle. We were two young kids, ready to take on the world.

Jewish custom dictates that the groom is not allowed to see the bride the day of the wedding, so Richard stayed with my father's brother Uncle Sam, and Auntie Ethel, the night before and the day of the wedding. Our best man, my Uncle Joey — my dad's other brother — drove me to the synagogue in my father's new white Pontiac.

*Walking down the aisle with my father
in the Emmarentia Shul*

The Emmarentia Synagogue in Johannesburg looked warm and inviting, washed in the soft lights of candles. The plush red carpet, red velvet seats and arc cover gave everything a rich and luxurious feel.

It was a beautiful ceremony. My long white gown of slipper satin had beading just under the bustline. A full veil covered my face. My big smile hid the pangs in my stomach as reality started to hit me between the eyes. As my father walked me down the aisle, looking dapper in his tuxedo, my grip on his arm was as tight as that of a little girl who was afraid to let go. That grip also sent an unspoken message to him: *No matter how far I may go, I will always love you.* I was grateful for the strong role model he had been in my life.

As my eyes traveled forward to the "chupah", I saw Richard there waiting for me. I couldn't wait to stand next to him under the marriage canopy. I realized at that moment that the qualities that had attracted me to him — his warmth, love of family and common sense — were all qualities that I loved in my own father.

Richard was standing, facing forward, as instructed by the Rabbi. It was only when I was standing next to him that he glanced at me, and smiled that smile that had started the whole thing.

I turned my head to look at my dad, and noticed his habit of biting his lower lip whenever he was trying to fight back a tear. I don't remember much that the rabbi said, but I do remember that I clearly heard him say; "I now pronounce you husband and wife. You may kiss the bride."

I had told Richard before he left the States that the highlight of any South African Jewish wedding was the groom's speech at the reception. I made sure that he had enough time to prepare something eloquent.

While Uncle Joey drove us from the shul to the reception, Richard took a pen and paper out of his pocket and started writing.

"What are you doing?" I asked, somewhat surprised.

"You said I have to give a speech," he casually answered.

"What? You mean you're writing it *now* — on the way to the reception?!"

———◆———

"Wish me luck," Richard whispered to me.

It was Richard's turn to deliver his speech. He stood in front of the microphone and said, "I'd like to thank all those who traveled from far away to be here." That opening line was followed by an outburst of applause and laughter. I'm not sure if it was his American accent, or the fact that *he* had traveled the farthest to be there, but whatever it was, he was an instant hit. He went on to thank my parents for the faith they placed in him by giving him their daughter, and he promised to do whatever he could to make me happy. I held back the tears as best I could for two reasons. I didn't want to upset my parents any further, and I didn't want mascara running down my cheeks!

When the reception was drawing to a close, people came to kiss us good-bye. They were, in fact, saying farewell — I was leaving South Africa, and had no idea when I would be back. My grandmother said, "Lorraine, I'm an old lady, and I don't know if I'll ever see you again." We clung to each other. I kept telling myself *don't cry, don't cry.* Again: it was the mascara thing. Deep inside I felt devastated at the thought that I might never see Granny Eva again.

The whole night was a merry-go-round of excitement and sadness, each surfacing in turn. Although I was marrying my Prince Charming and riding off with him into a sunset on the other side of the world, I was also leaving behind my family and everything that was familiar to me. Looking back, I now know that I was too young and too naïve to be aware of the enormity of my decision.

My departure would, for instance, mean my parents' loneliness. They came with Selwyn to the airport to see us off. Through his tears my father pulled Richard aside and said, "Please look after my little girl."

"I promise I will."

As the plane lifted off the runway of Jan Smuts Airport in Johannesburg, I grasped the seat with one hand and my new husband with the other. I couldn't look out the window. I didn't want to see Jo'burg get smaller and smaller as we soared upwards, becoming an insignificant speck in the rear view mirror, and then disappearing.

Richard started to talk about all the European cities we were going to visit on our honeymoon on the way to the States: Rome, Amsterdam and Athens. The airlines allowed us to make as many stops as we wanted on the way "home" as long as we didn't retrace our steps. It was a perfect opportunity for two young people with no money to visit all these cities in Europe.

I will always be grateful to my parents for supporting me, and allowing me to find my own dreams. They gave me roots and wings.

WHEN LORRAINE MET RICHARD: A photograph taken at the Maccabi Games Stadium in 1965.

SPRINTER LORRAINE MARRIES

SWIMMER RICHARD —

SPORTS WEDDING OF THE YEAR

A romance that started at the Maccabi Games in 1965 culminated at the Emmarentia Synagogue in Johannesburg on Sunday when Lorraine Lotzof, the South African sprinter, was married to top American swimmer Richard Stanley Abramson. They w.ll honeymoon in Europe and settle in the United States.

Miss Lotyof met Mr. Abramson when both won gold medals in their respective sports at the 1965 Maccabiah. She now holds three Maccabi world records (in the 100, 200, and 400 metres) and he is the holder of a Maccabi World swimming record, hving prviously gained gold and silver medals at the 1961 Maccabiah.

A lieutenant in the United States Air Force, Mr. Abramson has retired from competitive swimming but coaches swimmers at the U.S. Airforce Academy.

He has two brothers who are also top-notch swimmers and have won Maccabiah medals at different times.

Lorraine, who is a nursery-school teacher, has gained many Maccabi and South African honours and, in 1965, was awarded the "S.A. woman athlete of the year" title. She was also nominated for the much-coveted American Helms Award.

After a two-year lay-off from competitive running, Lorraine plans to go into serious training once she has settled down in America and to defend her titles at the 1969 Maccabi Games where, incidentally, she will still be a member of the South African team.

Lorraine is the daughter of Mr. and Mrs. David Lotzof of Johannesburg, formerly of Reitz, O.F.S. and Richard is the son of Mr. and Mrs. Jack Abramson of New York, who are both prominent Maccabi officials.

A newspaper article following our wedding

CHAPTER *Twelve*

An Air Force Wife

"Morning ma'am," said the guard at the gate, in a deep voice, as he eyed the Air Force sticker on my car. His hand flew up in a salute to the peak of his cap, fingers straight and tightly held together with his thumb tucked under. He stood at attention in his khaki uniform, and the salute gave me the signal that I could enter the Base.

An hour before, I had kissed my new husband good-bye as he left for work at Hanscom Field Air Force Base, just outside Boston. His light brown hair was short, in accordance with regulations, and his shoulders and smile were both broad. He looked handsome in his uniform. I had given him a mock salute, clicking my heels and singing, "Off you go into the wild blue yonder, flying high into the sky!" He was on his way into the crisp fall air of New England.

WE HAD SETTLED into the life of newlyweds, in an environment that was unfamiliar to both of us: an Air Force Base. But it didn't matter, because we had each other. And we had a song. It was "our song". The song was by the Seekers and the words of the first few lines were:

There's a new world somewhere they call the Promised Land
And I'll be there someday if you will hold my hand
I still need you there beside me, no matter what I do
For I'll know I'll never find another you.

We played the tape and sang along while driving in the car. Everything felt right. I knew I had made the right decision in marrying Richard. When I glanced at his profile while he drove, the tingling at the base of my spine was still there. My thoughts drifted to both sets of parents.

Richard's parents had said: "You're bringing a foreign wife here — what if she gets homesick after you're married?" Mine had said: "He has his family, and you'll have no one." But we were committed, and determined to make our marriage work and to prove our parents wrong. Fortunately, we didn't have to work that hard.

I knew Richard loved and respected me; I could tell by the proud way he introduced me to everyone. Whenever they heard me speak, they'd ask where my accent was from, and how on earth Richard came to meet a girl from Africa. He would immediately tell the story of our meeting at the Maccabi Games, and then tell them about my achievements. He sounded proud of me, and that made me feel special.

"You're a great asset to me," he told me once, while touching my cheek. "Your background is so different from everyone here, and that makes you unique and interesting." He was kind, and he never missed an opportunity to compliment me for something or other. Before we'd go out, he'd look at me and say, "You look great. You wear clothes well." It meant a lot to me to hear his praise, and his warmth reminded me of my father.

RICHARD HAD GRADUATED from the Academy with a four-year commitment to the Air Force. Many people that we met in the Air Force had been transferred to different locations every year or two, so I was grateful that we were going to be at Hanscom Field for all four years. It wasn't just the convenience of being in one place the whole time; it also meant that Richard wouldn't be called up to go to Vietnam.

He was perfectly willing to go and fight for his country if he was called to duty. He was a trained officer and that was part of his commitment. It was I who was greatly relieved when he came home one day and said that he had been assigned a project that would keep him at Hanscom for all four years. It was as though a weight had been lifted off my shoulders. His job was a sensitive one: to negotiate the contract for the AWACS (Airborne Warning and Control System) and then build the plane.

FALL WAS UPON us, and as I drove onto the base, the trees burst into reds and yellows. Some leaves were still holding on to the branches, while some had started to fall off and were engaged in a flirtatious dance with the wind along the sidewalk. Other leaves were doing cartwheels as the wind whisked them head over heels. Fall in New England was magical. In South Africa we basically had two seasons, winter and summer. Because there was no snow, the winters were brown and dry in the area where I grew up. The leaves simply shriveled up, died, and fell to the ground; we trampled them with our bare feet and they made a crunching sound. That was it.

On the car radio, I listened to the latest summaries of American casualties and deaths in Vietnam. My stomach churned as I heard the climbing numbers. I thought about the families getting the news. For each cold statistic, I knew there were flesh-and-blood loved ones who were grieving. It was 1968; America, it seemed, was not getting any closer to victory in that war.

I pulled into a parking space at the Base Exchange supermarket and tightened my sweater around me. As the plunging temperatures nipped at my bones, a thin wind began to whine. With my price clicker in hand, I made my way through the automatic doors.

The BX prices were cheap compared to the "outside" supermarkets, but on a Second Lieutenant's salary, we were still on a tight budget. The price clicker was a device that I used every time I put something into the shopping cart, recording the price. I shopped for the most important items first, like meat, bread, eggs and milk. Then, with whatever amount my budget allowed, I bought cookies, ice cream and soda, while recording each purchased item on my clicker. I watched as the dollar amount added up, and when I reached my limit, that was it. With my packages in the back seat, I waved to the guard at the gate as I exited and drove to our modest apartment in Lowell, about 30 minutes away. We didn't yet qualify for free base housing, because a Second Lieutenant was at the bottom rung on the ladder.

I walked down the stairs to our basement apartment and, once inside, glanced up toward the windows that were at street level. All I could see were boots and shoes walking outside. After unpacking the groceries, I sat down to write a letter to my parents. There was irony in our situation: *they* were now the ones eyeing the mailbox every day to see if there was a blue aerogramme with the American stamp on the front!

I smoothed open the blue tissue-like paper and began.

Dear Mom, Dad and Selwyn,

You won't believe how patriotic these Americans are. Every day at five o'clock on the Base, the national anthem plays, and everyone has to stop whatever they're doing and stand at attention with their hand over their heart. Cars stop and the drivers get out and everything comes to a complete halt.

The Vietnam war is weighing heavy on me and I'm always thinking of how hard it must be for the wives I meet whose husbands are overseas. I'm strongly against this war and yet I'm living in the military, so I can't say too much. My friend Susan, whose husband is fighting over there, needs my support, not my condemnation of our being in Southeast Asia. I feel the way I did in South Africa. I disagree with the government's policies and yet I have to live by their rules. I know that you understand that stifling feeling.

I dropped the letter in the mailbox the next afternoon, on our way to Boston for a Sunday walk along the Charles River. On the way back to the car, Richard and I saw an angry crowd that had gathered for a protest. They were carrying signs and yelling, "Stop the war now!" Hippies with

213

long hair and tie-dyed T-shirts carried large peace signs; the girls had brightly colored flowers in their long hair. Their voices rose in unison as they filled the chilly Boston air with the song "Kumbaya." I thought back to the protest march I had witnessed in Johannesburg, with police lining the streets, taking photos of the students. I knew that their goal had been to keep those photos, as evidence that those students were a threat to the security of South Africa. The opposite was true here. The police were there to protect the protesters and to make sure things remained peaceful. I wondered if the students realized how fortunate they were, to be able to protest openly without fear of repercussion from the authorities, as protesters had faced where I grew up.

Back in the car on our way home, I asked Richard, "Why are Americans fighting and dying for the Vietnamese?"

"We're fighting Communism," he answered. "The Commies want to spread their philosophy everywhere. If we don't stop them in South Vietnam, they'll continue their plan to take over the world."

"Don't you think we should bring our soldiers home?"

"Definitely not." His knuckles tightened on the steering wheel. He was speaking like what he was: a true officer in the military.

"I guess I don't understand. Neither do those people out there on the street," I said, crossing my arms as I looked out the window.

A bit further on we saw flames darting up from the ground. A group of students were burning an American flag. I glanced at Richard. I noticed that he was clenching his jaw as he looked straight ahead.

"Our soldiers are fighting and dying for their freedom," he said, "and they're burning the flag that is the very symbol of that freedom."

"I agree it's disgusting to burn the flag. The flag belongs to the American people and not the government. It represents the freedom that I never had in South Africa."

Watching them burn the flag showed me their disrespect for the country as a whole. I said, "I bet those people burning the flag of the United States have never lived in any other country for any length of time. If they had, they would appreciate what they have in America and what that flag stands for."

"You're right, Lorraine; they don't realize what they have here."

When we drove back onto the base, the guard once again saluted us, and we made our way back into our secluded cocoon-like environment, with the uniformed soldiers on the open field training to be sent over to Vietnam.

As we drove through the gates I had a flashback of going back behind the walls of Eunice High School, and of what it had felt like to be secluded from the outside world. It seemed as if my life in South Africa had prepared me well for this Air Force life. I was used to living by strict rules in my country and in my boarding school. I found it easy to obey authority, which in the Air Force meant the higher-ranking officials. Richard was a second lieutenant, which meant everyone had a higher ranking. I wondered if those hippies could ever adjust to this strict military life. But for me, it was just something I had grown up with. I was used to being structured and living by strict rules; I was also used to keeping my political views to myself when I had to.

Everyone in the military had been trained to believe they were doing the right thing by fighting in Vietnam. Were they? It was all so complex.

The country was torn apart. The more I thought about the cost of the war both in lives and in dollars, the less I liked it. I found myself once again on the other side of the government's position, just like in South Africa. But at least this time, the government wasn't about to imprison me if I expressed my views on the subject.

⟶◆⟵

WHEN I FIRST met Richard's boss and his wife at a restaurant, they seemed like a really nice couple. He reached out his hand to me, looked me in the eye, and said, "Nice to meet you, Lorraine."

A perfectly natural greeting.

So why then was I trying to keep the smile from fading from my face, and trying desperately to calm the quickening of my heartbeat? It was because Richard had failed to tell me one minor detail about his boss, Maury Conner. He and his wife were African American.

I realized that this would be the first time in my life that I'd be sitting, *not* on an overturned tin can outside our house in Reitz eating with the servants, but in a restaurant on a completely equal basis with an African American couple. Well, not exactly equal. *He* was my white husband's boss!

The tables had turned completely for me. I was in a new world. If only my friend Sybil could see me now. I suppressed a smile as I thought about that.

Maury and his wife were charming. They told us about their children and about some of the trips they had recently taken. Within no time at all, I was completely relaxed. It was a perfectly normal conversation. Then he asked me which country my accent was from, and I felt a twinge in my stomach. When I said "South Africa," I was afraid he would associate me with the apartheid government. Maybe they were thinking, "Hmmm, a white South African. I wonder if..." If those were their thoughts, however, they didn't show them. We had a lovely evening and immediately made a date to have dinner again.

Back in the car, I asked Richard, "Why didn't you tell me that Maury and his wife were African American?"

"Because I didn't think it was important. Is it?"

"No, of course not."

I was reminded that I was now in a world where skin color was not the most important thing about a person. It felt right.

———⟡———

ON MONDAY MORNING I made my ten-minute walk to work. I had gotten a job at the Lowell Early Childhood Center, a facility for children from ages three to six. I remembered the conversation at my interview.

"Where is your accent from?" the principal had asked.

"South Africa."

"South Africa? I didn't know there were any white people in Africa."

I had smiled and tried not to roll my eyes; I'd heard this reaction many times. Sometimes I'd tell people I was Jewish when they had this reaction, just to watch their mouths drop open. "Hey, come and meet this white Jewish African," they'd say. I noticed, too, that Americans always pronounced the name of my country in two separate words, South (pause) Africa, whereas South Africans slurred the two words into one: Southafrica.

Lowell was a town famous for its textile industry, located in the northeastern part of Massachusetts, just 40 minutes from downtown Boston. I liked working at the Early Childhood Center.

Mom and Dad, everyone is so friendly and welcoming at my new job. Americans in general have an appealing casualness. Every day they ask me, "Are you from England or Australia?" Then after I answer, they say, with raised eyebrows, "South Africa! No kidding. But you're white."

Speaking of accents, you should hear the Massachusetts accent.

I asked a little boy in my class how old he was and he held up four fingers and answered "I'm fourwa". Every one-syllable word now has two; for example, the children sit on the "floorwa" and they open the "doorwa". Yesterday I asked the custodian for some batteries for the torch. He had no idea what I was talking about; eventually he said, "Oh you mean baddaries for the flashlight."

—◆—

I joined the New England Liberty Track club, and after work each day I drove to the Lexington High School, where I ran with the team on the track. I had a hunger in my heart to defend those titles from the 1965 Maccabi Games, and I was training to try out for the 1969 team. This time I would be representing the United States if I were selected. A few months after I started training again, I competed in the New England Championships and won the 100 meters. I felt truly thrilled, and there was a great sense of satisfaction knowing that everyone in New England had had the opportunity to compete if they wanted to. Many years before, when I had won the South African championships, there had been a nagging feeling that my title should have really been "*White* South African Champion." The only way I could claim to be the best in the country is if *every person* in the country who wanted to, was allowed to compete. Unfortunately that wasn't the case back then.

As soon as the weather got colder we moved to an indoor track. I had never seen or heard of an indoor track, but I realized that in countries where the weather is not perfect all year long, like it is in South Africa, the athletes move indoors. I had to learn to run around the banked lanes of the much smaller track. For hours I practiced leaning into the sharp bends. The best indoor track I ran on was in Madison Square Garden in New York, when the Liberty Track Club competed in the Milrose Games.

In November, big fat snowflakes started to descend slowly and gently down to the earth. One morning we couldn't see out of our sidewalk-level windows; we were buried! The snowstorms here crept up softly, quietly blanketing everything, and, I assumed, creating a surprise for everyone as the town woke up.

"A foot of snow fell last night," said the matter-of-fact weatherman on TV, as though this were nothing particularly unusual.

This kind of weather was so different from the fierce electric storms I had grown accustomed to in South Africa. In a strange way the weather in South Africa had mirrored the climate (no pun intended) of the country. Most of the days were gloriously sunny and warm, just like the life of a person on the right side of the color line. Then came the brutal thunder and lightning storms, fierce and loud. The clouds hung heavy and dark over us, ready to burst into rolling thunder, and lightning zigzagged across the sky — just the way the laws of the land hung over us...brutal and fierce.

Mom, Dad and Selwyn,

I walked to school today in snow up to my knees. Yesterday I bought my first pair of boots and they are keeping my feet warm and dry. Because the temperatures fell to below naught degrees, everything is frozen. It's four o'clock in South Africa, so right now you are probably being served your afternoon tea while sitting in the garden amongst all your beautiful proteas, pansies and honeysuckle, enjoying the warm sunshine. I can almost hear you sipping the tea. It's dark here before I'm ready, and I'm looking at trees and plants encased in ice. When the weak sun shines its rays on them, they look like glass. It doesn't look real. There's actually great beauty in its coldness.

Do you know what I do each morning? For the first time in my life, I start each day by listening to the weather forecast.

Except for the occasional rainstorm, the weather in South Africa was like a string of pearls, one perfect day after another. The sun showed its face like an expected family member; it was just always there. The weather forecast would go like this: "Today it will be sunny and mild to warm, and tomorrow will be cloudy and mild to warm." That was it. In America I had to learn new words like wind chill factor, barometric pressure, and snowdrifts measured in feet. I learned a new way of dressing for the cold: "layers" of clothing.

———◆———

SPRING ARRIVED ONE blossom at a time in New England, until the trees were a bouquet of pink. The warm May sun smiled on all the new sprigs of grass. A million buds had been lying patiently under the blanket of white, and were now pushing their way out from the earth. I was never too engrossed to miss the first signs. The daffodils, tulips and irises arrived on cue. The wind stirred up the fallen pink blossoms instead of snowflakes. How reassuring to know that the world was once again being reborn!

I had had a few good months of running on the indoor tracks, competing in numerous indoor meets in the Boston area. Now the Liberty Track team, like everyone else, was ready to venture outdoors, and I was eager to fill my lungs with real fresh air as I sprinted around the track.

It was late afternoon in mid-April 1969 when I arrived home from work. There was a bone-chilling wind in the air, and I still needed to turn up the collar of my coat. The days were still too short. When I got to the front door of our apartment, I heard the shrill ring of the phone through the closed door. I quickly unlocked the door and rushed to pick up the receiver. The voice on the other end said, "Congratulations, Lorraine. This is to inform you that you've been selected to represent the United States at the Maccabi Games in Israel in August." It had happened! "Wow, thank you so much," was all I could say.

I put the receiver on the cradle, then quickly picked it back up again. My heart was pounding hard and I immediately phoned Richard at work to tell him my exciting news. I was going to represent my new country. My dream of running for the United States had come true!

"That's great news," Richard said. "You deserve it, because you've worked so hard all winter."

"I wonder what it will be like to march behind the U.S. flag in the opening ceremonies. It will be so great to see my South African teammates again. I wonder if I can come close to the times I ran in the 100, 200 and 400 meters four years ago." I rambled on, and he listened patiently. Eventually I replaced the receiver, with a big smile on my face. With a song in my heart I started to prepare dinner. I realized that I still had my coat on! My mind was swirling as I hung it in the closet.

Wow — the United States of America. I've come a long way from bare feet and the dirt track in Reitz. I couldn't wait to phone my parents, but it was the middle of the night in South Africa. I welcomed the warmth of the kitchen and tried to focus on preparing the vegetables for dinner. I had bought a new wok, and I had planned to try it out that night.

As I washed and chopped the vegetables, I was vaguely aware of The Donny and Marie TV show in the background. *I'll phone my coach in the morning, and we can prepare a program to peak by the summer.* Then I started to sauté the garlic, broccoli and carrots in olive oil. How lucky I was to have this opportunity once again. I'd be defending my titles from four years ago.

I was so deep in thought that I jumped when the phone rang again. I heard Doctor Dennison's familiar voice saying, "Your tests just came back, and congratulations, Lorraine — you're pregnant."

I froze.

"*What!*" I said to myself — but to the doctor I said, "Thank you, Doctor Dennison," trying to keep the shock out of my voice. "I'll make an appointment to see you next week." I was desperately trying to keep my voice steady. My hand was shaking as I hung up the phone. Then my legs buckled under me and I collapsed into the nearby chair and sat paralyzed, staring at the wall opposite me. I cupped my hand over my mouth in shock and disbelief. My head was spinning. I was completely stunned.

Oh my God! What am I going to do? What on earth am I going to do now?

I was pregnant. That changed everything. I had gone from exhilaration to devastation in less than one hour. The smoke from the burning vegetables jerked me back to the present. I watched in horror as the black plumes rose up from my new wok. I scraped the burned and ruined vegetables from the wok and threw them into the garbage.

I had a little time before Richard got home, and I used that time to think things over. Before long, I knew what I had to do. I had to withdraw from the Games.

An hour or so later I heard Richard's key in the door.

"I'm not going to go to the Maccabi Games," I blurted out flatly, before he even had a chance to say hello.

"I'm withdrawing from the team." A tear found its way down my cheek.

He shot me a curious glance.

"Excuse me? Did I hear you correctly?" he said taking off his coat.

"Yes."

"What happened?"

"I got some news right after I spoke to you. You'd better sit down."

"What are you talking about?"

"You're going to be a father."

"What?"

"You heard me."

It was now his turn to collapse into the nearest chair. His hands rested on the arms of the chair; he sat motionless, and his eyes pierced mine like laser beams. As he leaned forward, I saw the color drain from his face.

"But I don't know if I'm ready to be a father."

"Well, in nine months time, you'd better be. I've had some time to think about it since that phone call from Dr. Dennison, and I've calmed down a bit. I've decided that this baby is more important than a track competition. I'm not going to do anything to jeopardize this pregnancy." I knew that there were a few women who had competed in the Olympics in the very early stages of pregnancy, but I wasn't about to take the chance. I decided to put the Games out of my mind and focus on being a mommy-to-be.

———◦———

THE MINUTE I heard the word "pregnant" I started to crave tomatoes. Not just tomatoes, but anything remotely related to a tomato. Tomato soup, tomato juice, ketchup, sun dried tomatoes; I ate lots of pasta just to have the tomato sauce. As the weeks turned into months, we watched my flat stomach turn into a basketball. I was feeling great, and the doctor said I could keep doing whatever was normal for me. So I continued jogging and playing tennis right until my eighth month. We knew this was going to be a live wire of a baby judging by the way it was kicking and moving constantly. When Richard felt the baby kick he reacted in shock.

"Oh my God. Doesn't it hurt?"

"Not at all. It's the baby's way of saying, "Hi, I'm here, growing and doing well.""

I was so preoccupied with preparing for the new baby that I hardly thought about the Maccabi Games. I vaguely heard about the results of the events that I would have competed in, and I remember thinking that the winning times were not out of my reach, but that it was okay because I had something more exciting and special to look forward to.

Dr. Dennison came highly recommended, but I needed to have a serious conversation with him before deciding to use him as my obstetrician. Because he was Catholic, there was an issue of concern to me.

"Doctor, there's something I need to discuss with you." I went on to tell him that I knew that in the Catholic religion, if there was a complication in a pregnancy and the doctor had to choose between saving the life of the baby or the mother, he was supposed to save the baby. The reason for this, I had learned, was that the baby hadn't been baptized yet. But in the Jewish faith, the mother's life is to be saved, because there is a husband and probably other children.

"If this is an issue for you," I said, "then I understand, but we need to be on the same page with this before I become a patient."

"Lorraine," he said, taking off his glasses, "It's no problem. I've had many Jewish patients and I respect my patients' wishes."

I was relieved, and he became my trusted doctor from that moment on. Nine months went by relatively quickly.

On January 11, 1970, the World Trade Center was under construction in New York and was to become the tallest set of buildings on earth. Preparations were underway for the first New York City marathon, which would be run on September 23, 1970, with 126 runners. Sesame Street was a year old. And on that day, I got my first contraction at around 5:00 am. By 6:00 am, the contractions were coming every five minutes. I patted Richard on the shoulder, and said, "I think this is it."

It was a sunny Sunday morning when Richard and I drove to the hospital; the contractions were coming every three minutes. I was expecting Richard to be the stereotypical panicked father-to-be, but he was surprisingly calm, and even stopped to buy the Sunday Boston Globe newspaper on the way so that he'd have something to read. *Sure, I'll be in labor and he'll be catching up on the latest news.*

I had had every intention of having natural childbirth, but as it turned out, I was no hero. After a few hours of intense shooting pain from the contractions, I said, "bring on the epidural." From then on it was smooth sailing.

Dr. Dennison, who was convinced I was having a girl, got ready to deliver our daughter. He said: "Congratulations! It's a ...boy!"

Gregg, our surprise baby, was born at 8pm on Sunday night, January 11, 1970 at Emerson Hospital in Concord, Massachusetts.

Gregg's first cry was heard all the way to Johannesburg. The nurse wheeled me to the phone twenty minutes after he was born. He cooperated with several loud cries, and my parents heard the voice of their first grandchild. I held him at my side, stroked his soft cheek with the back of my forefinger, and said, "There's no medal in the world that could compare to this."

—◆—

WHEN WE BROUGHT Gregg home, I would stand and watch him sleep in his crib and marvel at the wonder of it all. It meant a lot to me that my son was born in a country that would embrace him as a full citizen along with everyone else, unlike South Africa where the country belonged only to a segment of the population, the Afrikaners. In America he could fulfill his dreams and goals to the full extent of his imagination, desire and abilities. What's more, he'd be free to disagree with his government openly, unlike his mother who — by virtue of living in a police state — was forced to be complicit in a society I disagreed with.

Eight days later, we had the traditional Jewish "bris"— the circumcision ceremony. Gregg's Hebrew name was Leib Michel. He was named after three grandfathers who were all named Louis or Leib: my father's father, my mother's father and Richard's mother's father! The Michel was added because my dad's father had two names, Michel Leib. Richard's parents came from New York to the bris, as did his brother Allan, our sister-in-law Carole, and two year old Roger. There was an empty place in my heart because my parents and brother weren't there at this milestone event, but the plan was that I'd visit them in South Africa when the baby was a bit older. When spring finally arrived in Massachusetts, the track started calling me again. When our little boy celebrated his first birthday, a thought crossed my mind: Since I had missed the Games in 1969, maybe I could try out one more time in 1973. I rejoined the Liberty Track club and started serious training once again. My cheering squad consisted of two people: Gregg in his stroller, and Richard. They sat at the side of the track at each meet every weekend.

One day, when we got home from practice, there was a letter from my parents. My mother wrote:

"I just found out that the government is allowing South Africans to send money to family members overseas if they're experiencing financial hardship. However, we have to show them proof in writing that there has been a request for money. So I had an idea. Why don't you write a letter explaining that things are tough and you would like help from us?" She was still bent on sending money out of the country in case they ever had to leave in a hurry. I heard her voice in my head saying, "the German Jews said it could never happen to them."

The plan was that we would open an account for them in the U.S. and deposit the money when it arrived. So I wrote a letter about how hard it was making ends meet on a Second Lieutenant's salary, and how, since Gregg was born, things had gotten even harder.

The next week my phone rang and I heard my mother's voice. She was sobbing uncontrollably.

"What's the matter?" I asked, holding my breath and bracing to hear bad news.

"I just got your letter," she said. "It was so heartbreaking to read the things you wrote."

"But mommy, you *asked* me to write that letter."

"I know, I know, but seeing it in your own handwriting tore my heart out."

In the next letter she said;

"We can't stand it anymore. We want to meet Gregg. We're sending you plane tickets."

In April, I took my three-month-old infant son for his first visit to South Africa.

228

Richard couldn't get off from work, so I took a deep breath and made the 17-hour flight without him. I was lucky during the journey — I was blessed with a happy, contented baby, and the flight was uneventful. When I walked into Jan Smuts Airport in Johannesburg, I saw my parents standing on the other side of the glass divider, waving their arms frantically to get my attention. I asked one of the officials if they could hand the baby to my parents while I waited on the customs line. She carried him through and gave him to his grandparents. My mother was crying so much, it took 10 minutes before she could see him. My father's first words were "He's so pale he looks blue."

I smiled. "Daddy," I said, "It's been winter in America."

⟵━◆━⟶

I had been away from South Africa for two years. One night, after I had put Gregg to sleep, I sat with my parents in the living-room and asked them about the headlines I had been reading in the American newspapers.

"I read that international opposition against South Africa has intensified and that the United Nations has imposed strong sanctions, while many countries have divested their holdings," I said, waiting for their response.

"Yes," my mom replied, biting her thumbnail. "Ever since Sharpville, our image overseas has been on a steady decline."

She was referring to the peaceful protest march that had taken place years earlier in an African township near Johannesburg called Sharpville. On March 21, 1960, a few hundred Africans marched in protest of the laws requiring them to carry a pass wherever they went. A hail of bullets rained down on them from the police. Some of the protesters were shot in the back while running away.

The police thought they were making a powerful statement: "Don't try this again or you'll get more of the same." In reality, they were giving the resistance a statement to share among themselves and with the world: "Apartheid is brutal and deadly and must be turned back."

This incident, which gained currency as the "Sharpville massacre," signaled the start of armed resistance against apartheid and the police reaction prompted worldwide condemnation. The government believed that the African National Congress (ANC), the principal anti-apartheid organization at the time, was behind the protest. After the Sharpville massacre, this organization was banned, and its leader, Nelson Mandela, was sentenced to life imprisonment on Robben Island just near Cape Town. He was accused of treason, but somehow this only brought him and his movement more credibility and more attention.

I heard the tension in my mother's voice as she recounted the long-term consequences of these events.

She continued: "Our passports are filled with the names of countries that won't allow South Africans entry. We're hated by the whole world." My dad didn't say much, but I noticed his furrowed brow.

I thought, "Thank God I don't have to bring up my son in this country."

Gregg at eighteen months and me
in Bedford, Massachusettes

CHAPTER Thirteen

A Crack in the Apartheid Armor

"Should we stay in or get out?"

Richard's four-year commitment to the Air Force was coming to an end in June 1972.

He had to make a decision. Should he make the Air Force his career for the next twenty years, live a good life with a secure and steady income ... or should we venture into the "outside world" with its larger risks and larger rewards?

Richard and I knew he could make a much larger salary and be more competitive in the for-profit workplace, but he also knew that the job security was nothing like what he was enjoying in the military. We eventually opted for the outside world and headed straight for Wall Street. He was offered a job at CBWL Hayden Stone, in the "Big Apple", also known as "Noo Yawk, Noo Yawk." Bayside, Queens, became our new home.

Our happy, ever-smiling little boy took his tricycle and put his pedal to the metal as he rode miles and miles around the track, burning up

233

the rubber of his small tires as his Mommy worked out on the running tracks at St. John's University and Post College. When Gregg was three, I tried out and was selected once again for the Maccabi Games in 1973. My chance had finally come —I was going to represent the United States!

Of course, this was the year after the 1972 Munich Olympics, when a group of Palestinians terrorists broke into the village and murdered eleven Israeli athletes. The shock and horror were indescribable. Jewish athletes around the world resolved not to allow such an act of cowardice to deter us from going to Israel the following year. The murderers needed to know that they couldn't intimidate us, and that life would go on.

Richard's father, Jack, was a member of the Maccabi Committee and an official of the AAU (Amateur Athletic Union), and was selected to be the overall manager of the American contingent in 1973. The plan was that Gregg and Richard would move in with Richard's mother for the few weeks while my father-in-law and I were away in Israel. While he was staying with his grandmother, Gregg would go to a summer day camp called Rolling Hills.

With a big hug and a kiss, I waved good-bye to my husband and son the day I boarded the plane with the rest of the team. This was such a different send-off than my previous trips to the Maccabi Games, where I was an excited single woman. Now my emotions were mixed as I left my "two guys" behind. There was also a huge difference in the atmosphere in Israel at that time.

The Games opened with a tribute to the murdered Israeli athletes at the Munich Olympics the year before in 1972. As I expected, there was a somber mood at the opening ceremonies that year.

234

UNITED STATES COMMITTEE
SPORTS FOR ISRAEL, Inc.

Suite 53
STATLER HILTON HOTEL
33rd STREET & 7th AVENUE
NEW YORK, N.Y. 10001
(212) 947-4815

June 12, 1973

Mrs. Lorraine Abramson
215-16 - 15th Road
Bayside, New York 11360

Dear Lorraine:

It is my very great pleasure to advise you that you have been selected as a member of the 1973 U.S.A. Maccabiah Track and Field Team.

Selection is contingent on your maintaining practice and good condition through the period of the 9th World Maccabiah Games ending July 19th, 1973, and your agreeing to abide by all the rules governing the U.S.A. Maccabiah Team and the 9th World Maccabiah Games.

Whatever assistance you can enlist through your family, friends, neighbors, etc. would be very helpful. Contributions should be payable to the U. S. Committee Sports for Israel, Inc. and earmarked "TRACK".

Please let us know promptly whether this selection is acceptable to you so that we may proceed with such steps as public announcements, etc. We ask that you do not release the news of your selection (formally or informally) until you have further word from us.

We know that you will be proud to be a member of our Team and that we, in turn, will be proud to have you among our representatives of American Jewry.

Sincerely,

Nat Holman
President

The United States Committee Sports
for Israel, 1973

I was marching in my new country's uniform of red, white and blue, behind my new country's flag and I was reveling in the joy of representing the U.S. Then I saw the South African team in their familiar green and gold uniforms.

I have a jacket like that in my closet at home.

A lump found its way into my throat. Seeing the South African team was bittersweet; as I watched them in the opening ceremonies, I knew that a piece of my heart would always be with them. I was relieved that there was no South African woman in my races for me to compete against!

Being at the Maccabi Games brought back a flood of memories, but there was a great emptiness at being there without Richard. While I was warming up for the 100 meters final, I felt the soft grass against my bare legs as I sat and did a few stretches in the center of the field. I heard my opponents talking and giggling about the cute boys from the other countries. They were going to a party after the competition was over. For a brief moment I thought about the beach party with Richard eight years ago. I had no interest in joining in their conversation. I missed my husband and my son.

I looked around at the other girls jogging and warming up for their races, and I realized that I was probably the oldest woman there, and most likely the only mother in the track competition. At that moment it struck me: not only would this be my last time at the Maccabi Games, but the two upcoming races were going to be my last.

When I lined up for the 100 meters final, I shook my arms and legs out, to keep my muscles loose and my nerves calm. I waited for the starter's command to take our marks. When the gun sounded, I had a good start and once again felt the exhilaration of the wind brushing my face. I

36 SUNDAY EXPRESS, July 1, 1973

Free State girls runs in Stars and Stripes

A FREE STATE girl will be competing in the Maccabi Games in Israel next month in the colours of the United State — Lorraine Lotzoff Abramson, who has the finest record of any athlete at the Games.

As Lorraine Lotzoff she was chosen for South Africa for the first time in 1961 as a 15-year-old schoolgirl from Eunice College, Bloemfontein, and won two gold medals in the junior 100 m and 200 m and a silver and bronze medal in two senior sprint events.

In 1965 she was chosen again and became the star of the Games, winning three events — the 100 m, the 200 m, and 400 m — all in record times.

It was the first time she had run the 400 m.

She met her husband at those Games. He was in the American air force, and they were married.

Lorraine left South Africa to settle in America in 1968 and in 1969 was chosen for the United States for the Maccabi Games. But she had to withdraw because she was having a baby.

Now she has been chosen again for America — and this time she will run and will again compete in the three events.

According to reports, she has not lost her speed and should do well.

Lorraine has an unprecedented record in the Maccabi Games — she has been chosen for it four times, twice for South Africa and twice for America.

In all, she has won five gold medals, one silver and one bronze. No other athlete can match that feat.

The year 1965 was her greatest. In addition to winning the three gold medals in Israel, she won both the 100 m and the 200 m at the first South African Games in Johannesburg and was chosen as the "South African Woman Athlete of the Year."

She was nominated for the Helms Award — for the best sportsman or woman on the African continent — with Karen Muir and Kip Keino, the great Kenyan athlete.

Her parents, Mr. and Mrs. David Lotzoff, of Johannesburg, will be attending the Games next month and will be cheering her — the only South African athlete competing at the Games.

South Africa's athletes have been excluded from the Maccabi Games because of their suspension from the International Amateur Athletic Federation.

They are allowed to compete overseas as individuals, but not as a group.

The Maccabi Games falls under the direct jurisdiction of the I.A.A.F. and is one of the organised meetings which South Africa's athletes cannot take part in even as individuals.

A South African newspaper

crossed the finish line a close second: a silver medal. About fifteen minutes later, when the announcer read the results and called us up to receive our medals, he didn't say Lorraine Lotzof from South Africa — he said Lorraine Abramson from the United States. It felt so strange — a whole new identity.

I knew that the following race, the 200 meters, would be my very last. But the competition was tough; when it was over, I was grateful and relieved to win a bronze medal. As I crossed the finish line for the last time, my emotions were mixed: exhilaration at having won a medal, nostalgia, and relief and gratitude for the many ways track had enriched my life: the people I met and the discipline I learned. Competitive track had kept me in shape, both physically and mentally, for most of my life; but now it was time to hang up my spikes for good, and to let the curtain fall. My mind drifted back to the day when I won my first race in Reitz at the age of five — the day the boys accused me of cheating because I beat them. I had been competing in track meets for twenty years. Running had been in my blood and in my soul; it was the essence of my very being. But my hunger had now been satisfied.

It was time to move on, and I was ready. It was time to start working on a sibling for Gregg.

I felt the sun setting as I took the spikes off my sweaty feet for the last time. I held those trusted spikes in my hands for a few minutes, just looking at them. Those spikes had stood me in good stead during every race, and I stroked them a few times before I put them in my kitbag. I would never put them on again. *To everything there is a season* (sang the Byrds, following the Book of Ecclesiastes) *and a time for every purpose under heaven.*

One chapter closes and another opens.

———⊰◆⊱———

In 1974 the country was dealing with President Nixon's resignation, and we were waiting for the arrival of our second baby. As soon as the doctor confirmed that I was pregnant, I heard myself say, "I have to have a tomato." The tomato cravings came rushing back like a raging river.

I started to worry: *Will my heart be big enough to love two children? How could I possibly love another child as much as I love Gregg?*

While Gregg came to us as a big surprise, Jill's conception and birth were planned to the day. On June 13, 1974, exactly nine months after my visit to the doctor, our beautiful daughter was born at Long Island Jewish Hospital. When I first set eyes on her, a wave of love washed over me. Her thick dark hair was so long that I could have made pigtails before I left the hospital. Her blue eyes were a big novelty in our brown-eyed family. My fears were unfounded: There was lots of room in my heart for both of my children.

People mentioned how cute it was the way three-month-old Jill lay on her stomach in her crib or carriage, with her two little feet next to each other facing the same way. "So ladylike," they'd say. But something didn't sit right with me; the way her one foot turned inwards concerned me. Most babies lie on their stomachs with their toes facing outwards. That foot that turned inwards raised a red flag for me. I made a mental note to point this out to the pediatrician at her three-month check-up.

Dr. Berman examined her foot thoroughly, turning it this way and that way. He looked at me and said, "Mrs. Abramson, there's absolutely nothing wrong with Jill's foot. She has full flexibility; everything is fine." When he saw that I wasn't fully convinced, he said, "If it will make you feel better, I can arrange an appointment with an orthopedist." There was an ever-so-slightly condescending tone in his voice, as though he were indulging a panicky mother.

"Thank you Dr. Berman. I'd like that."

The following week, the orthopedist took an X-ray and came back with the diagnosis: "Mrs. Abramson, your doctor was right; there is nothing wrong with Jill's foot. However, her hip is out of its socket. That's what's causing her foot to turn inwards."

"What?!"

That was the furthest thing from my mind. But he assured me that it was not uncommon for a baby to be born with a hip out of its socket, and that the condition was more common in girls. He also said it was completely correctable. In defense of Dr. Berman, he explained that it was a very easy problem to misdiagnose, because in these situations there is no discomfort and the babies have full movement in their legs and feet.

"What would have happened if I hadn't insisted on seeing you?" I asked.

"Well, it would have become noticeable when she was supposed to start walking and she couldn't walk or stand up. By diagnosing this so early, she'll wear a plastic brace, which comes on and off easily. She'll wear it over her diaper for about nine months, and by the time she's about a year old, she'll be fine."

I drove home with tears streaming down my cheeks. The sad tears were because my baby had to wear a plastic brace for nine months; the happy tears were because we had picked the problem up so early in her life.

240

Jill at her second birthday party

The moral of this story is: Never dismiss the instincts of a mother.

Looking back now, I see this as another important example of my trusting my own judgment and instincts. I felt satisfied that I had stood up to authority when I knew something was really important. The other time was when I knew Richard was the right guy for me, and I stood up to my parents and family for the first time.

AT JILL'S SECOND birthday party, I ate my last piece of meat. After many years of cringing and gagging at the thought of eating animals, I finally decided to give up fish and meat permanently. I had read an article about the protein contained in certain vegetables. My father had been incorrect; I didn't need to get my protein from animals. I could get it from beans, rice, tofu, and any number of other sources. I became a happy vegetarian. (I still am.)

———◆———

I LEARNED VERY early on not to be fooled by Jill's innocent-looking big blue eyes. While she gave us lots of hugs and kisses, this young lady was full of confidence, had a mind of her own, and had a strong will to match.

I found that out the hard way at an indoor pool near where we lived. Jill was four years old. She insisted on going up the high diving board, and she wanted to jump into the deep diving pool. I felt certain that when she actually stood on the top of the diving board and looked down, she'd never jump off. So Richard and I allowed her to go.

She climbed up the ladder; slowly her tiny legs went up, one rung at a time. She stood at the top, looked down and ... jumped! I inhaled fast and held my breath. Then she came up and doggy-paddled to the wall and proceeded to go up the ladder again. The lifeguard sat forward in his seat. She repeated this about four more times — and the fifth time, she didn't come back up!

I flew out of my seat as Richard dove into the pool, followed by the lifeguard. Richard pulled her up. She was crying hysterically. *We should*

242

never have allowed her to do that. We're her parents and we should have known better. Now she'll be traumatized about swimming for the rest of her life. When she finally stopped crying, sitting with the towel wrapped around her, she looked at me with those big blue eyes and said, "Why did Daddy pull me up? I was trying to see how long I could stay under the water."

I realized that she was crying because he had pulled her out of the pool — and not because she was in trouble.

That night I said to Richard, "We're going to have our hands full with this one."

The good news is there certainly wasn't any lasting trauma connected to the pool incident. Jill went on to become captain of her swimming team in high school.

———

THE HEADLINES NEARLY leapt off the page: "Black students protest in Soweto, South Africa."

It was June 1976. I was giving Gregg and Jill their breakfast of oatmeal and milk in our home in North Woodmere, New York. They were ages six and two. After Gregg left for school and Jill settled down in front of the TV to watch Sesame Street, I sat down with my cup of coffee and studied the newspaper more closely.

I read that the African students in Soweto were protesting the Afrikaans Medium Degree of 1974, which forced all black African students to use (Dutch-derived) Afrikaans as the language of instruction, rather than their own African languages. They resented this decree deeply, and simply couldn't accept the new order. To them, Afrikaans was the language of the oppressors; they refused to be forced to study in that language. "The protests quickly spread to other cities in the country," the article said. It went on to describe how the police began firing into the crowd and the students responded by throwing stones at the police. The violence escalated. The police came down on them with great brutality and started shooting indiscriminately.

I completely understood the point that the African students were making, but I was also worried about the safety of my family. "There was a ground swell throughout the country," the news article said. There was also a ground swell in my stomach. Nausea rose in my throat.

I glanced up at the kitchen clock. Yes, it was still early enough to place a call to my parents.

"What's going on?" I asked my mother, trying desperately to keep the alarm and concern out of my voice.

"It's too terrible," she said. Then added, "What's this bloody government thinking?"

"Shveig!" I heard my dad's voice in the background talking to her in Yiddish, warning her to keep quiet because the phone could be tapped. I remembered how careful I had always been about what I said over the phone when I lived in South Africa.

My mother ignored him and continued.

She told me that a few months earlier, the students had gone on strike, refusing to go to school; they had organized a march, which ended up numbering in the thousands. "Even the police were surprised at the power and strength of the demonstrators." I could hear the slight tremble in my mother's voice. She told me how the students carried signs that read, "Down with Afrikaans," and "If we must do Afrikaans, Vorster must do Zulu." (Vorster was the Prime Minister of South Africa at the time.)

Then my dad came on the phone. "Daddy," I told him, "maybe Mommy was right all these years; maybe it's time to think about leaving the country."

In the past his response to this kind of suggestion had always been a curt, "I'm not leaving!" Not this time. Now there was a hesitation in his voice as he said, "Hopefully it will blow over and things will calm down." We both knew this was wishful thinking. There was a crack in the armor of apartheid. The situation was now dangerous for everyone.

I thought about the young African boy in the café that day, many years ago, when I had had coffee with my friend Sybil. I remembered how he was escorted out of the café to drink his soda outside the building because it was a "whites only" café. Was he one of the protesters in Soweto?

My cousin David, who was a doctor in Cape Town, told me how the violence had spread to the students in that city too. He was working in a maternity hospital in District Six, a Colored/Cape Malay section of Cape Town. They heard loud firecracker-like sounds right outside the hospital. "When we looked out the window, we saw the police shooting into the crowds, sending them screaming and running. The students had put car tires in the middle of the road and set them on fire as a barrier so the police cars couldn't get to them. We saw the flames of the burning tires, and the smell of the melting rubber was overwhelming." He continued to tell me how people carried wounded students, one after another, into the hospital. All had been shot. "It was the worst thing I've ever seen," he said.

I was covering my mouth with my hand as I listened. My mother had always believed that the country was on the brink of disaster. Maybe what was unfolding in Soweto was what she had feared all these years.

The whites all over the country, he told me, were panicked. They knew that if this avalanche of ill will continued, they would be completely overrun by the black populace. We ended our call. As I slowly put the receiver on the cradle, I said to myself, "This Soweto uprising is the beginning of the end of apartheid."

The fallout from Soweto was indeed impossible to ignore. International sanctions started to intensify, and they inevitably had their effect on the country, notably in the world of sports. The boycotts that kept overseas teams from coming to South Africa, and kept South African teams from competing in other countries, continued to hit the sports-crazy nation hard.

———◆———

A NEW FAMILY moved in across from our house in North Woodmere, New York . They were Asian; their son and Gregg became friends. When I saw the two boys riding their bikes together, laughing and having fun, I thought about how different his childhood was from mine. Gregg would never have been allowed to have an Asian friend in South Africa. It would have been called "socializing across racial lines" — a criminal offense. When I was a child, I never knew any children from other races; yet, here was my child, who saw the new boy across the road merely as a new friend.

246

What a privilege to bring up our children in a country where they can choose a friend by the content of their character, and not by their race or skin color. We watched Gregg play soccer matches against teams with kids of all colors and sizes, and I was reminded of how my Olympic dream was shattered because of my "old" country's racial policies. But that was another world, another time, another life. Now Gregg was playing wing, and as he flew down the field at lightning speed, the only color difference he noticed was the difference in the color of people's uniforms. The other parents took this completely for granted and didn't even think about it, but for me it was a very huge deal.

I had made a promise to myself that I would always be there to encourage my children in whatever interests they had. I remembered how my mother supported me in my track career many years ago, and I wanted to do the same for my children. Doing well in my running gave me the self-esteem and self-confidence that is so important for a young person. I wanted my children to find their own passion, and to go with it.

———⊰◆⊱———

"Mommy, how come that girl has a brown face and brown hands?"

I was in the supermarket when Jill, who was sitting in the shopping cart, asked me this question in a loud voice. She was pointing to the little girl standing behind us in the check-out line with her mother.

"Well," I said, "How come you have a pink face and pink hands? And how come I have brown eyes and you have blue eyes? It's because everyone is different, but everyone is special."

247

I was pleased to be able to give my child that message. I also felt a vast personal distance between the answer I had been able to offer to her (natural) question, and the messages I had received when I was her age, from my teachers in my segregated school.

⟶◆⟵

APARTHEID REALLY STARTED to unravel in the 1980's. I could tell from the news coverage that the writing was on the wall. It was only when my father said to me during one of our phone calls, "This is not the white man's country anymore," I knew for sure that the end of the apartheid era was in sight.

My cousins Marcelle and Sonny told me by phone that talks were going on outside the country. These talks were between the members of the underground organization, the ANC, which was headed by Nelson Mandela (even though he was in jail) and prominent whites, like the heads of large businesses and the heads of banks.

"We don't know exactly what's being said, but the speculation is that they're negotiating with the black leaders for some kind of non-violent takeover," Sonny told me.

I couldn't believe my ears. Were the words "takeover" actually being uttered? The Prime Minister at the time was P.W. Botha. He was a staunch apartheid proponent, and was (it seemed) unwilling to yield an inch to anyone. Botha's approach had been "toe the line or pay the price."

There was agitation in Sonny's voice as he told me, "We read that Botha was preparing a 'speech of note.' We were all hoping he was about to take a step in the direction of reconciliation with the blacks. But to everyone's disappointment, his speech was the same old rhetoric. In fact, he ranted and raved so much that even his supporters became concerned about his mental state. Apparently, he was becoming senile."

Shortly after this disastrous speech, Botha's own caucus forced him out of power. He was replaced in 1989 by F.W. De Klerk. In that same year, De Klerk made an astonishing speech announcing that Mandela would be freed after twenty-seven years in jail. The crack in the armor was now wide open and, according to my cousins, the jubilation from the black community could only be matched by the fear of the whites.

"Marcelle," I asked, "can you tell me what's going on?"

She said, "You can't imagine the anxiety amongst the whites. We're hording candles, canned food products, batteries, gasoline and water. There are rumors that the Africans are going to poison the water supply! So we're stocking up on bottles of water."

"They have a lot to be vengeful about," I said. I thought about my father's oft-repeated line: "They'll paint all the whites with one brush." I thought of what my mother had been telling me for years: "God help us if Mandela is ever released." "Have you ever thought of leaving?" I asked. Marcelle's answer was a familiar one. "I would leave in a minute, but Sonny is making a good living here, and he's worried about what he'll do in another country. We enjoy such a high standard of living, it's hard to throw it all away."

———⸺◆⸺———

FORTUNATELY FOR EVERYONE, F.W. De Klerk turned out to be the right leader at the right time. He and his advisors saw that apartheid simply couldn't continue. He met with Nelson Mandela and secured a promise of a peaceful takeover.

The whites were terrified, promise or no promise. At the time Mandela emerged, no one knew *how* he would emerge and what his mindset would be.

In another phone call, Marcelle told me; "We're all taking shooting lessons."

"What?" I gasped. "What are you talking about?" I felt my heartbeat quicken.

"Yes, we've all bought weapons. The first time I went for a shooting lesson my hand was shaking so much that I could hardly hold the gun. Anyway, we have the gun unloaded and locked in a safe, and I'm sure we'll never take it out. It's just a means of comfort." Then she joked, "If a burglar ever breaks into our house, I'll have to ask him to wait a minute while I put the bullets in the gun!" We both laughed, but before I hung up, I said, "Please be careful."

When Richard came home from work that night, he could see that something was bothering me. I told him about my conversation with Marcelle. "I can't believe it's come to this," I said. I was trying to concentrate on making dinner, but my mind kept drifting back to the disturbing thought that everyone I knew in South Africa was buying weapons.

I was witnessing a revolution from a distance — and I knew now that my family was on the wrong side of that revolution.

MY FATHER DECIDED to retire at the age of seventy-five; he and my mother announced that he was finally ready to leave the country, and wanted to immigrate to the United States. Certainly, the political situation in South Africa had helped to change his mind. A few years before, he had started to gather twigs for his retirement nest. My brother and his wife Trish had moved to the United States a few years earlier, not far from us, and we wanted our parents near us as well. It didn't take much urging. Both their children and all four grandchildren were in New York. Now my parents would be following suit. It was a chance to make up for lost time.

They bought an apartment around the corner from our house on Long Island. They got to spend time getting to know our kids, Gregg and Jill, as well as Selwyn and Trish's children, Evan and Kaylie. My father would stop by our house before the children went to sleep, to tuck them in and give them his special Grandpa David's good-night kisses.

———※◆※———

RICHARD AND I were blessed with two good kids, and I'm happy to say that our life as parents was, by and large, a smooth one. I loved being a mother. We survived the early years as well as the teenage years with little incident, and before we knew it, our children were applying to college — and we were the ones who had to learn to let go of our children when they needed to be free.

The University of Wisconsin was the school of choice for both of them, and we all became Badger fans.

Our lives had been so consumed by our children's activities that there was hardly time for anything else. I wouldn't trade those years for anything, but when Gregg and Jill were both out of the house, Richard and I looked forward to the next phase of our lives, with more time together alone.

Once again, a chapter closed and a new one opened.

CHAPTER
Fourteen

The Double Gift and Free Elections.

They came into this world on September 23, 1998, weighing 2 lbs 4 oz and 2 lbs 10 oz.

My eyes scanned their tiny bodies, lying in their incubators. I had never seen babies that size before. Despite being hooked up to tubes and monitors, their faces, with perfectly formed features, looked peaceful as they slept. The one thing they each had plenty of, was a full head of dark hair.

Gregg and my daughter-in-law, Lauren, had been married for three years. I still remember the beautiful wedding. As Richard and I walked our son down the aisle, it had brought back a rush of memories of the day I had clutched my own father's arm, a young and nervous bride getting ready to start my own new life. Now here I was, clutching my son's arm as he took that same walk. At the reception, I danced with Gregg and then with my dad, and I thought about how I had stood on my father's shoes at five years of age as he taught me, for the very first time, how to waltz. The memories all flowed together, with images swirling over each other as I pondered the dance of my own life. At eighty-two years old, my father

Emma and Leah sharing an incubator
at The Schneider Children's Hospital

still looked vibrant and handsome in his tuxedo, and he could still glide
me around the floor with steps as smooth as glass.

Then three years flew by, and before we knew it, we were presented
with the most special double gift in the world. Sometimes gifts arrive on
time, sometimes they're belated, and sometimes, as with our twin grandchildren, they're a bit early.

"Well, Gregg," I said as I stood outside the delivery room, "your twin daughters just couldn't wait to meet you, so they decided to make their appearance eight weeks ahead of time."

I could tell that my son seemed to appreciate my attempt at humor, but his smile never reached his eyes. He was uncharacteristically quiet and pensive. I had never before been in Gregg's presence where he didn't have a joke or a funny comment.

On the day the babies were born, we were all trying to be brave and strong for each other. Yet I didn't feel brave at all. We only seemed tranquil because our anxiety was so paralyzing that it translated into calm.

The neonatal unit at the Schneider's Children Hospital on Long Island was a new experience for me. The extraordinary nurses and doctors with the stethoscopes around their necks were hovering about, checking the heart monitors every few minutes. If one of the monitors made an unusual beep, the nurses were there in an instant. These angels in white were saving precious little lives every day. How blessed we were to have such a fantastic children's hospital nearby, and such an outstanding staff for the twins.

"Why do all the babies have tubes down their noses?" I asked one of the nurses. She explained that these babies were not yet strong enough to suck a bottle *and* breathe through their noses at the same time. So a feeding tube went down their nasal passages to their stomachs. During my visits to my new granddaughters, I found my eyes glued to the screen of the heart monitor, watching the jumpy little beats to make sure their hearts remained regular. On their heads they wore special preemie-sized caps that covered their silken dark hair. Volunteers knitted these caps, with love in every stitch. Pinned to each one of their sleeves was a piece of paper with their names: Emma and Leah. They left their tiny handprints on my heart. During one of my visits I saw that the nurse had put them both into *one* incubator.

They were so tiny that there was still room to spare around them. They were lying facing each other. Their small pink hands had found each other's, and they were holding hands. When the nurse pointed to the heart monitor, I learned the power of touch. Both heartbeats had calmed down significantly at the closeness and touch of the other. I focused the lens of my camera and snapped away, and the resulting photos are among the most precious I have ever taken.

Finally, after the babies had been in the hospital for two months, the good news arrived. Lauren called and said, "Mom, we're bringing Emma and Leah home tomorrow."

My heart soared.

"To live to see your great-grandchildren is the biggest blessing of all," said my mother as she stroked the hair of her great-granddaughters. Emma and Leah became the third generation to get Grandpa David's special kisses.

Today they're two beautiful, active eleven-year-olds with long dark hair and sparkling dark eyes. They're chatterboxes who want to tell me all their news, riddles and jokes at the same time. They fill my heart to overflowing and have enriched my life in ways I could never have imagined. These girls will be growing up, like my children, in a country where their freedoms are guaranteed, and where they'll have opportunities open to them; a country that will embrace them equally as Americans, along with every other citizen in this country — unlike their grandmother, who was

*Emma and Leah getting
Grandpa David's kisses*

always told that despite my being born in South Africa, the country didn't really belong to me, but to the Afrikaners.

A decade ago these girls were too weak to suck a bottle, swallow milk and breathe at the same time; today, Emma is the fastest runner on her traveling soccer team, and we love to watch as Leah does back flips with her graceful gymnastics body. After being able to hold them in the palm of one hand, I smile as I notice on their class photos that they're the tallest in their class.

They're the miracle of today and the promise of tomorrow.

As I WRITE these words, apartheid is no more.

The historic event happened in 1993, five years before Emma and Leah were born. The peaceful transition of South Africa from one of the most repressive societies into a democracy, is one of the twentieth century's most remarkable success stories. That same year Nelson Mandela and F.W. De Klerk were jointly awarded the Nobel Peace Prize.

In 1997, the year before our twins were born, the Truth and Reconciliation Commission began hearings about human rights violations that had occurred between 1960 and 1993. The commission promised amnesty to those who confessed their crimes under the apartheid system.

The following year, the nation held its first true democratic elections — in which all South Africans, regardless of race, color or creed, could cast their votes. I thought about my nanny Gracie and her family; about the Afrikaner farmers; about my teachers and Mr. and Mrs. Muller. I'd have given anything to see their reaction. What did they say now about the Bible and God's mandate regarding white superiority over blacks? Had God changed his mind?

It was my cousin Marcelle who gave me the most excited account of election day.

"Everyone felt privileged to participate in this historic event. We stood in a line that snaked for four miles! Yet no one complained. There was great exhilaration in the air. There was a group of Africans in front of me and behind me and we chatted together."

She told me how a friend arrived and wanted Marcelle to let her get in line behind her. This would mean that she would be cutting the line in front of an African. "No," Marcelle said, gesturing to the Africans behind her. "These people have been waiting here for hours just like I've been. You need to go to the back of the line like everyone else."

She told me how some of the Africans had dressed in their Sunday best for the occasion. Some old African men wore suits and hats, and the women wore their best dresses and high-heeled shoes.

I heard the news on the TV the day Mandela was released from jail. He had walked along Long Street in Cape Town wearing a broad smile; TV reporters had interviewed him. His message to the country was clear from the onset: "No violence, no bloodshed. Let us get this together. Let us work for a peaceful unification of the country."

This calmed everyone. Mandela parted the waters and led his rainbow nation through. He was an icon to the Africans. If his message had been to go out and kill — that's what they would have done. He was the savior of the country. There was no doubt about that.

My mother had been wrong. Mandela was not the monster he was made out to be. "Let's all share in the bounty of this beautiful land," he had said. I wish I could have shaken his hand and told him about the years that I had spent terrified, envisioning a bloody uprising of the blacks against the whites, led by him!

After the elections on May 10, 1994, Nelson Mandela became the first black President of South Africa, with F.W. De Klerk as his deputy in the Government of National Unity. Mandela's term as President cemented his reputation as one of the world's most magnanimous statesmen. He had gone from imprisonment in a tiny jail cell for twenty-seven years, to being the most honored man in the world, received by leaders of countries everywhere.

I now realize how thoroughly the apartheid regime had done its job: instilling fear in all of us. We whites had believed everything they told us about Mandela. Looking back, I can't berate myself too much for believing it. How was I to find out the truth back then? We lived in a police state that was ruled with an iron fist. We played by the rules or we went to jail. Yes, I was complicit like everyone else, I had been driven by fear.

The following year, in 1995, the South African rugby team hosted the rugby tournament against the New Zealand team called the All Blacks, due to the color of their uniforms. It was a watershed moment in the post-apartheid nation-building process. Nelson Mandela made a surprise appearance on the field to wish the South African Springboks good luck. Not only that, but he came out wearing a Springbok Rugby jersey with the number six (the number of the team captain) on the back. The eruption from the crowd was earsplitting! They went wild. Rugby had always been an Afrikaner obsession. Reaching out in this way was a masterful gesture, a sign of political genius on Mandela's part. At the end of the game, which concluded with an upset win by the South Africans, Mandela presented the trophy to the team captain, Francois Pienaar.

Today, Mandela is a retired elder statesman, and the country he saved is facing all the challenges of a young democracy. There are lots of growing pains and monumental hurdles to overcome. Unemployment has skyrocketed and with that has come the rise in crime. South Africa now has one of the highest rates of AIDS in the world; this disease has orphaned countless black children.

When I ask my family and friends who are still living there what they see for the future, I get two responses. My young cousins say, "This is still a great country, with gorgeous weather and natural beauty, and it needs time to come into its own. We have faith and we're staying."

On the other hand, my older uncles and aunts, who are in their eighties, say: "We handed over a thriving country, and they've made a mess of it. Look at all the crime and incompetence. It's become a third world country." I suppose there is truth in both viewpoints.

I'm keeping my fingers crossed for the success of South Africa. I hope my young cousins are right. I wonder what the opinion of my paternal grandparents, who moved to South Africa in 1920, would have been?

CHAPTER *Fifteen*

Walking In The Footsteps Of My Ancestors

In 2001, the world had embarked upon a new century. Most people's eyes were on the future, but my family's eyes were on the past. We were about to walk in the footsteps of our forefathers. We left for Latvia in July of that year.

———◆———

TWO YEARS EARLIER, I had received a phone call from my cousin Franklin in San Diego.

"How would you like to go on a "roots trip" to Ludzin?"

"What?"

I caught a glimpse of my astonished expression in the bedroom mirror as I held the phone to my ear.

Does he actually expect us to go there?

Ludzin, Latvia, near the Russian border, was the birthplace of my father, grandfather, great-grandfather and Franklin's grandfather. Our

263

grandfathers were brothers. I had literally *never* thought of actually going to this "schtetl", a Yiddish word meaning little village. It's not that I wasn't interested; it's just that the thought never occurred to me!

Ludzin was a name that belonged to the past.

"It would be a great legacy to leave our children," Franklin continued. "And just think how much it would mean to your dad if we took him back to his place of birth. My friend gave me the name of a Russian historian who will get information about our family from the archives in Latvia, and she will be our guide while we're there. What do you say, Lorraine?"

I noticed a hint of excitement and urging in his usually calm and gentle voice.

I said, "Franklin, this could be a wonderful legacy to leave our children ... but the thought had never crossed my mind to go to that part of the world. I think of it as our family's past, part of our history," I said. "I'll talk to Richard and see what he says, and I'll get back to you."

I hung up, went upstairs, and found Richard working on his computer. I told him about Franklin's suggestion. He swung the black leather swivel chair around, and as his face brightened, he looked at me and said,

"What a fantastic idea. Of course we have to go. It could be the best gift we'd ever give to your father."

Well, when he puts it that way, well then ... okay.

We drove the five-minute ride around the corner to my parents' apartment. My mother and father had immigrated to the United States in 1987 after my dad retired; we'd found an apartment for them around the corner from us, and about an 18-minute drive from Selwyn and Trish, who lived in Queens. Although my mother never fulfilled her dream of moving to Israel, she was pleased to be out of South Africa and near her children and grandchildren.

My parents were now proud American citizens. I'll never forget the day I took them to the Immigration Department for their citizens' test. They had been studying and agonizing over the Constitution for months. I took every opportunity to ask them questions about the flag, previous presidents and the history of the country. When the day arrived, they were ready. We walked into the crowded, sweltering waiting room, and my mother and I found two empty chairs next to each other. My dad sat opposite us. We were all a bit anxious about the test.

What if they don't pass? They've studied so hard.

My father turned to the black woman next to him and asked if she had heard anything about the questions they'd be asked. He asked her which country she was from. She smiled and said she was from Jamaica. "No," she said, she knew nothing about the questions. They chatted. I couldn't hear what they were saying, but I marveled at how far my father had come. He went from having Thomas and Piet look down on the ground while he spoke to them, in accordance with the apartheid laws, to sitting and having a conversation with a black woman, recognizing her as an equal. Same person; different country, different situation. He was completely comfortable on American soil and I smiled to myself. I was proud of him.

There were about five different rooms. The examiners all had stern expressions as they called the next person into one of the rooms. We decided to time each person as they went in. Each took about six or seven minutes.

"Mommy," I said, "*please* don't get into a conversation with the examiner or ask about his family. Just answer the questions and let's go home. Okay?"

"Okay," she promised.

My mom had the habit of befriending everyone she met, but this time I just wanted to get out of there. It was hot and stuffy ... and I was nervous for them.

If they don't pass the test we'll have to go through this all over again.

After what seemed like forever we heard, "Sadie and David Lotzof?"

"Good luck," I said as they stood up.

After about six minutes I started to look at the door expecting them to appear soon. Ten minutes passed. Then 15 minutes went by. *What's going on? Why are they taking so long?*

After twenty minutes I started to feel the palms of my hands get clammy as panic started to grip my stomach. *I wonder what happened.*

After about twenty-five minutes, the examiner came out and in a loud voice called, "Lorraine Abramson." My pulse rocketed. I raised my hand. "Please come in here."

What on earth ...?

I stood up and walked into the office. My parents were sitting there, calm as a lake. The examiner pulled up a chair for me and said, "I hear you're a runner."

I can't believe it. I told her not to get into a conversation about the family.

I shot my mother a look, and then answered. "Yes," We chatted for a while and then he said, "Mr. and Mrs. Lotzof, just so that I won't be fired, I need to have you write a sentence in English on a piece of paper so that I can make sure you're both literate." Then he took the paper from them, stood up and shook their hands. "Congratulations. You'll be notified when the swearing in will take place."

When we were safely outside the building I turned to my mother, "Mommy you almost gave me a heart attack. You were in there for so long. I told you not to get into a conversation with him."

"I didn't. All I said was that he must be very thirsty."

"What! Why in the world did you say that?"

"Because he had a very big bottle of water on his desk. He said he wasn't thirsty; he was hydrating his body for a road race that weekend. So I just told him that my daughter was also a runner. He wanted to hear all about you, and I told him how you met Richard and that was why we were here. He wanted to meet you and I said you were in the waiting room."

That was when he had bellowed my name, sending me into shock.

"See Cooks, I told you she'd be cross with you." My dad was right. I was.

It cost me a few gray hairs, but my parents became citizens of the United States.

———◆◆◆———

THE SIGNIFICANCE OF that moment back in 1987 was not lost on me. My thoughts went back to the time, many years earlier, when my parents were shocked and horrified that I was contemplating moving to the United States with my "American." Now they, too, were citizens of my adopted country. It spoke volumes about the value they placed on family, and the importance of being near their children.

Something similar had happened once before, even further back in

267

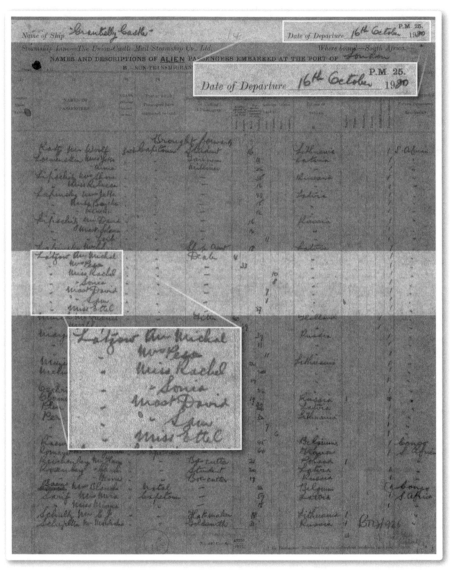

*The passenger list of immigrants
on the ship bound for South Africa*

our family, when my grandfather's brother made the trip from Latvia to South Africa, and then the rest of the family followed. Now I had paved the way to America: my brother, Trish and now my parents followed. Who would have thought? I had Richard *and* my parents and brother right here. I felt blessed.

———⊰◈⊱———

WHEN RICHARD AND I entered their apartment to ask my father about going to Latvia, we found them eating their dinner of chopped herring, tomatoes, pickles and Challah bread with butter. My father had bought a grinder and took great pride in grinding meat, liver or herring himself. Richard and I pulled out the other two chairs from the table and sat down.

"Daddy ... how would you like to go on a trip back to Ludzin with Franklin and Jean Gaylis and us?"

His blue eyes shot at me like an arrow, as if to make sure he heard me correctly. He was clearly astonished. There was a long silence. Then, tears overflowed and he said with a tremor in his voice, "I never thought I'd ever go back to see the house that I left eighty years ago." He pushed back his chair, and walked over to Richard and me. His gratitude and excitement could only be matched by the big bear hug he gave us. He almost squeezed the breath out of me. At eighty-seven he still had the strength of a much younger man. My mother, though, wasn't as strong as she used to be, and because we weren't sure what to expect on this trip, she said, "You go. I'll be fine here at home. Selwyn is not far away if I need him." He had just started a new job, and we knew he wouldn't be able to join us.

A map of Latvia

And so, as if we were called back in time, we heeded the summons, and in 1999 our planning began.

———◆◆◆———

TATIANA, OUR HISTORIAN/TOUR guide, began gathering information about our ancestors. Her archival research started to produce documents, which had — miraculously — not been destroyed during the war. We were all amazed when the mail arrived with names, addresses

270

and even photos of our family, who had lived in Ludzin. Tatiana included her English translations about the family from the time they lived in this "shtetl" until they immigrated to South Africa. It was a massive undertaking to find all of this information, and the amount she gathered over time astounded us.

The entire project took a year and a half.

<hr />

MY FATHER, DAVID Lotzof, was born in Ludzin, Latvia, on June 18, 1913, to Pessa and Michel Leib Lotzof. He was the third of eight children and the first-born son.

In October 1920, at the age of seven, he left Ludzin with his parents and siblings for South Africa. There were only four children at the time: Rachel, Sarah, David (my dad) and Sam. The next four were born in South Africa: Gertie, Lili, Joey and Cyril (Sikki).

"Why did your parents leave, Daddy?" I had asked him one night when I was in my early teens.

"Because life in Latvia had become very difficult for the Jews under the Russian rule. Amongst many other things, they were levying heavy taxes on the Jews, and the Russian police started to force the Jews to desecrate the Sabbath by making them work on jobs like sweeping the streets, knowing that we are not allowed to work on the Sabbath. The other issue was that if you were called up for the army, you would have to serve in the Tsar's army for life."

There were other stories that surfaced too. One, which Auntie Gertie,

Avsey (Isiah) Lotzof, my paternal
great-grandfather in Ludza

my father's sister, told us, was that one of my grandfather's brothers got into

an altercation with a Cossack and killed him. So the family had to leave.

Another story claimed that one of the brothers got a gentile girl pregnant

and his life was threatened, and so that was why the family had to leave.

Regardless of which story is true, my grandfather's brother Frank was the

first to arrive in South Africa; he entered the country on July 19, 1920.

Next came my grandfather Michel Leib and grandmother Pessa with their

*Michel Leib and Pessa Lotzof, my paternal
grandparents in Reitz*

four young children, who arrived in South Africa dreaming of a better life
for themselves and their children; they were looking for the fabled streets
lined with gold and diamonds. They didn't find those streets. Michel Leib
became a farmer and a horse trader on a farm near Reitz.

My dad was in his story-telling mood and I wanted to hear more.

"Daddy, do you remember much about your childhood in Reitz after you arrived in South Africa?"

"Even though my parents were very strict, we had great respect for
them," he said, nodding his head. "Oh yes, we had respect." As he was

talking I glanced up at the framed photo of his parents hanging on the wall. This was the same photo that each one of his siblings had hanging on their walls in their own homes. There was obviously great love for their parents. Then his expression changed as he recalled a painful memory.

"When I was sixteen my father had a very bad car accident and broke his back. I was the eldest son, so I had to leave school and work on the farm to help support the family."

I could tell from the crack and quiver in his voice and his furrowed brow that this was a tremendous burden placed on a young boy's shoulders. He looked somewhere into space as he recalled the memory.

"My parents and younger brothers and sisters had moved to Reitz, and I had to go back to the farm to run things all by myself. Sometimes I lay in bed in the old farmhouse at night and cried. It was too much."

I felt a dull ache for that sixteen-year-old who had shouldered so much so long ago. As the years went by, he learned all about farming from his father, and it became his profession, too.

The eight Lotzof siblings:
Left to right: Gertie, Joey, Sarah, Sam, Rachael,
David (my father) Lili and Sikki (Cyril)

CHAPTER
Sixteen

Ludza

Our excitement grew as the day of our departure to Latvia drew nearer.

Our group consisted of Franklin, his wife Jean, our twenty-seven-year-old daughter Jill, Richard, I and, most special of all, my eighty-eight-year-old father.

Franklin and Jean's children were in high school and couldn't go, and my son Gregg couldn't take the time off from work, so he and Lauren also couldn't go. So our group numbered six.

We went with no expectations at all. We were fully prepared to find nothing left of the original town. We had heard that the Nazis had completely destroyed many of the villages in that region. We agreed, however, that it was still worth going on this "roots" trip, even if everything had been rebuilt. We would see where the family houses *used* to be and we could walk the streets they *used* to walk on.

A week before we were to leave, Richard and I had dinner with our friend Gabriel Erem. We told him about our exciting upcoming trip to

Latvia. In a nonchalant voice, he asked, "Would you like to meet the President of Latvia? I can arrange it for you."

Richard and I glanced at each other and then almost simultaneously asked, "What do you mean?"

Gabriel explained that President Vaira Vike-Freiberga, one of Latvia's first women Presidents, used to be a teller in a bank in Toronto, Canada, where Gabriel had an account. He became friends with her and remained so when she returned to her native Latvia to enter the political world, and when she subsequently became the President. We thanked him a million times and gave Tatiana another task: to arrange, with the help of our friend, a meeting with the President of Latvia!

After two years of correspondence, the day finally arrived when we boarded the flight to Riga, the capital of Latvia. Tatiana was waiting for us as we cleared customs.

She greeted us with a welcoming smile, holding a clipboard with our name. She had a short, modern, highlighted hairstyle and clear skin. I immediately recognized her voice and soft Russian accent from our numerous phone conversations over the past two years. A few minutes after shaking hands with us, she flipped the clipboard over and said,

"Mr. Lotzof, yesterday I received this photograph of your mother as a young girl, from the archives."

She allowed us a moment of emotion. We crowded around my dad's shoulders to get a better look. Tears welled up in my father's eyes as he gazed at the picture of a beautiful young woman whom we all recognized as his mother, Pessa Weiner Lotzof ... my grandmother. My daughter Jill's Hebrew name is Pessa, after this grandmother. Jill put her arm around

Granny Pessa as a young girl in Lithuania

my dad's shoulders in a comforting gesture, and we composed ourselves
enough to walk to the red minivan Tatiana had rented for us.

———✦———

FROM THE WINDOW of the minivan, Riga looked like any large and bustling city in Europe. Rushing cars and people were everywhere. This surprised me. I wasn't expecting anything so cosmopolitan in this Baltic city.
On the way to the hotel we stopped at the Jewish Community Center,
which was run by the Joint Distribution Committee. The JDC is one of
the overseas arms of United Jewish Appeal, an organization that Richard
and I have supported for many years. It was comforting to see the familiar
emblem on the wall. Inside, my father spoke Yiddish to a woman who

279

explained that they were preparing two hundred meals for the needy to be delivered later that day. It was good to see the program in action.

Tatiana told us that she was half Russian Christian and half Jewish. "I consider myself Jewish but I'm proud of my Russian heritage," she said. "However," she continued, "It doesn't say "Russian" on my passport. I prefer to maintain an Alien status."

"Why is that?" asked Jean.

"Well, if my passport showed that I was a Russian, my sons could be called up to the army and sent to Chechnya."

A mother is a mother no matter which part of the world you live in.

———◆———

THE NEXT DAY we woke up at the first glint of gold on the horizon. We were pumped up and ready for our adventure. My father came down to breakfast wearing a striped shirt and checkered shorts. I knew it was going to be a big "photo day," and the striped shirt and checkered pants simply didn't match, but I could never say anything that might embarrass him or hurt his feelings. So I let it go.

After a delicious breakfast of fresh eggs, herring, smoked salmon, yogurt, warm rolls and fruit, we all clambered into the red minivan ready for the four-hour ride to Ludzin, which was situated in the southeastern part of Latvia near the Russian border. Tatiana had assured us that one full day would be more than enough time to see this small shtetl. I thought, *we probably won't even need a full day from what I'd heard about it.*

Our minivan took us out of bustling Riga, and we passed through many little towns on our way: Kruk, Tukums, Ventspills, and Sabile — the names of these Baltic towns made strange music to my ears. The devastation caused by the Nazis during World War II was everywhere. We saw memorials in many towns commemorating the people who had perished at the hands of the Nazis.

"I wonder what is left of Ludzin." I said.

Everyone was wondering the same thing, including Tatiana who had never been there either. As the miles rolled by, we watched the timid daylight grow stronger, and my father's face was lit up in anticipation, like a little boy on the morning of his birthday. He was once again in his story-telling mood, and when Franklin asked, "Uncle Dave, what do you remember about my grandfather Frank?" My dad answered, "Your grandfather was the one who met us at the docks when we arrived in South Africa. He had gone ahead of us. I remember him as being a real gentleman. A "mensh", a real decent person."

Franklin was hanging on his every word, as he connected in this special way with the grandfather he never knew. His grandfather Frank had died before Franklin was born; he had been named after him.

The Latvian countryside was lush and fertile, and the sun shone brightly in the Baltic sky, casting its welcoming rays over us. A carpet of green lined either side of the road. Our minivan passed peasant farmers cultivating their small plots of land with a horse and a primitive plow. The cows mooing along the way seemed to welcome the farmer from South Africa back to his beginnings.

Each telephone pole that flashed by brought us closer and closer to our past. I was excited but anxious. What if there is nothing left of the town? Even though we were prepared that this might be the case, I knew that I'd be disappointed, especially since we had the actual addresses of the families' homes. What if all the homes have been destroyed? My father's only concrete memory of his childhood home was that he had lived in a red house near a large body of water. He remembered ice-skating on that water in the winter, and he had a clear memory of his mother pumping water from a pump across the road. But that was all. Because Tatiana had never been there, she arranged for a local guide to meet us and show us around the town.

And then we saw it! The big signpost read LUDZA.

That was our first surprise. We saw that the name of the town was *not* Ludzin but Ludza. Ludzin was the way the town's name was pronounced in Yiddish and the only way we had ever heard it. When we saw that sign, the trip suddenly became astonishingly real to me; we were crossing three generations, my father, my daughter and me. The four-hour drive on the bumpy dirt road in our cramped minivan had done nothing to dampen our excitement.

"Stop! Stop!" we all shouted at once to the driver. We scrambled out of the van and stood in front of the sign as Tatiana took photos of us. We continued on the final short leg of the ride to the town.

———⋙⋅◆⋅⋘———

I HAD TO blink my eyes a few times to make sure I was seeing what I thought I was. When we entered Ludza, we had left the twentieth century behind and driven back in time — right into history. It seemed as if

Entering Ludza, Latvia

nothing had changed since my father left eighty years ago. It was as if we had taken a leap backward through space and time.

There were no paved roads; our van bumped along the gravel. The chipped and peeled paint on the wooden shingles of the small houses suggested that they hadn't been painted since my family left. The little shack behind each house, we learned, was an "outhouse." There was no indoor plumbing in the town and therefore no running water. There was, however, a recent addition: electricity. We saw a few women lugging cans of water to their houses.

It was as though a time machine had brought us back to the year of my father's birth.

After the van stopped, Richard got out and started talking to one of the women. She was wearing a long skirt and a headscarf. The lines on her face and the lack of expression reflected the hard life she had endured.

She became indignant at Richard's offer to help her carry her water as if to make clear that she was perfectly capable of doing it on her own.

A group of men sat on the front steps of the houses smoking pipes, and seemed in no great hurry to go anywhere. My mind was transported momentarily to the little town of my own childhood, Reitz, where the pace felt just as slow as it did here in Ludza.

The men in Ludza all wore pants held up by suspenders, and shirts with the sleeves rolled up to their elbows. They watched our van drive by as though we were the entertainment of the day.

I had been so worried that everything would have changed, and yet it was clear that *nothing* had changed!

When the red minivan stopped, we slid the door open and stepped out. A pang of excitement and disbelief churned in the pit of my stomach. "Are we really here?" I asked myself aloud.

"Welcome back, Daddy," I said, taking his hand. He was too emotional to answer me. We walked along the unpaved roads, literally walking in the footsteps of my grandparents and great-grandparents, seeing what they had seen.

———◆———

THE FIRST HOUSE we found from my list of family addresses belonged to Faivish Lotzov, my dad's uncle. The present occupant, an old woman who looked Russian, met us at the gate. She was heavy-set with a simple dress belted at the waist, clunky black lace-up shoes, gray hair tied back in a bun, and a pleasant plump round face with ruddy cheeks.

"Excuse me" Tatiana said in Russian. "I have a group of Americans here who had an ancestor who used to live in your house. May we walk around the outside?"

Her cheeks flushed even pinker.

"Yes, of course."

As we began to walk around, she said excitedly in Russian, "I've never met Americans." The big, broad, welcoming smile revealed two dimples and a missing tooth.

She told us that she was born in Ludza in 1947 and had lived there ever since.

Oh my God, the "old" woman is a year younger than I am!

Her hard life showed in every strand of gray hair. She showed us the outside of the house, which badly needed painting. She was particularly proud of her strawberry patch, and picked a strawberry for each of us. I was apprehensive about eating unwashed fruit from that part of the world, but I didn't want to insult her. I said to Franklin, in English, "Franklin, I hope you have your doctor's kit handy because here goes..." (Franklin is a urologist. It was comforting traveling with a doctor.) The strawberry was delicious. There's nothing like eating fresh fruit straight from the earth; I know this from first-hand experience in Reitz.

We had other stops to make so it was time to move on. We thanked her, said das vedanya, and were back in the van.

Our next stop was the house of my grandfather's brother. The house had been converted into a grocery store. Jill had gone ahead of me while I was scanning the streets with my video camera, trying to capture everyday life in Ludza. Through the lens of the camera I envisioned my grandparents walking along these streets, the women in their long dresses and the men with their long beards. They had gone from one sleepy little town in Latvia to another sleepy town at the other end of the world, Reitz in South Africa. The difference was that in Ludza they were discriminated against because they were Jews, and their lives were made unbearable because of that. In South Africa they had faced a different type of discrimination. This time it wasn't so much against them but rather against the blacks, although they were still outsiders because they weren't Afrikaners.

I had so many questions I wished I'd asked them. I wondered how their lives in Ludza compared to living in Reitz. I would love to have heard how they felt about leaving Latvia to avoid the oppression of the Jews, yet finding themselves on the side of the oppressors in South Africa because they were white. Were there any issues of conscience? Or did one just accept the situation in the new country?

I would like to have asked my grandmother so many questions: "Granny, what was it like traveling on a ship for such a great distance with four small children? Did you ever wonder if you were doing the right thing? What was your biggest adjustment to your new country?"

I was too young at the time to even think of those questions. Their answers will always remain unknown, of course, but my sense, from my father's stories, is that being poor immigrants, they were simply happy to be allowed to practice their religion freely, make a living and live without fearing for their lives. Videotaping the streets of the town they left, I could see the victory in that. They had food to put on their table; no doubt they accepted the bad with the good in South Africa.

"Mommy, come quickly!" Jill shouted suddenly, breaking my reverie. "There's a Lotzof in here!"

"What!" I almost dropped the camera. "That's impossible." I felt my pulse quicken.

"It can't be", said my father.

Franklin added, "No way."

We all hurried into the tiny store. Shelves with unfamiliar household products lined the back wall. A bare wooden counter ran across the width of the store; behind that counter we found Oksana Lotzov. Tatiana said that was the Russian way of spelling our family name.

Oksana was a slim, twenty-seven-year old girl, with a modern short haircut and a shy pleasant smile.

"Ask her what she's doing here, Tatiana! Who are her parents? How can there still be family left in Ludza?"

We felt frustrated that we couldn't communicate with her directly; I could sense her frustration too. Tatiana acted as our interpreter, and we learned that her grandparents' names were Anna and Isaac (Itzaac) Lotzov. Anna was still alive and still living in Ludza. Anna and Isaac's son Valerie was Oksana's father. We noticed sadness come over her face as she spoke, and Tatiana told us that Valerie had recently been killed in a car accident.

Oksana's smile reappeared when she told us that she was engaged and about to be married in a few months. She urged us to go and visit her grandmother, and gave us her address. "Of course we will," we told her. Tatiana recognized the address. It was the very next house on our itinerary!

Oksana graciously walked out from behind the counter to pose for

Jill and my dad with our newly discovered
cousin, Oksana in Ludza

photos. First we took a group photo, and then one of just her and Jill. They looked at each other and smiled, distant cousins from different planets, each wishing they could talk to the other directly. As I watched them, I was suddenly struck by how fortunate we are to be living a privileged life in the United States. My children Gregg and Jill have every opportunity available to them. We can all proudly maintain our Jewish identity, while this lovely young girl was stuck in Ludza with her Jewish heritage all but gone. How different her life might have been if her branch of the family had also emigrated from Latvia.

I felt deeply grateful to my grandparents for taking that huge step to leave. At the same time, I wished we had had more time to spend with Oksana to ask her about life as a young girl in Ludza, about her schooling and about her dreams. I wanted to hear more about what she knew about the portion of her family who left. After about twenty minutes, though, it was time for us to move on. I glanced around the store, hoping to get a clearer idea of what Oksana was selling, but all the groceries had names written in Russian. If we had had more time I would have asked her about some of those products on the shelves.

"I'm sorry, but we have to go now," Tatiana said.

We kissed Oksana goodbye and exchanged addresses, and after big hugs made our way back into the red minivan to see her grandmother, Anna. She lived in the house that belonged to my dad's grandfather. When we saw the house, on Latgales Street, it triggered a memory in my dad.

"I remember this house," he said, pointing his forefinger and poking the air as we pulled up in front of the gate. "I remember coming here to visit my grandparents."

"Really, Grandpa?" asked Jill. "That's amazing," she said. We waited quietly for a few minutes, allowing him to absorb the moment.

Anna came walking out of the house. She had a puzzled look on her face as she scanned the minivan and its unfamiliar occupants. She was a woman in her eighties, short, stocky and jolly-looking, like many photos that I had seen of Russian women. She had smiling blue eyes and short curly white hair. At the moment, though, she looked confused.

She and Tatiana exchanged conversation in rapid-fire Russian. Then she beamed at us, and invited us into her humble home.

There was a musty smell in the house. Every room seemed to me to be crying to have a window opened. The kitchen sink doubled as the bathroom sink. I noticed a bowl of ripe red strawberries about to be turned into jam for the winter. A propane tank sat precariously in the corner. Flimsy yellow-

*The clock that Anna gave my father
in Ludza*

ing lace curtains with a rip here and there barely covered the windows. The furnishings were sparse and the worn blanket on the bed was threadbare.

As Anna escorted us into her small dark living-room/dining-room, she went to a drawer and took out a family album. Jean and I each pulled out a chair and sat down at the table to look at the photos. First she showed us photos of her son, Valerie, Oksana's father; through Tatiana, she told us how he was killed. I couldn't understand her words but I could clearly understand the pain in her voice. She dug her hand into her sleeve, pulled out a white handkerchief and dabbed her eyes.

"Sy gaan nou huil," Jean said to me, forgetting that Anna couldn't understand English and she didn't need to tell me in Afrikaans that Anna was about to start crying. Then she turned the page and showed us family photos. The expression on my Dad's face matched the excited feeling in my stomach as our eyes came to rest on the familiar family names. The names matched my family tree, name after name after name. A wave of disbelief overwhelmed me. *This can't be happening.*

In the album, Anna pointed to the part of the family that had gone to South Africa. When we told her that *we* were that family, her eyes grew large and her hand involuntarily flew up to cover her mouth in shock. Tatiana had originally told her we were Americans. A well of tears filled her eyes again as she walked over to my father and embraced him, and they clung to each other. They were both crying. Their tears spoke the same language. We all reached for our tissues. She walked to the shelf and took down a plastic clock, painted gold, and gave it to my father. He turned to me and said, "How can I take this from her? She has so little?"

"Daddy, you can't insult her by not accepting her gift. You have to take it. "

At that moment we realized that we hadn't brought any gifts for her or Oksana. Who would have ever dreamt we would be meeting relatives? We opened our wallets and took out all the money we had, a few hundred dollars, for my father to give her. As poor as she was, she refused to take it. Tatiana explained, "I'm not surprised she refused the money. You see, in our culture a woman never accepts money from a man who is not her husband. If one of you women stayed behind after everyone left, she would accept it." We decided we would try to give the gift that way.

Soon it was time to say good-bye to Anna. With heavy hearts we bade her farewell with promises to stay in touch. We elected Jill to stay behind, and sure enough Anna accepted the cash from Jill and then kissed her. As I got into the van, I was already planning in my head to send her sweaters and scarves before the winter approached.

The Baltic sun was rapidly moving across the sky. It was late afternoon by now, and the trees and their shadows seemed engaged in a dance in the slight breeze. We had not yet found my father's house. We needed to move on.

The directions led us to the street of his house. We parked the mini-van at the end of the block. I held my father's hand as we started to walk down the gravel road. Our footsteps crunched on the gravel of the street. The smell of burned wood coming from the chimneys filled the air. *Could this really be the same gravel my grandparents and great-grandparents walked on eighty years ago?*

"There it is!" my dad exclaimed. He was pointing excitedly.

"I told you it was a red house!" he said. His voice, an octave higher than normal, was filled with exuberance. My eyes came to rest on the small red house he was pointing out; it had peeling shingles. Two elderly men were sitting on the front step.

"And there's the water!" My father's excitement was almost childlike. Now he was pointing to a lake at the end of the road. "And there's the pump where my mother used to pump our water!"

My heart was beating wildly. We snapped our cameras as my father bent over to pump some water from the same pump that had been the source of drinking water for his family all those years ago. We walked toward the lake on which, as a young child, he had ice skated in the winter and fished in the summer. Its water was as flat as a mirror.

We wandered around the area; every step held memories and emotions for my father. We came across a large monument on the banks of the lake that read "In memory of the victims of the Fascists." At the lake we met up with the local guide, who introduced herself as Irina. She wore a black

My dad pumping water from the same
pump his mother used eighty years ago

suit with a short skirt and spoke only Russian. She was not Jewish, but she
gave us a brief history of the Jews of Ludza with Tatiana translating.

"The 4,000 Jews that lived in the shtetl before World War II made
up 72% of the population," Irina said. "It was an Orthodox community.
On July 3, 1941, the Nazis marched into Ludza, gathered up all the Jews,
brought them to this very spot where you're standing, and then marched
them across that little bridge, into the forest right over there, where they
shot them all. They were thrown into a mass grave in the forest. The pits
were open and were never covered."

We all gasped. I had an image of people going about the business
of daily life in a small town when their world was suddenly shattered, as
they were dragged from their homes to the edge of this lake — the same
lake that my father had ice-skated on and fished in eight decades ago. A

293

The street my dad lived on in Ludza

shiver crept down my spine, and I shook my head from side to side as I envisioned the horror.

Then she continued. "One woman pretended to be dead and later climbed out of the pit with a bloody nightgown. A Gentile family took her in because she could sew." She told us that she had since moved to Israel. Her name is Frida Fried.

I shuddered at the thought that, had my grandparents not made the brave move to leave, they would have surely been amongst those poor souls who were rounded up right across the street from their house. I was shocked to learn from Irina that Polish pogroms against the Jews also took place in Ludza in 1949 and as late as 1968.

"Oh my God," I said suddenly. "Do you know what the date is to-day?" I pointed out that it was July 3, 2001. We were standing there exactly sixty years to the day after the 1941 massacre had taken place. The coincidence left us speechless.

Irina told us that the Russians had sent five thousand Jews from Latvia to Siberia during the war. Amongst them was Isaac Lotzov. When the war was over, he worked his way down to Moscow where he met and married Anna, bringing her back to live in Ludza. That's the reason they weren't amongst the unfortunate who perished at the hands of the Nazis the day they marched into Ludza: the Russians had gotten to him first!

As I looked at the monument I noted that, just like all the others we had seen, there was no mention of the word "Jews", only "Victims of the Fascists." We had heard that the Latvians were not that great to the Jews, and that, during the war, Gentile neighbors turned on Jewish neighbors they had known for years. I asked Franklin, "What in a person's psyche can make them turn on people that they've lived side by side with for their whole lives?"

"It may have been a self-preservation and survival thing," Tatiana responded. "They themselves, or their families, could have been killed for failing to cooperate with the Nazis."

My thoughts went back to South Africa. Given the right set of circumstances, human beings can sink to terrible levels. I've seen it myself.

"Ask her about that building, Tatiana." I said, pointing across the street. The brick facade suggested the structure had been built after my family left.

Irina said, "I think it is an old synagogue, but no one uses it anymore. It's locked up and abandoned," she said. She was ready to move on.

Jill, however, had gone ahead of us to the back of the synagogue. She came running hurriedly back towards us. Her face was ashen. She looked as if she had seen a ghost, and there was great anxiety in her voice as she said,

"You've got to see this. Hurry, hurry!" she urged us.

"What is it?" Richard asked her.

"Just hurry up."

What on earth did she see that's so terrible that she won't tell us?

Not only was the door in the back unlocked, it was completely off the hinges and lying on the ground. This gave us easy access. I covered my mouth with my hand when I saw what lay inside.

The inside of the synagogue had been ransacked and lay in shambles. There was complete destruction everywhere. The seats were turned over and broken. The bimah in the center was broken and we had to step carefully on the creaky floorboards. Dozens of sidurim (prayer books) were strewn all over the floor. As I picked up a few of the prayer books, I saw that each one had a name written inside the cover.

Each filthy, moldy book represented a human being. The ones still on the shelves were covered with an inch of gray dust.

A hole in the ceiling had allowed rain in over the years, causing a musty smell. The doors were ripped off the wooden arc that held the Torah (Holy Scrolls). The Torahs were gone, but Torah covers lay on the floor, along with a Shofar, Tzedaka box (charity box), Talesim (prayer shawls) and other religious items, strewn all over the floor.

It looked as if the Nazis had interrupted a prayer service and dragged everyone out. Our mood went from pink to charcoal. We stood frozen, silent and transfixed, trying to digest the horrific sight. Then suddenly, we all began to speak at once.

The desecrated synagogue found in Ludza

"Look at this!"

"Oh my God, look here!"

"Look over there!"

"This is unbelievable."

I had never been confronted first-hand by such desecration of a holy place. I felt as if I had been personally assaulted and violated. A wave of nausea passed through me. It seemed that in sixty years, *no one* had entered this synagogue. Maybe the handful of Jews who lived in the town were too afraid to do anything about it, or maybe they were too old and poor to bother.

As we stood on the cracked floorboards in the center of the sanctuary, Richard asked, "What are we going to do about all this? We can't just walk away and leave it."

"Maybe we can pay to have it cleaned up," said Jean.

"Maybe we can help to make it into a museum," said Franklin.

"A museum for whom?" I asked.

The Nazis had trashed the vibrant synagogue's heart and soul; there was no way to bring it back. After much discussion we agreed that it would make no sense to try to restore the place. No one used it anymore. Our plan was to inform the Rabbi in Riga on our way back, so that it could be cleaned and closed up in a respectful way.

When everyone left, I took a few moments alone to look around once more. My eyes started to play tricks on me as I saw the dust lift off the prayer books and dissipate into the air. In my mind's eye, the books were once more clean and neatly lined up on the shelves. The doors on the arc were once again closed, shielding the Torahs safely inside. The seats righted themselves and were filled with old men in dark pants and white shirts. They all had beards, some gray and some dark. Their heads were covered with kippas or hats, and because there was no electricity, they hunched forward, their long beards touching the prayer books as they tried to read by candlelight. There was a warm glow in the room and the air was filled with the sound of their davening (praying) in unison. They rocked back and forth as they sang and prayed.

"Lorraine it's time to go."

I was back in the present, surrounded by dirt, dust and destruction.

I took Jill aside and asked her to record the scene into the video camera.

"We need to document this," I told her.

She stood in front of some broken chairs and started to talk into the camera.

"Now I'm going to cry," she said, as tears filled her eyes and her voice. Her words were a mix of sadness and anger.

"Why couldn't they have taken this building and at least used it for something? Why have they just left it like this? Look at all this." She gestured with her hands. Then she went on to describe in detail what we had just stumbled on. She was clearly as shaken as the rest of us.

I tried to imagine what the congregation must have felt as the Nazis came barging in, but I couldn't get my mind around the terror of that moment.

We took a few items with us to give to our synagogues, or perhaps to a museum, when we got back home.

———◆◆◆———

OUR LAST STOP was the cemetery on the outskirts of the town. The sun was starting to surrender to the evening, and the shadows of the trees cast a peaceful, mournful glow over all the graves. The silence of the cemetery filled my senses as I walked passed each grave, looking for the names of my family. We found the names of a lot of the Lotzofs on the family tree. We stopped a little longer to pay respects at the grave of Isaac Lotzov, Anna's husband. As I walked around the cemetery and touched each headstone of my forefathers and foremothers, I felt a strange, strong connection with them. As I reached out to each tombstone, it as if I was reaching right through the cold stone back into the past and touching them. All their faces greeted me, even though their eyes had long ago closed to this world.

We left Ludza in a somber mood. The day was too rushed. There were things we didn't have time to do. I wanted to go *into* my dad's house. I wanted to see his bedroom. I wanted to see the school. But there was no time. We thought that a full day in a sleepy little town would be more than enough, but had no idea how it would turn out.

The four-hour ride back to Riga in the red minivan gave us time to reflect.

"We should never take our good fortune for granted. And Jill, you'll have to make sure you keep this story alive for the next generation after we're gone," I said.

"Yup, I sure will," she said as she reached for my father's hand.

"Franklin, how can I ever thank you for initiating this trip?" I asked. "I will always treasure these memories."

I HAD WALKED with my Dad hand in hand on the streets of his childhood — my father, my daughter and me — three generations connecting with those long gone. But we had one last order of business to attend to.

We had a date for tea with President Vike-Freiberga the next afternoon. As a group we decided that we would let Richard lead the discussion. My father was not known for his political correctness, and I was afraid of what he might say to her.

When we entered the Presidential residence the next day, the guards searched us, and I had to remove the gift-wrapping from the Tiffany pen we had brought her as a gift. Then we were shown into the room. President Vike-Freiberga was friendly, and her smile was welcoming. She was of medium height with short red hair. Her green suit was stylish and flat-

Latvijas Valsts prezidents

Mr. Gabriel Erem
Chairman & Chief Executive Officer
Lifestyles Magazines International

Fax: 1-212-355-3633

Riga, April 2, 2001 *Nº96*

Dear Mr. Erem,

Thank you very much for your kind letter of March 20, 2001. I am also preserving best memories from our meeting last year, and I appreciate very much your efforts in promoting my country.

Regarding the visit of Mr. and Mrs. Abramson to Latvia this summer, I will be very glad to meet them on Thursday, July 5. Unfortunately, this is the only possible date I can offer. Please ask Mr. Abramson to contact my office to make all necessary arrangements.

Looking forward to have an occasion to see you again and wishing all the best to you and your family,

Sincerely yours,

Vaira Vīķe-Freiberga
President of the republic of Latvia

*An invitation to meet the President
of Latvia*

tering. After we had all introduced ourselves to her, we took our places at the round table, which was beautifully set with china cups and saucers.

When she heard about the purpose of the trip, her focus shifted squarely and solely to my father. We were all just there "for the ride". All her attention was on my dad. Her questions were directed at him. The tea had an unfamiliar taste, but I smiled and got down every drop. I was much more concerned about what my father might say than about the flavor of the tea.

We told her about the synagogue we stumbled upon, and we spoke about the Nazi invasion sixty years ago. Then we told her about the absence of the word "Jewish" on all the monuments and memorials. She cocked her head sideways in surprise, and said she would look into it. I'm not sure if she ever did or not, but I'm glad we had the opportunity to bring that to her attention.

We all had a photo opportunity with her, and after thanking her for seeing us, we were escorted out. Once outside the gates I said "Whew" as I mockingly wiped imaginary sweat from my forehead. We all laughed. My dad did just fine. We had gotten in and out without causing an international incident.

I thought about how my grandparents had left the country eighty years earlier as poor immigrants. Now their son and the next generations had come back to have tea with the President!

——◆——

AFTER LATVIA WE traveled to Lithuania and visited the birth towns of both of my grandmothers. My maternal Granny, Eva Kruger Faiga, was born in Ponevich, and my paternal Granny, Pessa Weiner Lotzof, was born in Tavrig (Traugue), both in Lithuania. My Granny Pessa died when I was very young; she didn't speak English very well, but I did spend a lot of time with my mother's mother, Granny Eva. While driving around the town of her childhood, Ponevich, it struck me how little I knew about my grandmother's childhood in that country. She had never spoken of it, and I had never asked. Why didn't I ask her about her childhood?

Back in Johannesburg she had lived at "Our Parents' Home", an attractive and well-run assisted living facility, supported by the children of the elderly living there. She stayed there until she died at the age of 88. Even in her eighties my grandmother was slim, with fine features and a pointed chin, gray hair, a ramrod-straight posture and a quick walk. Her fine gray hair was short and wavy; whenever I looked at my own fine hair in the mirror, I knew it came from Granny Eva. Years ago when I used to visit her, we sat in the garden outside her room and I told her about my day at college and about my track meets. She always listened with keen interest. Her English was excellent despite a heavy Lithuanian accent. Why didn't I ask her about her life in Lithuania and about her school days, her friends, her parents and siblings? I wish I had asked her to tell me how she met Louis Faiga, the grandfather I was named after, or about her reaction when she heard they were going to move to South Africa, or about her adjustment in the new country, and her feelings about apartheid, or about her wedding day. There is a photo of her taken on that day, dressed in a beautiful lace dress, standing behind my seated grandfather. Why was she standing while he was sitting? I never asked her any of these questions. It's not that I wasn't interested. It just never occurred to me. I missed the opportunity, which is something I'll always regret.

Now here we were in the land of her roots.

The country was lush and green, but it was as if every leaf on every tree in the Ponar Forest was watered with tears and blood. They cast their shadows over giant mass graves where the Germans rounded up the Lithuanian Jews during World War II and killed them all, dumping their bodies in these mass graves. Memorials with Israeli flags were everywhere; visitors came to pay their respects to those poor souls who were so tragically murdered.

We found a flicker of light in Vilnius, the capital, when we visited a Yeshiva there. We saw a group of nursery school children reciting a prayer before they ate. "Shma Yisroel, Hashem elohanu Hashem echad," (Hear oh Israel the Lord our God, the Lord is One.)

I've heard and recited those words a million times, but they had never had such an impact on me as at that moment. Hitler did not win. That little group of beautiful Jewish children in Lithuania was proof of that.

———⟫•⟪———

I GIVE MUCH credit to my grandparents, who ventured into the unknown, not only for themselves but also for their children. The pebble they threw into the pond has rippled for many generations.

On the flight back home I reflected on my reaction when Franklin first mentioned the possibility of this trip two years before. I thought that these places were part of the past: why did we need to go there? But now I know that the past is not really the past. It is part of us.

When we got back to New York, we couldn't wait to tell my mother all about our journey, and to show her the pictures of our day in Ludza. When I handed her the photos, we waited anxiously for her response to this deep and life-altering experience. She took off her eyeglasses, holding each photo close to her face, studying them carefully as if she didn't want to miss a single detail.

We waited and waited.

Finally she lifted her head, looked straight at my dad and said,

"David, how could you have worn *that* shirt with *those* shorts?"

CHAPTER
Seventeen

Sadie Was A Lady

An hour after hearing that she had been diagnosed with leukemia my mother went to the local diner for lunch with my father and me. Only the most wonderful and caring doctor could provide a patient with such a sense of comfort and assurance that, after hearing such devastating news, she could walk out of his office at Long Island Jewish Medical Center and order a tuna sandwich and a salad.

Dr. Kanti Rai, with his silver hair and the soft brown eyes behind his glasses, had leaned forward in his chair and looked at my mother. His gentle voice, tinged with a slight Indian accent and warm smile, said, "Sadie, there is a new medication on the market which will allow you to live a full life." He continued, "I will always be here for you, and please call me at any time if you have any questions or concerns." My father and I were sitting on either side of her and felt a deep sense of gratitude that my mother was in the hands of this remarkable human being, one of the leading cancer specialists in the country. As we left his office and walked along the stark, white, antiseptic-smelling hospital corridor, we were all wrapped up in our own thoughts. The only sound was the clicking of my mom's high heels on the hard marble floor as we passed long corridors that disappeared in all directions.

L'Oreal color shampoo had given my mom's hair a warm chestnut color: there was not a gray hair in sight. Amazingly, at the age of seventy-nine she didn't have a single wrinkle on her face. I searched her eyes behind her glasses to see if I could read her emotions, but Dr. Rai had done his job so well that she seemed comforted and confident in his hands.

We walked outside on that beautiful fall October day in 1997. The clear blue sky and warm embrace of the sunshine was like a message from above, to say that between God and Dr. Rai, my mom would be okay.

⇒◆⇐

Following that day, my mother had five and a half more quality years. She danced at the wedding when her grandson Gregg married his beautiful bride, Lauren; she saw the birth of her twin great-granddaughters, Emma and Leah; and she celebrated her 80th birthday on September 13, 1998. The videotape of that birthday celebration is the last photographic memory we have of her. She wore black pants and a cream-colored silk blouse. Her hair was short and curly and her eyes, behind her large framed glasses, were smiling as she took the microphone and spoke to her husband, children and grandchildren. The warmth and love in her heart came through in every word as she recounted the blessings in her life, and as she told about the decision that she and my dad had made to leave South Africa and come and live in New York in 1987, to be near to their children and grandchildren and now great-grandchildren.

My mother's 80th birthday

My mom as a young girl

Four generations of women:
Me, Jill, my mother and my maternal
grandmother, Eva Faiga

In 2001, after many weeks of constant tiredness and lack of appetite, Dr. Rai gave us the sad news that the medication that kept my mom's leukemia under control had stopped working. Her body was no longer responding. There was nothing any of us, even Dr. Rai, could do to help her get better. Her decline was fairly rapid. Her internist, Dr. Scheer, had recommended that she stop using the hair color shampoo. He said there was a danger of the chemicals getting into the pores of her scalp. So as it grew out, her hair turned snow white, like an unexpected early winter. In a very short period, I watched her go from an active, fun loving, good-humored person to someone so frail that she needed a cane to shuffle along. My heart broke.

I arrived at their apartment one day to find my father yelling at her, "How can you get stronger if you refuse to eat?" I knew that this outburst was a result of his paralyzing anxiety about losing her. He wanted her to eat to get stronger. I pulled him aside and whispered "Daddy, she's doing the best she can. Her body doesn't need so much food anymore. Stop yelling at her."

It was my husband Richard, with his kind and generous heart, who had suggested that my mother and father move in with us when it became clear that she needed more help than my dad alone could provide. When my grandmother had become ill many years ago, I had watched as my mother took care of her mom with love and tenderness. She had been a role model to me, and this was my chance to do the same for her. After spending her whole life being on every diet ever invented, here I was, buying her favorite chocolate chip mint ice-cream and strawberry milkshakes, hoping that maybe this would be the day she'd take more than just a few sips. One night at dinner I saw her sitting and looking at the food on her plate.

"Mommy, why aren't you eating? I made your favorite: roast chicken and potatoes."

It was then that it struck me, with a sting in my heart, that she simply didn't have the strength to cut her own food. Before long I was not only cutting her food, but also feeding it to her. Life had come full circle. She had fed me as a young child; then I had watched her feed her ailing mother, Granny Eva; and now here I was, feeding her.

SADIE FAIGA LOTZOF was born on September 13ᵗʰ 1918, in Benoni, a small town just outside of Johannesburg. Her mother, Eva Kruger, was born in Ponevich, Lithuania, the place from which the largest influx of Jews had come to South Africa. Eva came with her parents when she was a teenager, together with her three siblings, Minnie, Leah and Morris. My mother's father, Louis Faiga, was born in Praszka, Poland, on January 10, 1877. He went with his sister and her husband, first to England, then Rhodesia (Zimbabwe), and finally to South Africa. Both came looking for a better life, free from oppression. Eva and Louis met, and were married in Johannesburg on July 3, 1910.

One day as I was paging through a photo album I said, "Mommy, tell me about your dad."

She often told me stories about her mother, but seldom spoke about her father. There were only two things she ever mentioned about him.

One was that he was the co-founder of an organization called the Hebrew Order of David, or "HOD" in 1904. "The HOD was formed to raise funds to assist poor new immigrants with their medical needs, and to help a family with the burial expenses when a loved one died. It was a wonderful organization." Then she added with pride, "After my father died, Uncle Seymour became very involved in the HOD." I know that two of my cousins, Arieh Faiga and Colin Braude, are members of the HOD, which now has lodges all over South Africa.

The other story she often told about her father was that he died be-

My mom with a group of friends

cause he didn't listen to his wife and ate all the wrong food. He had died of a heart attack. I had a quick flashback of my own father in Reitz eating gribenes (deep-fried pieces of chicken skin) on a slice of bread, smeared with a thick layer of chicken fat and sprinkled liberally with salt.

I think she tried to sound proud of her father for my sake, but I knew her mannerisms and her voice, and I could tell that she didn't have many good memories or a close relationship with him. He had his favorite daughter, and it wasn't my mother. She lived with her parents and siblings in Johannesburg until she met — and then a few years later, married my father, on August 13, 1944.

⟞⬥⟝

As MY MOTHER's leukemia progressed and she could no longer get out of bed, I sat at her bedside for hours, singing all the songs she had taught me

Eva Faiga as a young woman

Eva and Louis Faiga
(my grandfather whom I was named after.)

when I was a little girl. We sang Irish lullabies, Yiddish songs and some Afrikaans love songs. The words came flooding back to me, along with the memories of car trips filled with singing as the miles and telephone poles flashed by.

Noticing the strain her illness was having on my father, I encouraged him to go out for a few hours each day to play cards with his buddies at the Five Towns Senior Center, and I sat at her bedside. We would play a "remember when" game, where we would each recall something from the past. At first my memories came back one drop at a time, but then, suddenly, the drops came quicker, like the start of a rainfall. Soon I was drenched as the memories poured down on me.

The delicate shade of her pink nightgown matched the frailty of her frame. Her body looked small and fragile under the covers. She was a tiny sparrow now with a broken wing. I thought back to how practical and strong a person she had been. She always had sensible advice for us, with expressions like "A stitch in time saves nine", "A penny saved is a penny earned" or "Every picture tells a story," and her favorite, in Yiddish, "Man tracht and Gott lacht." (Man makes plans and God laughs.) These were the orange markers on the highway of my days, the guidelines that had prevented me from making too many mistakes. I always heard my mother's voice in my head with her practical advice and wisdom.

The phone rang and brought me back to the present. It was Hospice; they wanted to know if I needed anything. They told me that, at Dr. Rai's request, they would be sending a nurse every day to bathe my mom and to keep her as comfortable as they could. There was a tug at my heart; I knew that what they were really saying was that there was no more treatment that could be given. They were kind and compassionate, angels from God, every one of them. When she could no longer tolerate any solid food, I discovered Ensure, a drink fortified with protein and vitamins. Like my father, I wanted her to eat and build up her strength.

My heart was grasping at any sign of hope. Sometimes she would manage a whole can, but before long she was down to a few sips. I started to feed her one teaspoon at a time.

My mother was dying. She was in death's grasp, but I wouldn't accept it. I felt powerless to stop death from claiming her, inch by inch, with unhurried ease. I continued to feed her water long after her body didn't want it anymore. Soon she stopped talking and just lay for long periods with her eyes closed.

———◆———

THE PHONE RANG.

"Lorraine, this is Dr. Rai. I would like to come over and see your mother."

I wanted to say, "But Dr. Rai, this is 2002 and doctors don't make house calls anymore."

Then I reminded myself that Dr. Rai wasn't just any doctor. He was a genius in the medical world and a human being beyond measure — a "mensch." He sat with my mom for a while, and then, as he got ready to leave, my Dad and I showered him with questions. I saved my most pressing and gut-wrenching question for last.

"Dr. Rai, how long does my mother still have?" I tried to keep my voice steady. Part of me didn't want to hear his answer. I'll never forget his words. He said "Well, if you want to know if it's months or weeks, then I'd have to say weeks." I felt as if he had just punched me hard in the stomach and knocked the wind out of me. I couldn't breathe.

From that moment on, I put my own life on hold. No more golf, committee meetings or dates with friends. I became terrified that she might die when I wasn't at home.

I sat for hours rubbing her back. The feel of the silk nightgown was soft and smooth under my hands, but her body was thin and bony. I could feel every rib and every vertebra. By then her eyes were closed most of the time, but I continued to sing, just in case she could still hear me. Occasionally I choked back a tear as I sang.

My eyes always returned to the unmoving, tiny, blanketed mound that was my mother. Looking at her small frame lying there, it was hard to believe that she had been the strong tree trunk in our family and we were the branches. She had made all the decisions about what was best for my brother and me. It was my mother who never forgot a birthday or anniversary of any of the extended members of the family. Her sensitive and sentimental side came through in the poems she composed in every card she sent. They were always written in her beautiful handwriting. Although my dad was the breadwinner in the family, at home it was my mother who made all the decisions, and my father mostly went along with her.

One evening, I walked into her room and noticed a change in her breathing pattern. A few hours later, Selwyn emerged from her room; through his tears he simply said, "Mommy's gone."

My mother died peacefully at 10.30 pm on April 14, 2002. As she left us, I had an image of the family on the "other side"— including her beloved brother, Seymour, who died 13 days before her — waiting with outstretched arms ready to welcome and embrace her.

Selwyn phoned his Rabbi, Rabbi Penne, who drove to our house at 11pm. He was kind and compassionate and told us how to prepare for her funeral. The first thing we had to do was to open the window so that the soul could go out.

In accordance with Jewish custom, a deceased person has to be buried as soon as possible, usually the next day. My mom's funeral took place on April 16. It meant a lot to us that family members came in from out of town to attend her funeral. But what moved me as much, was when I saw the Five Towns Senior Center's bus pull into the parking lot. My mom had touched so many peoples' lives in her adopted land that a whole bus full of her new friends came to pay their final respects. I knew that I wouldn't be able to hold it together enough to deliver a eulogy, so I asked Richard to read my comments. My brother Selwyn spoke, and then Jill started her eulogy by reminiscing about the day at her Nursery School when the teacher had asked all the four year olds where their grandparents lived. When she came to Jill she said; "My grandma and grandpa live at Kennedy Airport." The teacher raised her eyebrows in surprise. "Yes," Jill continued, "That's where we pick them up and that's where we take them back." The laughter that rippled throughout the funeral chapel created the right mood as we continued to celebrate my mother's life.

AFTER MY MOM died, it was difficult for my father to be in the apartment alone, with all the memories around him, so Richard and I told him that he could stay with us for as long as he wanted. A few weeks after my mother's death, I decided it was time for me to go to the apartment to start going through her clothes and clear out her closets. I unlocked the door to their apartment and sat in her favorite armchair. The air was filled with heaviness. The quiet engulfed me. As I sat there in the deafening silence, I reflected on how well my parents had adjusted to life in America. The last thirteen years of their lives here in New York enabled us to have all the holidays together: Thanksgiving, Passover, Mother's Day, and Father's Day and, of course, birthdays and anniversaries. Our children were able to have the memories of a loving and warm grandmother who always had a ready hug and a kiss, a story or a song. My thoughts focused on our family's good fortune; that my parents spent the last years of their lives here in America, near to me, my brother and our children. Their apartment was filled with all the familiar items they brought with them from South Africa, as well as a few souvenir metal ashtrays from Israel. The bookshelves were stacked with her books: Yiddish Folklore, Hebrew Lessons, The Jews and Israel, and books on spirituality. If you want to learn about a person, just look at the books on their shelves. My parents joined the Five Towns Senior Center and found themselves the center of attention. Everyone loved their accent. As I sat in the quiet apartment, a neighbor walked past the window. A smile crept across my face as I recalled how this neighbor had once said to me, with a chuckle in her voice "Your mother looks like a normal Jewish woman, but when she opens her mouth to speak, she sounds like the queen of England!"

I got up from the chair and started to fill garbage bags with kitchen items, each one holding a memory.

"Mommy, why don't you throw out this old junky can opener and get a nice new electric one?"

"What's wrong with it? It still works," she had said.

I went to the bedroom, and when I opened her closet door, I stepped into an emotional minefield. There I saw all the familiar clothes I had seen her wear. I took out all the mushed up tissues in her pockets and started to fill up the garbage bags with her clothes. Some clothes still carried the scent of her Estee Lauder cologne, and an occasional lipstick smudge or stain.

At the bottom of the closet, I pulled out a box. When I opened it, I found every single letter I had written to my parents during my five years at boarding school — stacks and stacks of letters neatly bound together by a strong piece of elastic. In a canvas bag she had put every letter that Uncle Seymour and Uncle Maurice wrote to her and the family during World War II, when they were fighting with the Allies in North Africa and Italy. I couldn't believe she brought them with her when they moved to America. I made a note to sit down and read them someday. I opened the top drawer and found her hairbrush. I noticed that it had strands of her silver gray hair. I took the brush and placed it in a zip-lock bag and kept it. I'll always treasure that hairbrush. It contains the only *real* part of my mother that I have left.

I returned every day to do a bit more. I tried to keep the project going for as long as I could, so that I'd have an excuse to go to the apartment and feel the connection to my mother, until finally the whole place was empty. Every drawer, every cabinet and every closet was bare. I swear I heard the walls give a soft sigh. I walked out and gently closed the front door. Every now and then I take out the brush and just sit and gently touch those silver strands of hair. Invariably my mind transcends the silver to a much younger mother, with brown curly hair, vibrant and laughing.

I recently came across a poem whose author's name I don't know, but since my mother was so fond of poems, I dedicate this one to her:

In Loving Memory
We little knew that evening that God would call your name
In life we loved you dearly; in death we do the same.
It broke our hearts to lose you, you did not go alone,
For part of us went with you the day God called you home.
You left us peaceful memories your love is still our guide
And though we cannot see you, you are always at our side.
Our family chain is broken and nothing seems the same,
But as God calls us one by one,
The chain will link again.

CHAPTER
Eighteen

Dance With My Father Again

Luther Vandros

"Lorraine, I can't breathe!" I heard my father's frightened call from the upstairs guest bedroom in our house.

It was July 3, 2002. The warm weather forecast was welcome news to everyone with outdoor plans for the holiday weekend. Richard and I were getting ready to go to the pool at our club.

My dad had been staying with us since my mother died two months before. The anxious sound in his voice made me bolt up the stairs two at a time. I found him looking pale and sitting slumped over at the side of the bed. His gray hair was uncombed and disheveled. His head drooped downwards.

"Daddy, lie down and I'll call an ambulance."

When he didn't protest, I knew he was in trouble. I tried not to panic, so as not to alarm him further, and rushed to the phone. My first instinct was to call 911, but I wanted him to be taken to Long Island Jewish Hospital, where Richard's brother Allan is the head of the Ear, Nose and

Throat department, and where Richard is a board member of the hospital. We have a history at that hospital, so that's where I wanted him to go.

I knew that a regular ambulance would take him to the nearest hospital, as they're instructed to do. So I opted for a private ambulance. My fingers ran down our list of emergency numbers and I scanned down to names of private ambulances. It was the first time I ever had reason to dial that number, and I was grateful it was there. I gave the dispatcher our address, trying to keep my voice clear, calm and steady. He asked, "What's your father's Medicare number and his social security number? Who is his doctor? We need the name of the doctor in order to put in the request to bring him to the hospital." I was frantic and started to feel a knot tighten in my gut.

"Sir, there is a person here who is having difficulty breathing. Why are you asking me all these questions instead of getting an ambulance here immediately? Dispatch the ambulance and then I'll answer your questions"

"We need this information and then..."

For the first time in my life I slammed the phone down on someone in mid-sentence.

The fear started in my lower spine and crept upwards till I felt a vice-like grip on my heart.

My next call was to my brother Selwyn's cell phone. He and my sister-in-law Trish were, miraculously, just a few minutes away — in a supermarket, buying soda on their way to the beach. After I told them what was happening, they raced to my house and together we got my father down the stairs and into my car. Richard and I drove him to Long Island

Jewish Hospital, with Selwyn and Trish following behind. I prayed for green lights and no traffic, and every few minutes I glanced over to make sure he was still breathing.

Oh God, please let us get him to the hospital in time.

We did, but my father never came home again.

—⟫•⟪—

THE DIAGNOSIS, THE doctor told me, was stage four pancreatic cancer.

"Stage *four!*" I gasped in disbelief. That means it had been in his system for a long time.

"How can someone who lived such a full and active life with no symptoms be diagnosed with *stage four* cancer?" I asked the doctor. "Surely there would have been signs along the way?"

The doctor couldn't answer my questions. They haunted me until my friend, Cynthia, offered some very poignant thoughts that meshed perfectly with my philosophy.

"Maybe your father had such a zest for living and was always so positive, that the disease remained dormant in his system for a long time," Cynthia said.

She might have been right. And the truth is that when my mother died, something happened to my father. He was so devastated that I believe his immune system went by the wayside, and the cancer, which had been present for some time, finally surfaced. I've always felt that one's stress level is a large component of a person's state of health and well-being, and here was a perfect example of that. After my mother died, my dad's stress level became unbearable.

⋖⊙⋗

AFTER WE LEARNED about the diagnosis, the doctor took my brother, my father and me into a small conference room at the hospital and gave us a chance to ask questions and listen to the treatment he proposed. We sat on one side of the table, the doctor, in his white jacket and stethoscope around his neck was on the other side. I noticed the knitted brow on my dad's worried face. Who could blame him? After all, we were discussing *his* life and death situation. I was caught up in a maze of emotions and unfamiliar medical terms.

The doctor was very candid with my father. He said, "Mr. Lotzof, stage four is not good a situation to be in, but I've had some success in slowing the spread of the cancer with chemotherapy." My father latched onto the words "slowing the spread" and agreed to have the treatment. It was very difficult to talk in front of him, so I waited for an opportunity later to ask the doctor the question that was on my mind.

In the hallway, I cornered the doctor and asked, "Since my dad is eighty-nine and since it is just a matter of time for him, why put him through chemo? Why not allow him to live whatever time he has left, in the best comfort we can provide him?"

"Mrs. Abramson, I can't discuss this behind my patient's back. Those are his wishes and I have to respect his wishes."

"But doctor, I can't very well talk like this *in front* of him. Do you really think he's thinking rationally? You told him that you could slow the spread of the cancer, so naturally he'll agree to chemo. But let's weigh the side effects of the chemo with the actual success rate in slowing it down. Slowing it down by how much time? A month? A few months? A few weeks?"

"I'm sorry, Mrs. Abramson," he said. "I can't discuss this with you."

My stomach knotted, and anger and frustration raged through my body like a fever. Talking to this doctor was like rolling a big boulder up a hill. He was so different from Dr. Rai, who had taken care of my mother. Dr. Rai was the epitome of compassion, and he had included us all in his discussion. This doctor had his own agenda.

That night I phoned my cousin, Franklin, the urologist in San Diego. I asked his opinion on treating my father with chemotherapy. He said, "In my opinion, Uncle Dave should be kept as comfortable as possible. Why put him through all the discomforts and side effects of chemo at this stage of the disease?" What Franklin said was as clear to me as a flawless diamond.

I tried once more to talk to the doctor, but again I was rebuffed. He simply repeated that he couldn't discuss his patient with me. With gritted teeth, I walked away.

———※◆◆———

THE ANTISEPTIC SMELL of Pine-Sol assaulted me whenever I entered the hospital for my daily visit with my dad. I was back into the routine of sitting at the bedside of my dying parent. This time it was my father.

On one of my visits the doctor pulled me aside to tell me that it didn't look good, and it wouldn't be too much longer. My father was suffering terrible nausea from the chemo, so he was given medication to control the nausea. Unfortunately, this medication caused him to hallucinate.

One night on my way home from the hospital, my cell phone rang in the car. It was a nurse who told me that they had had to restrain my dad. He was hallucinating that someone was attacking him, and was lashing about in his bed, striking out at everyone. The next day the doctor stopped that medication and gave him something else to counter the hallucinations.

Finally he agreed that he should stop all treatment, and allow my father to be left in peace.

To this day, I am furious at the doctor for causing my Dad's final weeks to be so needlessly traumatic and turbulent. Unlike my mother, who was weak and frail during her illness, my father looked deceptively robust and healthy. Once the treatment stopped, my father was fully aware of everything going on, and we talked a lot. I once again put my life on hold. One day, upon arriving at the hospital, I walked to the kitchenette to put the Borsht soup I had brought for him in the fridge. When I reached his room, I noticed that he was lying with his eyes closed. His bed was separated from the patient next to him by a flimsy blue curtain, offering some privacy from sight but not sound. I tiptoed into the room, trying not to disturb him, but he opened his eyes. When he saw me he said with a big, wide smile on his face, "Lolzy, I'm *so* pleased to see you!" Even under those awful circumstances, his eyes still had the familiar sparkle. Then he peered out from under his graying thick eyebrows flecked with white, and with a serious look on his face, he asked me a question that broke my heart.

"Tell me the truth. How much longer do I have?"

I knew from what the doctor and nurses told me that it was a matter of weeks, but I couldn't bring myself to tell him that. At the same time, I didn't want to lie to him. So I said, "Daddy, only God can answer that question, but it doesn't look good." And I left it at that.

"Okay," he said in a resigned voice, "If mommy wants me to join her that badly, then I'll go."

I didn't say anything. Instead, I turned my head away so that he wouldn't see my pain.

He found comfort in thinking that my mother was waiting for him. As he closed his eyes to take a nap, I noticed that even though the skin on his face now had soft folds like an old Basset Hound, he still looked remarkably young for his age. I sat at his bedside, and while he slept, I allowed my thoughts to drift to happier times in South Africa. My memory came alive, and I once again saw my strong, tall dad in his signature gray felt hat with its wide brim, and his wooden cane with the curved ivory handle that he carried to prod the cattle on his farm and at the cattle sales.

A nurse was carrying a teacup on a saucer. The rattle of the china cup clinking in the saucer called me back to another time.

"Gracie, we're awake."

That was the signal for Gracie to bring my parents their morning steaming-hot Rooibos tea in bed. They couldn't get out of bed until they drank their tea. I was awakened every morning to the sound of the famil-

*Dancing with my father at Lauren and
Gregg's wedding, October 21, 1995*

iar clinking of the china cups on the saucer, as Gracie carried the tray to
their bedroom. After that, my mother was ready to start her day of super-
vising the servants. Other than the general running of the house, there
wasn't too much for her to do in Reitz. My Dad was off to the cattle sales.

My mind pressed the "fast forward button" to many years later,
when we got the news that my parents had decided to move to America.

Soon after they arrived, I said to Richard, "I'm so happy to have them here, but I'm a bit worried about my father. What will he do all day? He has no hobbies or interests outside of his work. His work was his whole life." I was wrong. He got his second wind and it blew at gale force. He hurled himself at retirement, and it turned out that he had many interests, but had just never had time to cultivate them. He embraced a healthy lifestyle with as much gusto as a hungry baby clings to its bottle. He greeted each day by putting on his orange hat, the one my mother hated, and walked, jogged or biked through the winding streets nearby. I often walked with him and had to hustle to keep pace. Although I had long since hung up my running spikes, I had now entered a new type of competition. My Dad and I walked in charity 5K races. Before some of the races I bought a trophy, and asked the officials to present it to the oldest participant, knowing that it would go to him. He was always so proud to bring home the trophy to show my mother. He never knew that I had purchased it. He and my mother attended the Five Towns Senior Center every day, where he joined a card players' group and became addicted to poker. I would get a daily report of how many pennies he won or lost. Each night he'd put his winnings in a large bottle. Whenever I visited them I'd say, "Daddy, the bottle is filling up," and he'd laugh.

Twice a week he took part in a men's current events group. All the seniors sat in a circle, solving the problems of the world. Surprisingly, he became a synagogue regular. I think it was more for the social aspect than the religious component. He and my mother loved to go into New York City and go to Broadway shows. His favorite comedian was Jackie Mason. One day while driving with me in the car, I put on a Jackie Mason tape. He laughed so hard; he was snorting and wiping his eyes, saying "Oy." I actually had to turn off the tape for a few minutes so that he could catch his breath. He particularly loved the routine where Jackie talks about going on vacation and the husband has a tiny case and is given two hangers, while the wife has a huge suitcase and takes all the hangers in the hotel closet.

"I don't think it's that funny," my mother had said. That made him laugh even more. His laugh was contagious, and soon I was howling too. I couldn't see where I was driving. I had to pull over to the side of the road to compose myself.

Being warm-weathered species from the southern hemisphere, they migrated to Florida during the winter months. Life was good for him and my mother. I noticed a lot of handholding, and though there was still much bickering between them, they were both very happy with their lives in America.

—————◆—————

I FLINCHED WHEN the shrill sound of the phone rang next to the hospital bed. It was Richard, calling to say he was on his way from work to the hospital. That night, when Richard walked into my dad's hospital room, my father took his hand, looked at him, and said, "Enjoy your life and never take your health for granted." Those words are seared into my heart forever.

Before Richard and I left the hospital that night I said, "Daddy, how about your special good night kisses before I go home?" I leaned forward and he held my face in both of his big hands and kissed me on my forehead, just the way he used to every night when I was a little girl.

"Good night." *Kiss.* "God bless you." *Kiss.* "God look after you." *Kiss.* "Pleasant dreams." *Kiss,* "I love you." *Kiss.*

The next day he slipped into a coma.

⟹•⟸

EVEN THOUGH MY dad was so desperately ill, he still looked healthy, with his full head of curly gray hair, as if he were just sleeping. The nurse barely got a reading on the blood pressure monitor. She told me that it wouldn't be much longer. I accepted the news with numbness. Selwyn and I slept in the hospital that night.

Selwyn left early the next morning to attend morning services at the synagogue, and I stepped into the nurses' lounge for a few minutes to watch the news. Ten minutes later the nurse came into the lounge to tell me that my father had passed away. A surreal tranquility washed over me. I said "Thank you" with the same calmness as if someone had said "Mrs. Abramson, your table is ready." "Thank you." It was 6.10 am on July 15th.

I made my way into his room. The first thing I noticed was the straight line on the monitor. That warm, big, wonderful heart was now forever still. I asked the nurse to pull the sheet over his face. I couldn't do it.

I also couldn't touch his body. But that was okay because I had said everything I wanted to say to him, and I even got my special kisses. I had complete closure. She slipped his black onyx ring off his finger and handed it to me. My father had been in the hospital for just over three weeks. He had died exactly three months after my mother, at the age of eighty-nine.

Before I left the hospital, I walked to the fridge in the kitchenette and threw out the Borscht soup I had brought for him. I didn't want anyone else to have it.

There was a lot of organizing to do. I had to let my children and all the family in South Africa know, and I had to arrange for the Shiva, the seven days of mourning, sitting at home receiving friends and family. When I got home, the house was empty and quiet. I sat down at the kitchen table with a pen in my hand ready to start a "to do" list.

But instead, the walls of the dam broke.

With a throbbing emptiness in my gut, I put my head down on my folded arms and started to sob, loud uncontrollable sobs. I cried so hard that I thought something inside me would break. I couldn't stop. I have no idea how long I sat there but all I know is that when I eventually stopped, I felt like an empty overturned pitcher. My eyes were red and swollen and I was grateful that I was alone.

———⊰◆⊱———

We were back at the funeral parlor on July 16th, exactly three months to the day since my mother's funeral. As I glanced around, I noticed that the chapel was completely full, with some people standing at the back. It meant a great deal to me to see such an outpouring of support and love. Who would ever have thought that the farmer from a small rural town in South Africa would someday fill a funeral chapel here in New York? The

Cantor from my parents' synagogue asked if he could say a few words; he had had a special relationship with my dad. His opening remarks were;

"I couldn't believe it when Lorraine told me that David was eighty-nine years old. I was shocked. I assumed he was at least ten years younger."

I thought, "That's my dad. Robust and strong to the end."

If someone had told me that both my parents were going to die within three months of each other, I would have been convinced that I would never be able to survive anything like that. Yet I survived. I now believe that we're all much stronger than we think we are, when we need to be. The unbearable pain is now a bearable pain, but the bond of love which unites us can never be severed, not even in death.

My dad's black onyx and gold ring now has a new home, on the pinky finger of my brother Selwyn. My father would be pleased. In my house, on my desk, where I can see it every day, sits a special memento, a gold plastic clock. I often wipe away a tear as I remember the day Anna gave it to my dad in Ludza.

—————→◦←—————

EPILOGUE

*W*riting this book has been a most rewarding experience.

As I reflected back on my life, I came to see how very blessed I've been. Being a Jewish woman in the 20th and 21st centuries, I've been privileged to live in a time and in a country, the United States of America, where my freedoms have been guaranteed by the Constitution of the land. I've gone from blue aerogrammes that took ten days to reach their recipient, to faxes and instant messaging. The Internet and emails have made the world so much smaller. I've gone from dipping pens in inkwells, to playing bridge online with someone in Iceland. Along with all the progress, I've also unfortunately witnessed one of the most horrific tragedies.

On September 11, 2001, I found myself five miles from the biggest attack in our country's history, an assault launched by terrorist extremists. This attack, for me, was a familiar example of a religion being hijacked (no pun intended) and twisted to justify evil behavior. This time the religion was Islam; it reminded me of my growing up years, where it had been Christianity that had been twisted in the hands of my teachers and the preachers in South Africa, justifying apartheid as the will of God.

Throughout my childhood, my mother warned of an attack of gigantic proportions in South Africa. It never happened. Yet here in the mighty and powerful United States … it happened. It never happened where it was expected, and then it did happen where it was totally unexpected. Writing this book has helped me to gain some perspective on the times in which I live, and I am grateful for that.

I grew up witnessing injustice and oppression and was not allowed to say or do anything about it. As a result I've devoted most of my adult life to the world of philanthropy. Now I am able to reach out to those less fortunate. An organization called UJA-Federation has been a vehicle for me to say and do things for those who can't say or do for themselves. I've been privileged to be part of the campaign that successfully rescued about half a million Jews from behind the iron curtain of the former Soviet Union in the 1980's who settled in Israel and other countries. I've also been part of the effort to rescue thousands of Ethiopians and bring them to freedom, in Israel. I'd like to point out that bringing these Ethiopians out was the first time in the history of Africa that blacks were taken to another country for freedom and not for slavery.

I've been able to use the process of writing this book to learn a great deal about myself and my family. My parents gave me the best examples of graceful aging I have ever known. I learned from my father a zest for living and a positive attitude. From my mom, I've learned never to compromise my values. My debt to them is impossible to describe or repay.

I've watched with profound satisfaction as Gregg and Jill have grown into remarkable human beings, and I know that I would be a lesser person if not for them. Their quick wit and sense of humor always puts a smile on my face. My daughter-in-law Lauren, whose warmth and caring, have led me to refer to her as my "other daughter," has fit into our family seamlessly. I love her.

I accepted the baton from my predecessors and ran with it. There

338

have been minor stumbles along the way, but for the most part the track has been smooth and in good condition. As I pass this baton on to you, my children, I hope you will carry it with pride, courage, strength and self-sufficiency, so that you may do well in your own journey. Hold on to that baton and all that it represents, and then pass it along to your children. You are the ones most capable of carrying it forward.

May you, my children and grandchildren, see a world where human beings treat each other with dignity and respect, within households and across borders with other countries.

I wish for peace. That is the biggest gift we can give the next generation. They deserve to grow up and grow old in a world at peace.

May ours continue to be a family of love and good values. Count your blessings and always remember those less fortunate.

To Richard, who is the star in the book and in my life; without you there would be no story. Words on the printed page cannot adequately articulate my gratitude and love for Richard. This is quite a journey we've shared! He embraced the Lotzof family as if they were his own, and called my parents "Mom and Dad" with genuine love.

Last year, I suggested to Richard that we go to Israel for our 40th wedding anniversary, with our kids and grandchildren. "Let's take them back to where it all started." Emma and Leah attend a Jewish day school and many of their friends had already been to Israel.

The decision was quick and immediate, and our planning began. Next to Ludza, it was one of the most special trips we've ever taken. Our granddaughters were ten years old, the same age as I was when I had to learn the New Testament in school; and here they were rattling off Hebrew with such fluency that they surprised us all.

We took them to the Ramat Gan stadium where I ran my races forty four years ago! The stadium no longer has a track; the area where I ran is now a soccer stadium. But Emma and Leah wanted to run on the grass that their grandmother ran on. They raced with speed and long lanky legs; both have a beautiful running style. I smiled and shook my head, wondering; where have the years gone?

Should our next family trip be to South Africa?

Sometimes, I feel as though I'd like to take my children and grandchildren for a visit to show them where I grew up, and to walk the streets of Reitz again. I'd like to see the school where the Bible ruled the day, the roads where my tough, bare feet walked over rocks and stones, and the road in front of Anita's house where I ran and won my very first race at

At the Maccabi Stadium with Emma and Leah. Israel June 2009

age five. And sometimes I don't want to go back at all. Whichever path I eventually decide on, I'll keep my memories intact and keep looking forward, always forward, as my journey beyond South Africa continues.

Emma and Leah, I wrote this book for you, my two angels. And if I'm blessed with more grandchildren in the future, this is for you too.

One of the luckiest things I ever did — forty four years ago — was to step out onto that terrace in Ramat Gan, Israel, in August 1965. When Richard slipped a note under my door, asking me out, I'm so glad I said "yes."

GRATITUDE

My deepest appreciation goes to the many people who have helped me bring this book to fruition.

My thanks go to the Gotham Writers Workshop teachers and classmates, for helping me to get started and for their honest and helpful critiques.

I am grateful to all those who were kind enough to read some chapters or the whole manuscript.

To Susan Sabreen, thank you for helping me with the punctuation, and for making sure that all the commas are in the right place. To Randi Kreiss, thank you for reading an early version of the first chapter. Phoebe Damrosch, the book doctor: your insights and suggestions were most helpful.

Auntie Gertie, I appreciate your patience and help in answering all my questions about the previous generations. You are my link with the past. You're the anchor and the glue in our family. I treasure our special relationship and I love you.

It was Paul Cheifitz, who was so helpful with all the information on the Lotzof family tree, photos and other items of our ancestors.

Peter Rich, my work-out buddy, I appreciate your input and your encouragement.

Franklin and Jean Gaylis, your idea of going to Ludza, became an important chapter in my book. Thank you for initiating and sharing the most meaningful trip of my life.

To Edna Ritzenberg, Adrienne Lurie, my sister-in-law Carole and

Steve Bookbinder, thank you for reading the manuscript and for your support and comments.

It was Steve Bookbinder, who introduced me to my editor, Brandon Toropov of iWordSmith. Brandon took my book to another level. He helped me open my memory bank, and I found everything still there. He guided me through my story with unerring vision and sensitivity, and made every page better. Brandon, there are no words to express the depth of my gratitude to you.

Thank you to Donald Prutzman for your legal advice and help.

To my friends, thank you for your encouragement and for wanting to know "How's the book coming along? I can't wait to read it." To all of you, I want you to know that your words gave me the motivation to keep forging forward.

To Richard and my children, thank you for your ongoing interest and support, and especially to Jill for reading the early draft. Your input in the first chapter and the conclusion was invaluable.

Thank you to Gregg for adding your helpful comments, including the choice for the title of the book.

A special thank you goes to Bill Boik and Joyce Burnett at DBM Press for their support and faith in this book.

Finally, thank you to Michelle and Jerry Dorris of AuthorSupport who put it all together and turned it from a manuscript into a beautiful cover and interior layout. Michelle and Jerry it was a pleasure working with you and thank you for your caring, patience and professionalism.

INDEX